Happy Birthday from
Mother + Charles
Mar. 26, 1992

Simply Halston

Simply Halston

THE UNTOLD STORY

Steven Gaines

G. P. Putnam's Sons

New York

G. P. Putnam's Sons
Publishers Since 1838
200 Madison Avenue
New York, NY 10016

Library of Congress Cataloging-in-Publication Data

Gaines, Steven S.
Simply Halston: the untold story / Steven Gaines.
p.   cm.
Includes index.
ISBN 0-399-13612-6
1. Frowick, Roy Halston.   2. Costume designers—United States—
Biography.   I. Title.
TT505.F76G35   1991   91-13850 CIP
746.9'2'092—dc20
[B]

Printed in the United States of America
1 2 3 4 5 6 7 8 9 10

This book is printed on acid-free paper.

CONTENTS

INTRODUCTION

I n early 1980, with the assistance of a Studio 54 bartender
named Robert Jon Cohen, I wrote and published a roman
à clef about Studio 54 called *The Club,* in which one of the
major characters was a brilliant and but self-destructive fashion
designer named Ellison who had a ruinous cocaine habit. Ellison's best pal was a talented but desperately unhappy enter-
tainer—Jacky, "with a *y.* "

"You'll never get away with it," Andy Warhol warned me
after reading an advance copy of the book, and I didn't.

The Club incurred the immediate wrath of Halston and Liza
Minnelli and Steve Rubell and many of their powerful friends.
What might have only been a cynical way to make money was
turned into a tempest by the New York gossip columnists.
Threats of multimillion-dollar lawsuits were rattled in the
press, and I became persona non grata at any place where
Halston or his tightly knit group of friends had any influence.
Even some other writers were suggesting that I had taken the
art of the roman à clef one slice too close to the bone. And
after reading the book Liz Smith, the syndicated columnist,
called to say that I should "brace myself" for the shock

waves—and that I had to be "philosophical" about what was coming.

What was coming was that the book sold out on both coasts. However, the long-term effects were not as profitable. *The Club* became a milestone in my career that no one would forget—or forgive—and has much to do with my authorship of *Simply Halston.*

I first met Halston in late 1969. I was part of a small entourage that had been invited up from Andy Warhol's Factory on Union Square to help populate a poetry reading by Gerard Melanga, one of Andy's "superstars," at Halston's East Sixty-eighth Street salon. I had then only vaguely heard of Halston and was surprised to find myself in a lush, junglelike environment of overstuffed furniture done up in batik prints, fabric-shirred walls, and potted palm trees, the air pungent with scented candles. The other guests ranged from elegantly dressed society women to cool fashion models and disheveled artists and painters. Tennessee Williams was there, too, as well as Candy Darling, the transvestite *nonpareil,* who broke a tooth on a pecan in the cheese, which a maid in a black uniform and starched white apron served with crackers and white wine.

In serene command of it all was Halston, so tall and thin in his black cashmere turtleneck and sport jacket that he looked like a giant exclamation point, stern and final. He moved smoothly around the room, smoking a cigarette with great affectation, chatting with each of his guests. I had been there only a few minutes when he sidled up to me. He was friendly, but his beautiful, catlike green eyes were coldly assessing. He asked what I did and why I was at his party, and when I said I was an acquaintance of Warhol's and an aspiring writer he had ready advice: "Steal from yourself," he said. "Find your forte and build on it."

By the mid-seventies I had taken Halston's advice. I had published several books and was also the "Top of the Pop" columnist for the *New York Daily News.* As a pop columnist, the discotheque circuit was part of my beat, and I had an unusual vantage point from which to observe Halston. We were often at the same place at the same time and we shared several mutual acquaintances, including Warhol and Steve Rubell. I saw Halston particularly during his Studio 54 period, when for a time things seemed so decadent and debauched that it appeared as if everyone had temporarily lost their minds. I certainly did when I wrote *The Club* about it.

The Club was also why in 1984 I was approached by Halston's long-time lover, Victor Hugo, to collaborate with him on a tell-all book about Halston, which I declined to write, and the details of which are discussed in this book. *The Club* was also, in part, the reason why in 1987 I was asked by Tina Brown, editor in chief of *Vanity Fair* magazine, to write an in-depth, feature-length article about Halston. It was for this unpublished article that several key interviews for this book were initially conducted, and I owe Tina Brown and *Vanity Fair*'s executive literary editor, Wayne Lawson, a great debt for the genesis of this book.

It was during my extensive research for the *Vanity Fair* article that I first began to realize just how dynamic and compelling the real Halston story is—far more so than any roman à clef could ever be. I came to learn that Halston was a loving human being who was a delight to his friends and family. I came to learn that Halston was probably the greatest American *haut couturier* who ever lived, and that he defined American fashion in an epochal phase. I came to realize that his business story is perhaps one of the great morality tales to come out of the corporate board-rooms of the eighties. Most of all, I came to regret that I had insulted one of the great artistic talents of my time.

Yet this book still has as its central character a fashion de-signer who ruined his beautiful life, in part, because of a drug problem. I wish I could have rewritten that part of the story.

I especially wish I could have rewritten parts of this story for the sake of Halston's family: his brothers, Robert Frowick and

Donald Frowick, and his sister, Sue Watkins, whose help I tried to enlist in my writing. Although I spent the day with Sue Watkins and Bob Frowick at their homes in Santa Rosa gathering familial and childhood information for this book, spoke with Donald Frowick in New York, and conferred for many hours with Bob Frowick on the phone, I am not able to thank them for their endorsement of this book, rather for their benign indifference.

I am, however, pleased to be able to acknowledge my great debt to Halston's attorney, Malcolm I. Lewin, of the firm Morrison Cohen Singer & Weinstein, for his many interviews and access to important documents. A tenacious advocate of Halston's rights, even in death, Lewin wanted Halston's side of his business struggle to be told at last. There are several other intimate sources associated with Halston, both in his business and private life, who contributed greatly to this book as well; however, they prefer to remain anonymous. I thank them for their help.

Happily, I am able to acknowledge the following people without whose assistance, interviews, and various indulgences this book could not have been written.

IN EVANSVILLE:

Jack Benjaman
Richard Hyatt
Tess and Ron Grimm
Don and Ann Partridge
Dana Jo Scism Holleman
Betty Jean Bradford
Madeline Hatcher
David Nurrembern

Harriet Bourland Douglas
Lester Watson, Jr.
Louis Wittmer
Marilou Berry *(Evansville Courier)*
Walt Lowe
Carol and Howard Primm

IN DES MOINES:

Phyllis Wolfe *(The Des Moines Register)*

Cheri Summers *(The Des Moines Register)*

Mark Horstmeyer (Des Moines school system)

Des Moines Museum of Art

IN CHICAGO:

Lucia Perrigo Myers
Peg Swecker
Sieglinde Sayles
Gerde Sayles
Ernest Settles
Dale Blood
Walter Gros
Rick Kogan

Medford Lange
Dorothy Manhart
Andrew Ryan
Marjorie Sawyer Goodman Graff
Chicago Historical Society
Chicago Institute of Art
Thomas Swift, Esq.
Rick Karlin

IN SAN FRANCISCO:

Dick Grosboll, Esq.
Richard Hauptman

Linda Rapp, Esq.

IN NEW YORK

David Mahoney
Patrick McMullan
Victor Hugo
Jacqueline Onassis
Paul Wilmot
Eleanor Lambert
Peruchio Valls
Connie Cook
Arthur Williams
John Fairchild
Joe Eula
Joanne Crevelling
Michael Pellegrino
Homer Layne
Alyce Finell
Paul Noble

Linda Wachner
Robert Kammerchen
Diane Sustendal
Chris Royer
Martin Snaric
Florence De Santis
John David Ridge
Don Friese
Fashion Institute of Technology
Barry Landau
Richard Townsend
Bert Keeter
Richard Cole
Casey Bush (Millinery Institute)
Peter Wise
Anton Perich

Walter Bregman
Robert Rogers
Alan Petrucelli
Crawford Mills
Myrna Davis
Edward Austin, Jr.
Joel Schumacher
Clovis Ruffin
Patricia Alexander ·
Patricia Bosworth
Ron Ferri
Milton Buras
Oleg Cassini
Andrew Goodman
Leonard Hankin
Gerald Shaw
Sam Bolton

Jeff Rodack
Tom Fallon
Julia McFarland
Michael Lichtenstein
Marjorie Ambrosia
R. Couri Hay
Jim Siewart
Women's Wear Daily library
Tony Freund
Andre Leon Talley
Christopher Makos
Richard Turley
John McMurray
Christina Costanza
Mildred Gilbert
Lisa Zay
Pat Hackett

My personal thanks to my dedicated friend and associate Martha Trachtenberg, for her great contribution to this book. Janet M. Chandler was also of tremendous assistance to me in the preparation of the manuscript, as was my dear friend Jim Williamson. I would also like to thank the following people for their kindnesses and support; Jeffrey Ulman, Esq., Paul Soloman, Steven Feldman and Susan Cohen Feldman, Sydney Butchkes, Stanley Posthorn, Pamela Booth, Gordon Robinson, and Joseph Olshan. Andrew Zeller at G. P. Putnam's Sons also has my great debt of gratitude. My special thanks are extended to Karen R. Mayer, Esq., at Putnam's Sons. Also, Sharon Friedman at John Hawkins and Associates has been a blessing to me, both for her wise legal and literary counsel and her boundless good nature. I owe a special debt of gratitude to Dr. Bernard Berkowitz as well.

I would like to thank my supportive publisher, Phyllis Grann; my agent, John Hawkins; James A. Urban, Jr., for his loving support; and my wise and savvy editor, George Coleman, for putting me back in the saddle again.

Finally I would like to dedicate my work on this book to my mother's courageous battle with amyotrophic lateral sclerosis, ALS (Lou Gehrig's disease), and my father's heroism in the face of it.

STEVEN GAINES
WAINSCOTT, NEW YORK, 1991

DES MOINES
AND EVANSVILLE:
THE HEALTHIEST BABY

"**I**f I ever wrote a book," Halston liked to say on those sunny northern California afternoons during the last few months of his life when he sat in the backseat of his brand-new $200,000 chauffeur-driven Silver Cloud Rolls-Royce as it tooled down the Pacific Coast Highway, "I know just how the book should start: 'You're only as good as the people you dress.'"

This was Halston's favorite truism: Fashionable people make fashion. "What good is it if your clothes hang in the closet?" he would demand. "It depends on *who* wears your clothes that makes you great." Of course, he had dressed the best of them, all the great and fashionable ladies of the world, from Jacqueline Kennedy Onassis and Elizabeth Taylor to Babe Paley and the wife of the shah of Iran. Halston was no fifteen-minute hotshot from the garment center who became famous by putting his name on the asses of tight-fitting blue jeans. He was an *haut couturier*. An *artiste*. A four-time Coty Award winner and perhaps the greatest American fashion designer who ever drew a breath.

Yet Halston's fame and influence went far beyond that of any mere dressmaker. Few celebrities have held the public and press so completely in their sway. He became an international legend in his own time, the personification of glamour and taste. He was the King of New York nightlife, a dramatic and compelling figure always dressed in black, his posture regally erect, his piercing green eyes hidden by mirrored sunglasses, a bland, "perfect" smile on his handsome midwestern face. Perhaps his greatest affectation was the Halstonettes, his band of merry models who seemed to float behind him as he emerged from the backseat of a limousine, the paparazzi surrounding them, strobe lights flashing like frantic fireflies.

But the man sitting in the backseat of the Rolls-Royce cruising Big Sur coastline was no longer the handsome and dashing designer the world knew so well. A two-year battle with AIDS had racked his body. His six-foot-two-inch frame had been stripped to little more than 150 pounds. His breathing had become labored and shallow, and his luxuriant brown hair had turned white and so thin in places that his scalp showed through. Radiation therapy had relentlessly weakened him, and, unable to walk unaided, he spent most of his day in a wheelchair. Yet despite all these ignobling horrors, his green eyes still burned brightly, and his dignity burned even more brightly. Not for a moment was there a hint of fear in his demeanor. He seemed devoid of self-pity, and the steadfastness of his calm gave courage and spirit to his family around him. To them, he was nothing short of heroic.

It was his family that held him together, his brothers, Robert and Donald, and his younger sister, Sue. Halston had moved to San Francisco a few months before to be near them at the end. On sunny days when he was feeling strong enough, the family would pack a picnic basket of Halston's favorite lunch, lobster salad, and the finest linen tablecloth and English china and best crystal goblets. They would all pile into the rich leather interior of the brand-new Rolls-Royce and take leisurely drives up and down the Pacific coast. It was on those sad, dreamy afternoons toward the end that Halston sometimes toyed with the idea of writing a book. "I might write a scathing book, or a nice one," he teased. "I've seen both sides of the sword."

Probably Halston never would have written a book, even if there had been time left to him. He was much too private a person, and anyway, during those last days, when he reminisced, it wasn't about his glamorous life in Manhattan, a city that had turned on him; or about the rich and famous women who had deserted him for untalented upstarts; or about the press, who had invaded his privacy; or about the friends and lovers who had betrayed him. When he reminisced it was about a little boy named Roy who had lived in Des Moines in a more innocent time. He remembered growing up in a warm and secure home across the street from an "enchanted forest," where friendly wild animals roamed and beautiful flowers grew. He remembered that even though he was a child of the Depression, he was always surrounded by relatives who made him feel loved and secure. He talked about his grandparents' big house, the polished wood floors and the wide staircase. He remembered the Thanksgiving dinners, when the house was filled with relatives and the smell of roasting turkey. He spoke of himself as a rosy-faced child of nine singing in the choir at the local Presbyterian church. Of visiting the Des Moines Museum of Art with his mother, Hallie May, and about the big department store downtown where he saw his first fashion show. He remembered that he had always been such a happy child, laughing all the time. He remembered that once he had been the healthiest baby in all of Des Moines.

DES MOINES IN the 1930s was a happy mecca of American normalcy. It was a God-fearing, industrious town, part cornfield, part growing metropolis, still reeling from the Depression. Only one in four people had a telephone, and plowing the snow from the streets after winter blizzards was the single biggest item in the city's budget. The city speed limit was thirty miles an hour, and a state income tax wasn't even enacted until 1935. Yet Des Moines was one of the world's great agricultural centers and, after Hartford, Connecticut, the insurance capital of the world. Most of all, it was a good place to live and work and a fine place to raise a family.

At least so thought Roy Frowick's grandfather, Edward James Frowick. Edward Frowick was born on January 1, 1880, in Haugesund, Norway, in a family farming area called Frovik. When he was a young man he and his family emigrated to Slater, Iowa, a little farm town of a few hundred people in Story County. There he not only built his own farmhouse but also all the furniture to fill it. Edward Frowick was six foot one, but he cut such a proper and imposing figure that people often assumed that he was several inches taller. "Ed," as he was called, was also a devout Christian Scientist who neither drank nor smoked. A former Des Moines Police Department captain and deputy state fire marshal, he became a Des Moines school custodian in 1928 until his retirement in 1949. He would live to be ninety-one and survive both his wife, Margaret, and his son, James Edward Frowick.

Born June 5, 1905, James Edward was also called Ed. The two Eds were nothing alike. Ed senior was a measured and dignified man who never lost his temper. Ed junior had a rebellious and angry nature and was given to great excess and extreme, both in terms of temperament and alcohol. When sober he seemed discontented and at odds with the world; drunk, he could be a terror. A bookkeeper by trade, he spent most of his life drifting from job to job, from city to city, until he died of cancer at age fifty-nine. When he was twenty-one he married Hallie May Holmes, who was also twenty-one, on June 24, 1926, at the Lutheran church in Des Moines. Hallie May, the daughter of Wilbur Halston Holmes and Mary Alice Merill, was a sweet and patient girl from good English stock who had grown up at 682 West Fortieth Street. Her father, Wilbur, was a fireman by profession, who, ironically, was badly burned by paraffin in a freak accident at home and forced to retire at the age of forty-seven. Halston was an old family name; Wilbur Holmes liked the name so much that "he wanted everybody in the family to be named Halston," according to a family member. The correct pronunciation of the name is *Hal* (rhymes with "pal")—*stone*. (At first, it irked his mother when the public started to call her son "Hall-stun," and she would correct strangers: "It's *Hal-stone.* I named him, I should know." Eventually, he got so famous as Hall-stun that she just gave up.)

Ed Jr. and Hallie May's first son, Robert Holmes Frowick, was born on the kitchen table of their ramshackle rented, two bedroom bungalow at 1809 Twenty-fifth Street on December 12, 1929. Their second son, Roy, was born nearly two and half years later on April 23, 1932, at the Des Moines General Hospital. He was named after his father's brother, an esteemed executive at the Bankers Life Company. A sister, Sue, was born July 15, 1937. For a while the three children shared not only a room, but also a bed. They grew up fiercely loyal to one another, but each very different. Robert was tall, lean, and handsome, an intellectual, who reasoned in the face of contention and took after his paternal grandfather, whom he greatly admired. Roy was a round-faced child with a ruddy complexion, moody and temperamental like his father and apt to get into mischief. He once set fire to the living room curtains, and Hallie May had to send for the fire department to put out the flames. Little sister Sue was a sweet and shy child, easily hurt, and like her mother, she tended to be plump.

"From the outset of our time together," Bob Frowick said, little Roy "was destined to attract attention." He made the press early in his life when at age two he was judged the "healthiest city boy" at the annual Iowa State Fair. On May Day, 1937, at age five, Roy made the front page of the Des Moines paper handing a little girl a May basket.

The children led a classic Iowa childhood—fishing, visiting

farms, attending soap box derby races. Roy went to the Callahan and Kirkwood elementary schools. The Kirkwood, allegedly built for the children of the faculty of nearby Drake University, had an excellent local reputation. When he was eight Roy began to sing in the junior choir at the local Presbyterian church at Grand Avenue and Thirty-ninth Street. Every Sunday a neighbor, Louise Thompson, along with her daughter Phyllis, would pick up Bob and Roy in a taxi and take them to Central Church. After church there were gatherings of the family clan at grandpa Ed's house, with aunts, uncles, and cousins to socialize with. "The children enjoyed the daily contact of three generations," said Bob Frowick. "We had a full, balanced, elegant, secure life."

Indeed, theirs might have been a storybook childhood had it not been for Ed Jr. "Dad was a strong personality," Bob Frowick put it gingerly, "and he had a temper." In fact, his temper was so extreme after a few drinks that the family dubbed it "the J.E. temper" and used it as a yardstick against which to measure anger all their lives. "We all have the J.E. temper," Sue said.

Because of his temper, and his alcoholism, Ed Jr. was never able to hold a job for more than a few years. Subsequently, Halston would tell friends that his father would have just one drink and be inebriated. His younger brother, Donald, disputed this: "He could drink a whole bottle and not show it," Donald remembered. "The next morning he would wake up as if nothing happened." It was Hallie May who often bore the brunt of Ed Jr's temper; over the years she buried her hurt by crocheting dozens upon dozens of afghans. Hallie May's pain did not go unnoticed by her children, particularly not by Roy, who adored his mother. In the years to come, through all his travels, he would continue to call her every Monday night of his life until she died in 1982. He would later commission Andy Warhol to make multiple portraits of her. As a child Roy began to despise his father for making his mother so unhappy, and as an adult he would never forgive Ed Jr. his meanness to the family.

Whatever demons haunted Ed Jr. were exemplified best by a quest that would elude his grasp his whole life: he wanted to invent some unique and wonderful gimmick that would sweep the nation and make him an overnight millionaire. He was forever tinkering, devising ideas for contraptions and building models, yet he never took out a patent with the U.S. Patent Office. Although he was clever with his hands, his ideas were gimmicky and not quite commercial. Bob Frowick remembered that his third-grade teacher at the Kirkwood School, Mrs. Wickstead, asked the class if one of the students' fathers could make a loom for the school. Bob told his father about it and in a few days Ed Jr. had created one from scratch, "functional and creative," according to Bob. But there was also Ed Jr.'s "Radar Sandwich": a microwave contraption that heated up a sandwich and sealed it in plastic at the same time. "He always had the desire to do something different," said his son. "When TV started he jumped on that too, but he was never able to capitalize on his visions." His growing sense of frustration and hot-headed temperament made for a hair-trigger atmosphere in the Frowick household.

It was in this environment that little Roy began to sew. Just as his mother lost herself in crocheting afghan after afghan, Roy took up needle and thread as a small boy. One neighbor who watched him as a child remembered that all she had to do to keep him contented was to give him a bit of fabric and a needle and thread; even as a tot he could sit for hours and sew. He saw his first fashion show as a little boy when his mother and grandmother took him to the Tea Room at Younkers department store downtown.

From the start, he showed a special interest in making hats, launching his first millinery creation by braiding flowers for his mother's hair. He also made his sister, Sue, a hat adorned with chicken feathers when she was only two years old, and on Easter Sunday of 1945 he gave his mother a homemade red cloche with a scouring pad pom-pom on it. Hallie May wore the hat to church that day, much to Roy's delight. "We all wondered how the hell and why he did it," said Bob Frowick. "But it was a smash and really flattered my mother."

"He always had a hat to try on somebody," said his grandmother, Mrs. Wilbur Halston Holmes. Years later, when his first hat appeared on the cover of *Harper's Bazaar* in 1960, Granny Holmes still didn't know what to make of it. "I don't think I'd care much for it," she said of the brown organdy sunbonnet, "unless I wanted to wear it in the backyard."

IN THE FALL of 1939, unable to pay the rent on his own home, Ed Jr. moved with his family to his father's house at 2127 High Street. The two-story house was roomy, rambling, with five bedrooms—and for a short time the children felt blissful and secure there. But two Eds under one roof amounted to a combustible mixture, and within a year Ed Jr. and Hallie May and the children left Des Moines and their family and close friends for good. The departure from Des Moines was a turning point, said Bob Frowick. Everywhere else after that was on the road for them, "Everywhere we moved after Des Moines was just a hick town," he said.

They wound up next in Carbondale, Illinois, where Ed Jr. got a job at the Crab Orchard Lake Ordnance plant as a defense contracts auditor and accountant. On December 8, 1941, Roy and Bob were sitting on the steps of the Bush School in Carbondale when FDR made his "Day of Infamy" speech.

In December 1943, when Roy was ten years old, the family followed Ed to Evansville, Illinois, a heartland city of 100,000 people where he found work as a comptroller at the Republic Aviation plant, which manufactured P47 Thunderbolt planes for World War II. Located 300 miles due south of Chicago, Evansville was a pleasant manufacturing center on the north side of a sweeping bend in the Ohio River. During the Frowicks' next nine years in Evansville, friends and family would remember at least four jobs that J.E. held, including one at the

Chrysler plant, Goad Electric (where he was a salesman), and the International Harvester plant, with the family living at at least as many addresses.

Evansville was a closely knit town where most of the neighbors had known one another for at least three generations. The majority of the townspeople were of German and Dutch descent. To rent as the Frowicks did was very unusual. In Evansville the streets were spotless, houses were well kept, there was no crime, and pennies were commonly pinched—which is how, natives say, they got through the Depression as relatively unscathed as they did. To this day, the Evansville banks are regarded by the local real estate businesses as especially prudent in terms of granting home loans.

The Frowicks first moved to a small house at 805 Villa Drive. Two years later, they were living at 1133 Joan Avenue, which Bob Frowick described as the "nadir of their existence"—a small, shacklike, one-story house on a lost little street, with a practically nonexistent backyard that faced a truck route. It was this pitiful backyard that many years later, in an interview, Halston turned into an "enchanted garden" from which he collected flowers for his hats. In 1945 Hallie May, at age forty, was pregnant again, and a fourth child, Donald, was born on July 28. Finally, the family moved to 812 Villa Drive, a much nicer house on a tree-lined street, and then eventually to a more modest place at 2325 East Michigan Street.

It was at the Hebron Elementary School that Roy began to show an artistic bent: in sixth grade he cowrote a school play and acted several of the parts himself. Then in seventh grade, at the Washington School, he choreographed the school musical in a very stylized, Kabuki-like manner. At age fourteen, already tall and boyishly handsome, he started at Benjamin Bosse High School, the premier, upper-middle-class school of the five high schools in Evansville. It was a big, handsome, two-story brick building situated on several tree-lined acres with its own stadium—home of the Bosse Bulldogs football team. In Roy's graduating class of just over four hundred students it was possible to know everyone's first name.

Although as a student Roy's grades were just barely passing, his teachers found him charming. "He talked to everyone, and he was very friendly," said Richard Hyatt, his music teacher. "I used to watch him in the cafeteria—so gregarious, a tablehopper, and fun loving." He was also, everyone noted, a terrific dresser—and although he did it on a constrained budget, everything he owned was always the best. "Roy had an incredibly innate taste for clothes," said brother Bob, "and all his money went into a fantastic wardrobe."

"He didn't have very many clothes, but what he had was lovely," remembered a close friend and schoolmate, Ann Holsclaw. "If he had one sweater it would be a cashmere." In fact, Roy was so discriminating about his clothing that during the war, when shoes were rationed, he spent months saving up six ration booklets until he could trade with a neighbor for penny loafers, the only kind of shoes he found acceptable. School chums also remember him strolling through the halls of Bosse High, looking somehow very glamorous at age fifteen, with the most peculiar habit of throwing his cashmere sweater over his back and knotting the sleeves under his neck.

He was also considered a little peculiar. "You knew after you talked to Roy five minutes that this was a nice, tall, well-built young man that was not a football player, if you know what I'm saying," said one high school friend. "He made it clear from the start that he always wanted to design women's clothes."

Said Les Watson, one of Roy's close friends in high school, "Not all the guys would run around with Roy because of a certain effeminacy that he had, certain mannerisms that were more delicate than others, but it didn't bother me. He was a really neat guy with a lot on the ball, and from our standpoint he was heterosexual as could be. He never hit on any of us or indicated it was any other way."

Indeed, almost universally his friends from Evansville so loved and appreciated him that his sexual preferences would not have mattered to them had they known for sure. To be certain, Roy's circle of friends was a rarefied group at Bosse High, for it was in high school that he first showed his propensity for the richest and most socially prominent people in any group. "In high school," said Bob Frowick, "my brother was driven around by rich girls in convertibles."

Roy's best friend through high school was Ron Grimm, the scion of Grimm Lumber, a large local company that supplied building materials for the postwar building boom of Indiana and Illinois. Grimm was Bosse High School's junior class president, too. Roy's circle also included Ann Holsclaw, a pretty and bubbly girl whose family manufactured the Holsclaw boat trailer, which was widely used during World War II and known by shipbuilders the world over. Holsclaw was Bosse's senior class secretary. Peggy Schwenker's father was Evansville Electric and Manufacturing, Harriet Bourland's family was Red Dot chemical. Their fathers all had late-model cars, their families all belonged to the Evansville Country Club, and "all those girls had cashmere sweaters by the dozens," said Les Watson, Jr., who later married Harriet Bourland.

Roy's girlfriend when he was at Bosse High was Dana Jo Scism, who, while not from a wealthy family like the others in the group, had her own special distinction in that she was the daughter of Darby Scism, the locally revered sports editor of the *Evansville Courier* who had been elected to the Baseball Hall of Fame. Dana Jo was great fun and full of energy, and when the group paired off, she and Roy would be together. Although nothing romantic ever transpired between them, it was Dana Jo to whom he gave an orchid and whom he escorted to the Bosse senior prom—but only after having given her dancing lessons so that they would look good together on the dance floor. Dana Jo remembers that he was a sensation in the senior play as the personification of the month of January, dressed in a white tuxedo and dancing the "Continental" with fellow senior Margaret Martin.

"Every morning of our senior year," said Dana Jo, "my

mother and I would drive by Roy's house and give him a ride to school in our Nash. He hated physical education. He cut his gym class and he had detention for at least a month to make it up. Every day when he got out, I'd be waiting for him. We'd ride the bus downtown and go to Walgreen's and stop up the salt and pepper shakers and share a Coke."

Saturday nights Roy and the girls sometimes played bridge. The girls adored him; he always knew how to talk to his girl friends and felt comfortable in what was basically a "hen party" situation. Once, when Ann Holsclaw and Patsy McConell were in a fender bender with a parked car and they thought they would have to give testimony in court, Roy was thrilled to orchestrate the whole thing. "Every day after school he would make us practice our testimony," said Ann Holsclaw. "He played all the parts, the judge and the prosecuting attorney. He arranged it all, right down to explicit directions on what I should wear on the witness stand." They were all disappointed when the case was settled out of court.

Summers, Roy worked at the International Harvester plant in the blueprint room with his pal Les Watson. They sorted mail and ran blueprints on a photostat machine, which they put to good use making phony driver's licenses for themselves and their underage friends. "They lasted most of us until we were twenty-one," said Watson.

Roy had some rather peculiar traits. One of the town's wealthiest women, Kitty Vanorman—the wife of Harold Vanorman, who owned the McCurdy Hotel, the big riverfront hotel in Evansville—held a special fascination for him. "Kitty Vanorman dressed like a million," Dana Jo remembered, "and Roy seemed to always be on the lookout for her, he admired her so much. He would always give her a big hello and I don't think she hardly knew him. Sometimes he would see her and he would come back and tell us everything she had on. He'd say, 'You're not going to believe this, Dana Jo, but I ran into Kitty Vanorman and let me tell you what she had on . . .' He would detail every last stitch of clothing, and his eyes gleamed as he did it."

Another time, just before Sue's thirteenth birthday in July of 1950, Roy wanted very badly to design a new fashion look for her. First, he took Sue down to the Wabash River where he made her lie in the sun to get very suntanned. It was a hot day, and Sue was miserable in the sun. Every few minutes she would ask plaintively, "Can't we go now?" and Roy would say no, he wanted her to have the "perfect" tan and made her rotate every fifteen minutes. On the day of her birthday Roy took Sue to a local dress store and bought her an entire outfit: a black-and-white dress with a pleated skirt, and red, three-inch high-heeled shoes. When Sue was all dressed up, he took her to the streets of downtown Evansville and paraded her around in circles, showing her off. At one point Roy made her walk a dozen paces ahead of him so he could watch the reaction of other people when Sue passed by.

Yet none of Roy's eccentricities prepared his family and friends for the day in his junior year when he was sixteen years old and he disappeared from Evansville for a week; he ran off to Florida with two boys, one of whom was Charlie Bradford—whose school chums suspected of being homosexual. Charlie came from a prominent and rich family; he was one of the sons of A. A. Bradford, who owned lumber mills and a nationally known building concern—and he had a late-model car and lots of spending money. One cold day in March, Roy, Charlie Bradford, and Louie Wittmer were sitting around the school cafeteria when Roy suggested they cut classes that afternoon and go downtown to window-shop. Wittmer said that if he was going to get "hung" for cutting classes, it might as well be for going to Florida. So the boys went home, packed their bags, piled into Charlie Bradford's 1947 fire-engine-red Mercury Town and Country convertible, and hit the road.

On the road they behaved like virtual outlaws. In Sarasota they stiffed the hotel by leaving behind an empty bag and saying they would be back to retrieve it when they paid their bill. At one meal where they skipped out on the check, a silver bowl with lemon water was put on the table; Roy dipped his shrimp in it, not knowing it was the fingerbowl. Eventually the boys totally ran out of money, and A. A. Bradford wired them just enough to buy gas to get home. The only thing they had to eat on the way back was a Pecan Log, which they had stolen at a gas station.

They were gone a total of one week, and when they returned home they found that they had become the scandal of the school. Louie Wittmer was given a long detention, Charlie Bradford defiantly quit Bosse High rather than be punished and went off to private school in Florida, and Roy, to the shock of all who knew him, was "expelled by request" for two weeks by the school authorities. There was hell to pay at home, too, and a good dose of the J.E. temper. Reportedly, from that moment on, J. E. cut Roy off without a penny, and Roy had to earn his own keep. "I went to work for a restaurant called the Merry-Go-Round," Roy said. "It was fun."

At least he had managed to buy a black sport shirt in Florida to set off his suntan to best advantage.

Charlie Bradford, who later owned the House of Charles Hair Salon in Evansville, reportedly died at the age of thirty-six.

ROY FROWICK LEFT high school in 1950 like a ghost. He did not have his yearbook picture, or any school pictures taken while he was at Bosse High. He did not "bequeath" anything silly or clever to the other students of Evansville as did the rest of the student body. Of all his friends, only one can remember ever having been inside any of the houses he lived in, and then just once. Only one of his friends remembers meeting Roy's father. None of them was quite sure exactly what J.E. did for a living. Roy would forever be the outsider for them, the poor boy with a secret at home, his nose pressed up against the windowpane of a richer life.

The fifties brought a miserable start for Roy. It looked as though his dream of becoming a fashion designer and leaving home was hopeless, yet he could not bear to live with his father any longer. With his older brother's encouragement, Roy went off to Indiana University in the spring of 1952 for one semester. According to Bob, Roy got all C's except for two A's in fine arts. He would liked to have continued school, but financial problems forced him to return to Evansville, his father's house, and the J.E. temper. Back home, he was so miserable that for a time he even considered doing volunteer work, just to be doing something positive and meaningful. Instead, he took a full-time job at International Harvester; there he was, back on duty at the copying and laminating machine. When, in 1952, he was laid off from International Harvester, he felt that he had reached yet another dead end.

Deeply depressed about his life and future, he went to sign up for unemployment compensation at the government office on the corner of Second and Court streets. There he wound up pouring his heart out to the lady behind the counter, Madeline Hatcher. Hatcher gave him some kind words of encouragement, and each week when he came by to sign for his unemployment checks they would chat a bit. Eventually, he asked her out to dinner. Although Hatcher was seven years older than Roy, and she had no romantic interest in him, "he wanted to take me to dinner and I went," she said. "We went a couple of times. One time I remember we went to F's (a local steak house). All during dinner all he could talk about was how he wanted to be a fashion designer. He even told me how to dress. I was short and he told me to wear drop-waisted dresses to give the illusion of height."

A few days later Roy showed up at the unemployment insurance office with a gift for Hatcher. It was a hat, a small hat done in ivory satin with three bunches of feathers and a trim of seed pearls. And inside, to say thank you for her words of encouragement, were the pressed leaves of a rose. It was a good-bye gift. Roy told her he was going to find fame and fortune in Chicago. His family was moving on again, and Roy wasn't going with them.

In late summer of 1952, Ed Jr. loaded up the family car with all Roy's clothing and possessions and took him off to Chicago. The rest of the family left Evansville, too, eventually heading for Kentucky and Florida. Roy's friends in Evansville never heard from him again, but they never lost track of him either. Except for Dana Jo, who moved not far away, most of Roy's high school friends still live only blocks away from one another in Evansville, their lives gently intertwined as they got married and raised children.

THIRTY YEARS AFTER Roy Frowick left Evansville, a man named Halston returned to town to orchestrate the second marriage of his sister, Sue. When Sue returned to Evansville for her Bosse High School reunion she ran into her old high school flame, Bryant "Bud" Watkins, to whom she had been engaged years before. Sue was in the throes of an unhappy marriage and when she remet Bud they fell in love again, divorced their respective spouses, and decided to get married at the Neu Chapel at Evansville College. Halston was returning to Evansville to host the wedding, for which he had designed many of the gowns, including Sue's.

Reading about the wedding in the local papers, Ann Holsclaw started to feel nostalgic about Roy and the old days and she decided she wanted to see him again and say hello. The morning of the wedding, she went to the church, hoping she would run into Roy outside. When she arrived, there was a long line of limousines, crowds of people and photographers and in the middle of it all, Roy directing the bridal party, putting to work his years of experience as a master of illusion and presentation.

But instead of going up to him, Ann Holsclaw hid behind a tree and just watched. It wasn't Roy. The man in the sunglasses was such an intimidating-looking stranger to her, she couldn't bring herself to say hello.

CHICAGO 1953:
A KEPT BOY

I t wasn't until Chicago that Roy Halston Frowick really began to invent himself, to become himself for the first time. Barely twenty years old, he rented a small, dark "English basement" apartment in a town house on Astor Street, with a roommate to help pay the rent. He enrolled in a night course at the Chicago Art Institute and took a job during the day at Carson Pirie Scott as a window dresser. Gay life was clandestine in Chicago then, but there were places one could go to meet like-minded people, or a certain circuit of discreet homosexual men, other window dressers and hairstylists and florists who all got together at weekly parties.

Now he was no longer Roy Frowick, but "Fro," as his new friends called him. Six feet two inches tall, slender and willowy, he was an optimistic and likable young man, yet he had a very grand and superior air about him for such a youth from the sticks. Even the way he moved was regal, his long limbs and big hands flowing with some innate poise. Then there was the way he held a cigarette, with the burning end straight up, the smoke curling lazily to the ceiling as he exhaled a long plume and went on and on in an dry midwestern drawl about all the grand things that he was going to accomplish. But it didn't take long to realize that all his grandeur was just a front—that there was a side to him that was quite soft and silly. Among friends, he liked to play the buffoon. He had a big, infectious laugh, and sometimes he got so carried away laughing that he would actually have to lie down on the floor and hold his sides to catch his breath. Then a moment later he would assume a cool and distant manner again.

This was the young man André Basil fell in love with when he was first introduced at a party of mutual friends in 1953. And although Basil was more than twenty-five years "Fro's" senior—easily old enough to be his father—there was something rather compelling about the legendary hairdresser; he kept Fro spellbound with his droll Germanic demeanor and his stories about the great ladies who had streamed in and out of his salon—everyone from Madame Chiang Kai-shek to Judy Garland. He had an apartment on Lakeshore Drive and a Lincoln convertible, and he had made twenty-one transatlantic crossings by liner—a voyage on which, he promised, he would one day take young Roy Frowick.

In some circles, André Basil was considered quite a catch for a young window dresser like Roy. Handsome and trim, he was also extremely well connected and something of a local Chicago legend. In Chicago in the fifties, if you were a celebrity passing through town, or one of the society ladies from the Gold Coast, or part of the Lake Forest crowd, Basil of the Ambassador did your hair. He had been at the top of the beauty field for three decades, first as a stylist for Charles of the Ritz and Michael of the Waldorf in New York, where he became the favorite hairdresser of ladies like Clare Boothe Luce and the Duchess of Windsor. Charming and well-spoken, he was hired by Elizabeth Arden to tour the U.S. after the war. Ernie Bifield, the owner of the Ambassador, invited Basil to move to Chicago and take up residence in the marble-floored arcade beneath North State Parkway that connected the east and west towers of the hotel. Within a few years Basil had become the city's foremost hairdresser.

By the early fifties Basil owned three other salons as well—one at the Bismarck Hotel, one at the Sherman, and one at the Canterbury Court. They all did quite well financially in what was mostly a cash business, but it was the salon at the Ambassador Hotel in which Basil himself worked that was the most famous and desired. It was a cozy, plush establishment just a few steps down from the hotel lobby. The pace was leisurely and the surroundings elegant. An assistant served tea and cakes and Basil encouraged the ladies to bring their dogs to the shop; sometimes it seemed as if there were a poodle in every private booth. Here Basil reigned supreme, social director as well as stylist, charming his patrons with an inexhaustible supply of urbane stories and amusing anecdotes as he smoked two or three packs of Pall Mall cigarettes a day and drank as many as thirty cups of coffee which flowed continuously from room service.

It was into this perfumed world of moneyed women that Basil invited Roy Frowick, about whom he knew very little. For all his commanding presence and authority, Fro let little be known about himself. He rarely brought up his family or his background, and when pressed, would recount only a sketchy history: he was born in Des Moines, the son of an accountant; his family eventually moved to Evansville, Illinois, and he later attended the University of Indiana; he was very proud of his older brother, Robert, who was in the Air Force, and he adored his younger sister, Sue. "Fro came from very good stock," one of his friends at the time assumed, "and his family belonged to all the best clubs."

Fro took up residence in Basil's fussy, antique-filled two-bedroom apartment in the old Reynolds mansion at 1445 Lakeshore Drive. He fit right in to his luxurious new life-style, as if he had always belonged there. Basil gave him a set of keys to the gray Mark IV Lincoln Continental, and the leash to Onka, a black standard French poodle that had been imported from Germany who would become Fro's constant companion. Basil's charge accounts were arranged to include Fro, and Basil's family remembers that he sent Fro to trade school for a short time. There were also sundry gifts of jewelry and trips, clothing, cash, and promises for the future. "Everything Basil had was Fro's," said Sieglinde Sayles, Basil's niece. She remembered Basil as the adoring teacher, completely in love with his young ward. "Money, possessions, it didn't matter to him; Basil just wanted to share everything with him . . ."

Fro, however, had a short attention span and was quick to bore. He had a roving eye, as well, and a hearty amorous appetite; Basil needed a way to keep Fro in line. Fro was not Basil's first younger lover. Part of Basil's lure for his younger friends was that he offered them not only a certain financial security and a beautiful place to live, but also the chance to start a career. It was simple for Basil to teach his boys the trade of hairdressing and turn them into his apprentices in the shop as well as in bed. But Fro didn't want to be a hairdresser. He thought hairdressing was *dreadfully* boring. Fro knew what he wanted to do—he had always known what he wanted to do— and he certainly didn't need Basil to tell him anything. Fro wanted to make hats.

Hats. He was nuts about hats. Hats made up a major part of Fro's every conversation. He was obsessed by women's hats: the shape, the style, the colors, the fit. He could sew hats, he could block them, he could make his own willows. Every moment he was not working at Carson Pirie Scott he was sewing hats on a secondhand sewing machine in his apartment bedroom. He said he had been creating hats since he was a little boy and that he had made his public debut with a red felt cloche his mother had worn to church on Easter Sunday.

Fro knew exactly how Basil could be of service; he could

finance him in the opening of his own millinery salon. As Fro was constantly pointing out, millinery was big business. In 1952, no proper lady left the house without a hat; hats were so important that entire outfits were built around milady's *chapeau*. "Hats were a very big business in those days," Fro later recalled, "especially in a windy city like Chicago."

Basil seized upon the idea. He would indeed back Fro in a millinery business, but they would start small. Fro would set up a small display area at the front of the Ambassador salon where there was room for just three hat racks. Basil would pay for whatever supplies were necessary to get Fro started and make room for him to work in the apartment's second bedroom. Basil also gave Fro one of the stations at the salon usually reserved for facials in which he could store his materials and sew. Fro could usually be found sitting on the floor with his fabrics and straws and colorful flowers spread out around him. If Fro could sell a hat every time Basil styled a woman's hair—well, then, a hat shop of Fro's own could easily follow.

Lucia Perrigo, the Ambassador's director of publicity, remembers seeing Roy Frowick for the first time. "I had a nine o'clock appointment every Wednesday," she said, "and one Wednesday morning, seated tailor fashion on the floor with his legs crossed—the longest legs I'd ever seen—was this good-looking young man. He was sitting in what looked like a garden of the most beautiful millinery flowers, sewing the most beautiful hats you ever saw in the world." Lucia cast a sly smile in Basil's direction and said, "What's this little extra added attraction?"

"This is Roy Frowick," Basil said, practically beaming with pride. "We call him 'Fro.' He's *very* talented. He makes *hats.*"

FOR A YOUNG man who had only months before arrived in Chicago from a small town in search of fame and fortune, the Ambassador was the cynosure of both. Landing at Basil's salon in the Ambassador Hotel in 1953 was an especially fortuitous bit of luck for Roy Frowick. The Ambassador was not just a hotel, it was a Chicago institution, the hub of many of the city's most glamorous events and the home to many movie stars passing through town. The Ambassador is actually two hotels, twin towers, east and west, with 738 rooms between them. In the hotel and travel trade it was said that Chicago was "New York's bathtub" where in the pre-jet-age world long-distance travelers would stop and spend a night or two and take a bath before continuing on their journey. The Ambassador also saw more than its fair share of celebrities, since Chicago was the gateway to the burgeoning midwestern media outlets in broadcast and publishing; every movie star with a picture to publicize or author on the road trying to sell a book would pass through town, often ending up having lunch at the glamorous Pump Room on the second floor of the Ambassador East with its famous "celebrity booth number one," where everybody from Cary Grant to Elizabeth Taylor and Judy Garland once sat.

Another reason the Ambassador was so popular was its director of public relations, Lucia Perrigo—a pint-sized, powerhouse of personality and wit. An inveterate Chicago booster and former newspaper woman in her forties, Perrigo had also been the midwestern director of publicity for Warner Brothers Pictures during the war and had often booked stars into the Ambassador before she went to work there herself in 1949. She continued to woo movie stars to the hotel, sometimes greeting the visiting luminaries arriving at the train station on the Super Chief with champagne and limousines. Once, when Joan Crawford stopped at the Ambassador, Perrigo put a sign on the door of her suite proclaiming "Headquarters of Joan Crawford."

Lucia Perrigo became a crucial ally and friend to Roy Frowick. "He was a young, loving, happy, upbeat young man," remembered Perrigo. "All the qualities that you liked in your fellow human being. He didn't have any sharp edges, and he was much loved by everybody." For Fro, she was a mother figure and confidante, a wise, older woman with a maternal tug. Lucia can remember him arriving at the hotel each morning, always dressed like a gentleman in tie and jacket, his arms filled with flowers and fabrics, ribbons and straw, the color high in his face from rushing around in the summer heat.

"Basil believed in him and pushed him," Perrigo said. "He believed that he had talent. When a client had her hair done Basil would look at her in the mirror and say, 'What you need is a hat,' and whisk her to where Fro sat. Fro would find just the right confection for Basil's 'do' from stock or whip one together right on the spot with seemingly magic fingers." Lucia was entranced by the way "he would conjure up the most fabulous hats and creations. It was like waving a wand and every woman felt beautiful," she said. "These women took one look at these hats and put them right on their newly sprayed and lacquered heads. They didn't care what happened to their hairdos. When he wasn't making hats, he was sketching them, and when he wasn't doing that he was walking the dog."

Walter Gros, the young man who preceded Fro as Basil's lover and remained good friends with him over the years, remembered that "in the beginning, Fro was shy. Fro was scared of presenting himself to the ladies and Basil literally had to shove him out there to talk to people, to go out there and show them what he could do." Basil also taught Fro how to charm and win over his customers. "Women," Basil often said, "bring their joys and their sorrows to their beauty salon. A really good stylist can revamp both spirit and coiffure." So Roy learned from Basil to gently stroke Madam's ego when needed, or gently deflate it when needed, too. He began to learn about the peccadilloes and peculiarities of rich women, how they lived, what their needs were. He soon began to give his customers advice about many aspects of their lives, about their clothing and shoes and handbags, and—much to Basil's chagrin—even about their hairstyles. It was all offered in a charming, droll way, yet with a rigid politeness underneath. Moreover, his taste proved to be uncannily correct. He was, unmistakably, a gifted young man.

It was a daily ritual for Lucia Perrigo to lunch in the Pump Room, where she would network with notable hotel guests and the press and generally spread her *bonhomie*. One Wednesday morning in Basil's salon while Basil was doing her hair, Perrigo was asked by Fro if she would wear one of his hats to lunch. Lucia gladly agreed. She no longer remembers what the hat looked like—only that it was a huge hit with the society ladies and that frequently thereafter she began to wear one of Fro's creations to lunch. On special occasions Lucia wore what she called "stunt hats" that Halston made for her; for Christmas, there was an emerald green satin Christmas tree two feet high; or, for an eighteenth-century costume ball, a tricorn of white fur and black chiffon was perched upon her head. Slowly his reputation grew by word of mouth, and the women from the Pump Room began to make their way down to the arcade where Fro sat sewing away in one of the booths. "The society women started to buy his hats like popcorn," said Perrigo. "And at about thirty-five dollars each—they weren't inexpensive in those days, even then."

It didn't take long for Lucia to realize that Fro had turned into a good story, so she rang up one of her old Chicago chums (and former sorority sister), Peg Swecker. At the time, Swecker was an influential Chicago newspaperwoman and gossip columnist who wrote a widely read column for the *Chicago Daily News* called "Fashionably Speaking." Perrigo told Swecker, "You should see what's going on over here in the basement of the Ambassador. It's the birth of a genius."

Shortly thereafter Swecker paid a visit to Basil's salon and spent the afternoon talking to Fro and observing him at work. "What was fascinating," said Swecker, "was that he could drape a silk print right on somebody's head and make a turban. He was very aware of what each individual customer should wear, what was right for her look. His attitude wasn't just that she was going to get some hat he picked out for her and she was going to like it. He was also concerned with what size purse she was carrying and the color of her shoes. I watched him for a long time, and he would select the hats he thought the woman should wear for her taste and her life. Then the lady would want to try on several others, but—without fail—she would always go back to his original suggestion. He was always right and always knew what was right for the customer."

Swecker began to plug his hats in her column, using, for the first time, his middle name, Halston, as his professional moniker; Roy Frowick, they decided, sounded too dowdy, although everybody who knew him in Chicago continued to call him Fro. Perrigo and Swecker also devised some rather brilliant press coverage for him. On the opening day of swimming season on Lake Michigan, they took three of the prettiest models they could find down to the Oak Street Beach and posed them coming out of the water wearing Fro's hats. "We had them drop their shoulder straps so they looked as if they were nude," said Lucia. "All you could see were bare shoulders and long necks and beautiful faces, all topped off by the most exquisite hats." The copy read, "Borne Upon a Wave" and caused a sensation when it ran in the papers. The next winter they borrowed the idea and this time had the models buried up to their chins in the snow, each wearing brilliantly red poppy-decorated hats for the spring. For increased exposure Fro supplied hats to any hotel fashion show that would have him, and on Easter Sunday he posed for pictures selling matching hats to women and their dogs. He made hats for Basil's poodle, Onka, too, and she was photographed with Fro for the papers wearing one as she picked out a pasty in a French bakery shop near the hotel.

The cumulative effect of the press could easily be seen in the increased volume of hats Fro was selling. Mrs. Philip Wrigley, Mrs. Brooks McCormick, Mrs. Byron Harvey, and Mrs. Michael Sewall became his clients. He began to cultivate a celebrity clientele as well. His first show-business client was Fran

Allison, the star of the National Broadcasting Corporation's popular TV puppet show, *Kukla, Fran and Ollie*. Allison had come to Basil's to get her hair done and bought a hat Fro thought was "terrible, just terrible," but a week later she was back and ordered eight more. Allison recommended Fro to a friend of hers who was the wife of the president of RCA Whirlpool, and she ordered four hats. Deborah Kerr soon followed as a customer, then Perle Mesta, Gloria Swanson, Kim Novak and June Allyson all made the pilgrimage to the basement of the Ambassador. It was Allyson who introduced him to Hedda Hopper, who of course was famous for her hats, and gave him his first national exposure.

As his charm and confidence increased, Fro became chummy enough with a few of his customers to occasionally be invited to a cocktail party or to tea. The young milliner would so charm his hosts and the other guests that a return invitation was practically ensured, as were several visits to his shop. Fro's biggest admirer was a wealthy eccentric in her late sixties named Annie Goodman, who claimed she was related to a famous Chicago family who owned theaters. "She was the embodiment of Auntie Mame," said Medford Lange, one of Chicago's top florists at the time and a friend of Basil and Fro's. Goodman wore her hair in a bowl-like haircut with jagged bangs and was always very dressed up, usually bedecked with large jewels or sometimes a trademark white cashmere sweater with a white fox collar. She lived with a servant at the Belden Stratford residential hotel in two apartments that had been merged into one large suite. In her later years, when she broke her hip, she would frequently entertain from her bed. "She always called Fro 'My darling Hal,' " Lange remembered. "He was really nobody at the time, but she'd buy a dozen of his hats at a crack at fifty bucks apiece and give them to anyone who would accept them, just to support him." Fro became one of Annie Goodman's favorite escorts, and they saw each other frequently for the next several years, often indulging in late, drunken nights on the town. One cold Chicago night one of Basil's stylists was walking by the Drake Hotel when he noticed a limousine pull up and and Fro and Annie and Basil got out of the back and stumbled up the front entrance together, drunk and happy.

WITH ALL ROY Halston Frowick's success, the one thing that seemed lacking in his happy scenario was money. Basil allegedly took 80 percent of the hat-sale profits on the theory that he had funded the millinery enterprise in the first place and was giving Fro free retail space. True enough, but perhaps more important to Basil was that control over the money also gave him some semblance of control over Fro—who was, indeed, a handsome young man with a wandering eye. As Fro became better known and started to turn into something of local personality himself, Basil couldn't help noticing how popular he had become with other, younger, men who would give Fro *those* looks and flirt with him at parties. So, Basil began to realize that, as his emotional hold on Fro became more tenuous, a way to keep a sure grip on his protégé was money.

For his part, Fro could be rather demanding in terms of tapping Basil's resources; he always did have grandiose schemes. Only the best was good enough for him, be it wine or shoes or crystal. By the end of their first year together, Fro decided that the two-bedroom apartment in the Reynolds mansion was too small for them: he needed more space for his millinery supplies. One day while walking Onka near the Ambassador he found the perfect place for him and Basil to move to: an enormous town house at 1250 State Street. It was four stories high with a two-car garage. The rent was extravagant, however, and Basil refused to pay it. But Fro was so in love with the idea of living in a huge mansion that he came up with a scheme: they could share the house with two or three other men who would pay a share of the rent. The house was so big, after all, he reasoned, that four or five people could live in it without hardly ever running into one another. One tenant would be Halston's former roommate from his basement apartment on Astor Street, Mark Lowell, who worked for Blue Cross/Blue Shield. Another would be Dale Blood, Basil's ex-lover, who still worked as a stylist in the Ambassador salon, and Blood's new friend, Ernest Settles, who at the time, coincidentally, also worked for Blue Cross/Blue Shield.

But Dale Blood was dubious about living with Basil and Fro and another person. "That many people wouldn't get along under one roof," Blood said, "and I told them that I wouldn't do it. Yet the place did have a two-car garage and I had a car. So I thought maybe I'd do it if I could have the master bedroom. There was one master bedroom with a little sitting room and fireplace, and I told Fro that I'd do it if I get the master suite. He acted surprised that I would even suggest it."

"But *I* get the master bedroom, of course," Fro told him. "I found the place and what with my sewing machine and hats and everything . . ."

Blood gave in—but he and Ernest Settles only promised to stay on for a trial basis of one year. "Within a few days it didn't look like things would work out," said Blood. "I had my idea of where to put furniture and Fro had his. He was terribly grand and liked the Empire look. We liked traditional. We worked it out in the end, only because I began to realize that he had much better ideas than I did."

The town house was run like a commune, with Basil in his role of "den father to everybody," according to one visitor. Household chores were divided Monday through Thursday. "I cooked on Monday," Blood remembered, "Ernest on Tuesday, Fro cooked on Wednesday, and on the weekends everybody went their own way." The den was Basil's private office, and he retired there each night to work on the books of the salon. "Basil claimed poverty all the time," said Blood, "but he made tremendous money."

Fro, when he was at home, could usually be found comfortably situated in an old Heritage armchair that belonged to Ernie Settles. "He'd sit in that damn chair every night with his stick pins," said Settles, "and he would whip up dozens of hats." Ernie also remembered that when he got bored or in a silly mood Fro used to like to dress up in drag and imitate female stars, especially Carol Channing, his favorite. "He'd love to get up and dress like her on Saturday night and he'd sneak down the alley in women's clothes to Mitchell's Restaurant on the corner and give them a good laugh."

True to their word, Blood and Settles pulled out of the arrangement after a year and moved to their own apartment for some peace and privacy. Unwilling to pay for the town house on their own, Basil and Halston moved into one of Chicago's newest and most glamorous apartment buildings. This impressive edifice was designed by Mies van der Rohe at 910 Lakeshore Drive, with wraparound views of the lake and the city skyline. Basil took a three-bedroom apartment so that there would be a workroom for Fro as well as guest accommodations.

When Basil and Fro first met, Basil had dazzled the young man from the Midwest with tales of his European adventures and the forty-two transatlantic crossings he had made by ocean liner. He promised that he would take Fro to Europe for his first time, and in 1956 he made good on that promise in a grand way. They set off from New York in late spring on the *Liberté*, bound for Le Havre. Dale Blood was left in charge of the salon, and he and Ernest Settles went to New York with Basil and Fro to see them off—as did Fro's older brother, Bob, and his sister, Sue. On board with them was a 1955 Cadillac convertible, Onka in a special kennel, and "a lot of luggage," according to Basil's older niece, Gerde Sayles, who was also with them.

It took eight days of food and drink and clear skies to reach Le Havre. There they had the Cadillac unloaded and, with the top down, they drove to Paris, arriving by nightfall for dinner and a stroll on the Champs-Élysée. A motor trip though the spectacular scenery of the Alps followed as they made their way to the family home, Erkheim, in the southern part of Germany near the Swiss border. It was in Erkheim that Fro first met Basil's niece, Sieglinde "Mausy" Sayles, then a pretty teenager. Mausy remembers how proud Basil was of his young friend and how deeply in love with him he seemed. She, too, found Fro captivating and hung on his every word as he sat on a bed in the guest room and told stories of growing up in the Midwest. At first Fro didn't even seem to notice Mausy was alive, but then later in the day he snapped her bra strap, which so mortified her that she didn't talk to him for the rest of the trip. A few years later, when Mausy moved to Chicago and joined Basil's business, she would become one of Fro's closest friends.

Back in Chicago, Basil and Fro each recounted their own version of the vacation. Basil told friends that Fro behaved like a prima donna, and that when they would arrive at a hotel, Fro would grandly walk out of the car with Onka on her leash and into the lobby while Basil struggled with the luggage and bellhops. When Dale Blood asked Fro what he thought of Europe, he sniffed out just one word: "provincial."

If the truth be known: Basil loved it when Fro was behaved in a grand manner. There was no wrong that Roy Frowick could do in his eyes. "There are no words to describe Basil's infatuation with him," said a close friend. "It was even more than an infatuation to Basil because Fro was partly his creation. Fro was already a personality as a milliner, especially for Chicago. He had *bloomed*." And once he'd seen "Paree," it was going to be hard keeping him down on the farm.

"But Basil was a Cancer," cautioned Walter Gros, another of Basil's lovers, "and once he got his hooks into you, he would never let you go."

IT WAS PEG Swecker who first arranged for Fro to meet Lilly Daché on one of her trips to Chicago, and although Fro was difficult to impress, he was thrilled at the thought of meeting the legendary French-born milliner. By then nearly seventy years old, Daché owned her own fashion "house" in New York on East Fifty-sixth Street in which she gave spectacular fashion shows in the great Parisian tradition. Born in Bèigles, France, she arrived in the U.S. when she was sixteen and got her first job when she saw a sign in a shop window that said MILLINER WANTED; she later bought the shop. Part of her legend was that she made her first hat—a turban, which became her trademark style—from scraps of material she found lying on the shop floor. The septuagenarian milliner and her husband, Jean Despres, an executive at Coty, Inc., were among the most esteemed figures in fashion.

Daché occasionally came to Chicago to make promotional appearances at the department stores that carried her hats, and Peg Swecker was one of her favorite journalists. Swecker had told Daché all about Fro and Daché promised that the next time she came to Chicago she would stay at the Ambassador Hotel and meet the young man who had all the fashionable women talking.

In the autumn of 1956 Daché was in town for a personal appearance at Marshall Field's and to attend one of the city's great annual society balls. The day of the ball, Daché mentioned to Swecker that she wanted to wear a ribbon around her neck that night. "It was years before women heard the word about face-lifts," Swecker said, "and some women wore ribbons to hide the wrinkles" Swecker seized the opportunity and brought Daché down to Basil's salon to meet Fro to see his hats and fancy ribbons.

"The first time I ever saw Halston," Daché said, "he was a baby. Innocent. Do you know what innocent means? He was wearing a navy blue sailor jacket in the cellar in the hotel in Chicago where there was a beauty salon. The salon belonged to a very grand man who had a big poodle. And Halston was just hanging around there. It was the first year Wallis Simpson came to the United States after marrying Edward and she was wearing a beanie. Everyone started wearing a beanie and there was Halston in the cellar making beanies in his little blue suit. He offered to come to my suite to sew for me."

Fro later appeared in Daché's hotel suite dressed in a conservative blue blazer and gray flannel slacks. "He was being very charming when he got to my suite," Daché said. Fro told her that he had brought with him the perfect ribbons to complement the colors of her dress. He produced a few, and he and Daché chose one. "But you know," he said to her confidentially as he fitted the ribbon around her neck, "your dress is too busy for this pin." He indicated a diamond brooch that Daché had pinned to the bodice of her gown. Then, unexpectedly, he plucked the pin off her chest and repinned it to the ribbon, which he had turned down in some clever manner.

Daché studied herself in the mirror and smiled. "I thought . . . I would invite Halston to come back with me," she said. "He was handsome and clean and simple. It was obvious he was from a good background. I needed someone like that to be polite to the clients. He was big, with blue eyes. He looked so much the part. Those Scandinavian types always do."

Fro said he had no plans to leave Chicago, but if he ever did decide to leave, he would look her up.

It was true that Fro had no plans to leave Chicago, but when Basil heard of Daché's offer he felt so deeply threatened that he was forever thereafter angry with Peg Swecker for having even made the introduction. Yet on the surface it didn't seem that Basil had any reason at all to worry about losing his young lover. Things were still unfolding splendidly for Fro in Chicago, and by 1957 his millinery business had outgrown the small space at the Ambassador and Basil opened up yet another salon for him, which they called the Boulevard Salon. This salon, on the second floor at 900 Michigan Avenue, devoted half of some several thousand square feet to Fro's hats. Decorated elegantly in black and green, it boasted a proper showroom for Fro's hats as well as a large workroom for custom work. The Boulevard Salon opened on February 18, 1957, with a gala attended by the great society women of Chicago. In Fro's first big out-of-town press, *Women's Wear Daily* noted the premiere of the "Boulevard Collection" by Halston, a "custom made line distinguished by fresh, sophisticated, wearable shapes," priced from $25 to $35. *Women's Wear* noted that "it is designed and sold by Halston in a twin-salon setup with Basil, hairstylist, under the theme of coordinating coiffures and millinery." The hats were described as bright pink and floral silk contrasting with white straw bodies and yellow chiffon scarfs. "Taffeta is worked as petals in layers," said *Women's Wear,* and one scarf that matched a silk hat in a peacock print was "swirled to a peak."

IT WAS AROUND the time when the Boulevard Salon opened that Basil discovered Fro was having an affair. One of Fro's friends from the time remembered that this new suitor was a "second string" Italian hairdresser named Ludi; another remembered that Fro had fallen in love with a French translator he had met on one of his increasingly frequent marketing trips to New York. Whoever it was, Basil was suspicious by nature and realized that something was amiss. After an angry, drunken confrontation just before Christmas of 1957, Fro admitted to Basil that he was in love with someone new. Yet, Fro protested, he still loved Basil and there was no reason for doom and gloom. He didn't want to leave Basil; he just needed to have this affair on the side. He asked that Basil be patient and even suggested that perhaps his new *amour* could move in with him and Basil and that all three could live together, just the way they had lived with Basil's former lover Dale Blood.

Basil went into a rage at the suggestion. He would not hear of such an arrangement. He was prepared to share Fro with no one, and he warned darkly that if Fro did not stop seeing this man immediately, there would be hell to pay. He reminded Fro that everything—the business, the apartment, the car, the bank accounts—was all in Basil's name, that on paper Fro owned *nothing*, and that if Fro did not disavow this relationship Basil would take everything away and turn him out in the street, just like that.

Fro, too, had a temper—the J.E. temper—and he did not take kindly to threats and stipulations about his life. He let it be known that he intended to continue to see his new friend and defiantly took to spending the night away from the Lake Shore Drive apartment he shared with Basil. When he and Basil ran into each other at the Boulevard Salon, there was blood in their eyes. The tensions of the impending Christmas holidays finally brought the situation to a head. One night at the apartment with the Christmas tree all decorated, distraught over losing Fro, Basil got very drunk and had a wild showdown with him. In the middle of a screaming argument, Basil produced a revolver and threatened to kill both of them. Fro almost died of fright.

But if Fro was frightened by Basil and the gun, he was mortified by Basil's next threat. Over the last few weeks, Basil had paid a private detective to follow Fro and his young lover. The two had been secretly photographed, and Basil produced a set of explicit photographs of Fro and his friend *in flagrante delicto*. Overwhelmed by despair and revulsion, Fro burned the set of photos Basil showed him, but Basil didn't care; Basil had dozens of sets of prints, and the negatives were safely stored in a safe deposit box. If Fro didn't come home to Basil and start behaving himself, Basil intended to destroy every last shred of Roy Frowick's dignity by sending the photographs to his family back home.

WHATEVER THREATS BASIL ultimately carried out against Fro are buried with him, for Basil died in 1984 at age sixty-seven. Certainly the blackmail threats clearly took their toll. Fro later told friends of "terrible scenes" and "a nightmare" in Chicago. Badly frightened and depressed, he met one last time with his dear friend and booster, Lucia Perrigo. "I have to leave town," Fro told her.

"But *why?*" Lucia demanded.

"I *have* to leave," Fro told her. "I'm kind of being run out of town."

Lucia couldn't believe what she was hearing. "Run out?" she asked, "By whom?"

"It's like a kangaroo court," he said. "Among Basil and his friends. I won't have any friends if I stay here. I'll be shunned." Lucia stared at him blankly for a second, and then Halston smiled sadly. "You don't even know what I'm talking about," he said, and Lucia said she didn't.

Lucia couldn't understand how anyone could be powerful enough to intimidate Fro that much. But their florist friend, Medford Lange, remembered the damage Basil was capable of inflicting. One day he was lunching with Annie Goodman at the Camelia House at the Drake Hotel when they were approached by a friend of Basil's. "Tell her the truth about Fro," the man demanded of Medford. "Tell her what an opportunist he is." But Lange kept his mouth shut. "Basil never got over him," said Med Lange. *"Never."*

Years later, when Basil died, Walter Gros tried calling Halston several times in New York to give him the sad news, but he could never get past Halston's secretary.

Fro left Chicago shortly after New Year's of 1959. However, for the rest of his life he would make this date a year or two earlier, almost as if by changing the year he could deny what had happened. On his penultimate trip to New York to make final arrangements with Lilly Daché, he had reserved a certain room at the Waldorf-Astoria Hotel that he remembered fondly from his various trips to that city with Basil. But when he arrived at the desk he was told the specific room wasn't available. In his grandest manner, he made a huge stink, saying that he had stayed at all the great hotels in Europe and how poorly the Waldorf compared and so intimidated the staff that they finally gave him a suite at the single-room rate to appease him.

Upstairs in the suite he looked around at the splendor and decided why let it go to waste? So he sat down and called every fashion editor and journalist he could think of in New York and set up a series of interviews to let them know, to let everybody know:

Roy Halston Frowick was coming to town.

3

THE HATMAKER

To dwell on the past, said Halston, "is to pull yourself down." Nostalgia, he said, was "dangerous."

So, a new beginning at seventy-five dollars a week. This time he arrived in New York with no fanfare—this time not expected at the Waldorf-Astoria, but at the apartment of a twenty-one-year-old window dresser named Arthur Williams whom Lilly Daché had sent to greet him at the Port Authority Bus Terminal. Williams was a small and wiry young man with blond hair and twinkling blue eyes. A native New Yorker who had attended the Parsons School of Design, Williams was destined to become Halston's best friend in New York. "Halston was the most charismatic, the most exciting, the most interesting man I ever knew," said Williams. "For the next ten years, I lived, ate, and breathed Halston."

"The day before I went to pick him up," Williams said, "Daché said to me, 'I found this wonderful boy in Chicago. He's just what I need,' she said. 'New, fresh, and young.' I asked her how to recognize him and she said, 'He's tall and plain'—that's how she described him. So I went off to the bus station and I saw this kid get off the bus. He was all done up. He had his blazer on and gray flannels and he was expecting to be met by somebody far more important than I was. He wasn't plain, but he had this midwestern sort of face—'puddin' face' is the only way to describe it. I introduced myself and said, 'Hi, I'm to take you to my apartment—which is a little forward—but as I understand it, you have no place to stay and I have a two-bedroom apartment.' And I did have just that, a two-bedroom at Sixty-third and Park, because I was a kept boy myself.''

Halston went home with Williams that night, consummated their friendship (''It was terrific,'' said Williams), and thereafter the two became fast friends. ''You had to like him the moment you talked to him,'' Williams said. ''You could immediately see he had charisma. Even in a city as devastating as New York can be to a stranger, he was totally in charge of himself. He was no bullshit, he was true, direct, and straightforward. And grandeur was second nature to him.''

The next morning Halston arrived at Lilly Daché's salon on East Fifty-sixth Street off Park Avenue. It was a beautiful sandstone building, with a dramatically elegant spiral staircase just inside the front doors. The interior was decorated in eighteenth-century-style furniture, accented with blackamoors and brass palm trees. A bastion of pleasure for wealthy women, it boasted not only Daché's famous millinery salon, but also a small *prêt-à-porter* department and a luxurious beauty salon.

Daché was a tough old hen who had worked hard to get where she was and expected total dedication from her employees. She had a good eye for talented young people, and over the years many important names in fashion worked for her, including the hairdresser Kenneth Battelle, who would later become known as Mr. Kenneth, and Arnold Isaacs, who later became world famous as the designer Arnold Scassi. ''She was often a wild, undisciplined, and neurotic woman,'' said Williams, ''but she could teach you everything about hats there was to know if you were willing to be used as an apprentice.'' And apprentices there were aplenty. Although the facade of Daché's was grand, behind the glamorous front working conditions were less than ideal. There was an un-air-conditioned workroom crowded with "a group of mostly French girls who were hunchbacked for life," contended Williams, "because they sat at their sewing machines on one level, then you had four little steps to a second level where there was a platform built right over the heads of the first one. After the hat was blocked below it was handed up and the next girl would sew on the top. They were all miraculously talented and really the only ones who knew how to make flowered hats and turbans," Williams said. "Daché was so frugal that at the end of each day we had to pick up the thread that was lying on the floor and knot it together so we had a full spool for the following morning." She would also test her design employees by giving them ten dollars and sending them out into the marketplace to see what kind of supplies they would get. When they returned with their purchases, Daché would shout at them, "Is that all you got for ten dollars! How stupid!"

Halston was given a place at a "design table." "Altogether I had eight designers," was the way Daché described it, "all of them at one large table, sitting together. Halston would schmooze with them. There were gloves and dresses and everything there to inspire him. He was innocent and willing," Daché said. "He knew nothing when he came to me, nothing. But Halston was a very, very fast learner. He watched everything. His eyes would soak in everything. In my shop there was an ambience you could learn from."

Halston quickly proved himself to be a hardworking and dedicated employee. "He was devoted to one goal," said Williams, "and that was to be successful." He was so seemingly dedicated it made others around him a little nervous. He arrived at work early each day and stayed long after the others had left, often past nine o'clock at night to fill back orders. When he was alone he would go through the design books of the other designers and copy their sketches. He did this not to plagiarize, but to educate himself and improve upon the sketches, as he invariably did. "There was such complaining about how he would copy everyone's sketches after the head designer went home," said Daché. "The staff didn't like him snooping around. But he was like a sponge. He was learning being there in the soup with them. He thought he deserved to see everything because he worked so hard."

After a short time he became something of a favorite of Daché's and she would invite him to have lunch with her—a travail for Halston, much to the mirth of his friends, because of Daché's "gas problems." All through their many lunches, Halston complained, the elderly Daché would pass gas uncontrollably. Halston was obligated to maintain a straight face while he kept up a stream of conversation. Halston said that Daché kept a large atomizer of her favorite scent nearby, and after she farted she would spray the perfume around. "I was never able to eat," Halston confided. "I was dying."

Daché's chief millinery designer was called Miss Emily. Miss Emily was the only one of the designers with a private office. She was a small, dour woman whose creations had been worn by all the great ladies of society. She was also a woman who understood that she owed her position of prominence to Lilly Daché. To her, Halston was an upstart, and sure enough before long Halston became determined to put together his own collection of hats, working on his own time, much to the chagrin of Miss Emily. "Miss Emily was deaf," said Williams, "and when Halston went on about the direction of millinery, Miss Emily turned her hearing aid off and continued making her turbans and flowers."

Halston finally convinced Daché to allow him to present to the public his own small collection of hats which Williams remembered as "oversized, overscaled, and very simplified." It included a "Sou'wester," designed so that the whole hat leaned east as if the wind were blowing the brim up, and many wide-brimmed hats with veils and big pins. The collection was an instant and smashing success with the customers. "We did more numbers with his hats that season than we had in five seasons," said Williams. "It would mean the alienation of Emily and the appreciation of Lilly Daché for a long time."

Indeed, after only a year with Lilly Daché, Halston was named co-designer with Miss Emily: nothing less than a triumph for a twenty-seven-year-old from nowhere.

Arthur Williams remembers that Halston "could take the dreariest day at Lilly Daché's and turn it into something glamorous and marvelous. He could be with you for just fifteen minutes and you would think that God had come into the room because nobody could contradict anything he said. He had some sort of authority that most people didn't have. He could totally captivate you. He could convince you the moon was made of blue cheese."

HIS FIRST APARTMENT in New York was a small, shabby walk-up above an art gallery on Madison Avenue between Sixtieth and Sixty-first streets, which he shared with a young French friend, Norbert Percell. This apartment was reportedly so rundown and poorly furnished that Halston never invited his friends there. But inviting people over wasn't Halston's idea of a social life anyway. "Halston knew how to cultivate," said Arthur Williams, and his climbing instinct to attach himself to the rich and famous brought him into many exotic circles in New York. "Halston had this proclivity," said Arthur Williams, "that the best was none too good for him. He wanted to know and assimilate the brains of the best, to understand how they ticked and what made them the way they are." One great personality and genius of his own time he befriended was Salvador Dali. Halston had been introduced to Dali by Nanita Kalachnikoff, a former Miss Spain (thirty years before) who was the *première vendeuse* at Lilly Daché's and an intimate friend of Dali's. Kalachnikoff "fell wildly in love with Halston," remembered Arthur Williams, and always took him with her when she went to visit Dali at the St. Regis, where he stayed every fall on his annual trip to New York. Along with his wife, Gala, Dali embarked on a social whirlwind in which Halston tagged along with Kalachnikoff. Dali was a rather shocking personality for Halston. He generally insulted people, causing a scene everywhere he went—and Halston loved it.

In time, however, Dali grew jealous of the attention that Kalachnikoff was showering on Halston, and one night at the King Cole Bar Dali decided to ridicule Halston in front of her. Dali, his wife, Gala, Kalachnikoff, and Halston were all getting drunk at a table when Dali disappeared for several minutes before returning with two sailors in white dress uniforms he had found on Fifth Avenue. The sailors recognized the great artist, and Dali promised them a drink and "a gift" if they accompanied him to the King Cole Bar. The sailors were marched up to the round table where Halston sat with Arthur Williams and Kalachnikoff.

"Here is the gift I promised you"—Dali announced very loudly and grandly, gesturing to Halston—"the best cocksucker in New York."

There was a moment of shocked silence. The sailors glared at Halston and then at Dali. Halston looked as if he wanted to kill. For a moment the tension rose so high that it seemed the sailors might take a punch at somebody. At that point, Halston let out a big horselaugh and said to them, "Sit down, boys, and have a drink. Have a *couple* of drinks." The two sailors then sheepishly sat down and got drunk with them.

Dali was an impressive friend for a young milliner, but in Halston's eyes he was only a footnote of his youth compared with the deep influence of the designer Charles James. James was then in his mid-sixties, and for Halston, James was the "Leonardo da Vinci" of dressmaking. Halston had first met James in 1958, having been introduced by Peg Swecker when James briefly passed through Chicago, the city in which James had also started his career. It wasn't until they remet in New York while Halston was at Daché's, however, that they "took each other up," in the words of one friend. It was James who introduced Halston to many important social and business contacts in New York, and it was James who was to become a profound—and prophetic—influence on Halston.

Born in England in 1908, James was a small man with thinning hair that he dyed shoe-polish jet black, two thin slashes of dyed eyebrows, and the features of a ventriloquist's puppet. Sent to America by his family to become a businessman, he instead began a fashion career in Chicago—as a milliner. James had gone on to become one of the great masters of the ball gown. There was a fantastical quality to his visions, and in his entire career he produced only 200 dresses. His seminal dress, the "Lampshade" was a long, strapless gown with a skirt so intricately laden with boning that it stood away from the body like a lampshade. His "Ribbon Dress" was a swirling rapture of ribbons six inches wide at the hem, narrowing to one-eighth of an inch at the waist. Perhaps his single most famous dress was called the "Four-Leaf Clover," designed in 1953 for Austine Hearst, with four distinct petals to the dress. James viewed his dresses the same way a great painter or sculptor would look upon his work. James was known to spend several years and twenty thousand dollars just to get the sleeve on a dress to hang the way he wanted it to. Balenciaga called him "the greatest couturier in the world," and he was perhaps one of the few designers to elevate fashion into fine art.

Alas, James was also an egomaniacal madman who destroyed his life and his career. When Halston first met him, James had already gone bankrupt several times and been involved in lengthy lawsuits with people who he claimed had stolen his designs. At one point he reportedly had seventy-five lawsuits going at the same time, and he spent so many years in court that he learned to be his own lawyer. An extended and celebrated lawsuit in 1955 had practically ruined him financially; yet he could not, or would not, come to recognize that the fashion industry was all about copying. James continued to lead a self-debilitating campaign against people who he believed had wronged him. Although he had won two Coty Awards and a Neiman-Marcus Award, he had returned all three. He was a man of spiteful whimsy who would sometimes deliver a gown to a woman in time for her ball, or sometimes not. He was also known to borrow back gowns that he had created for clients and lend them to other customers for a fee—or sometimes deliver a gown to a client after dancing in it all night himself. He once sent a flower box to fashion business publicist Eleanor Lambert, who had testified against him in one of his many lawsuits, and when she opened the box, hundreds of moths flew out.

He was, most of all, an *artiste,* and Halston was enthralled with him. For a long period they had dinner two or three nights a week. "Halston fed off Charlie," said Arthur Williams, and James became a confidant and mentor to the young milliner. James was grand, Halston became grander. James's favorite champagne was Moët and Chandon; it became Halston's favorite. James's favorite flowers were orchids; orchids would not only become Halston's favorite flower, they would become his trademark bloom. Halston began to look at cut and construction through James's eye, and his fashion vision broadened. "Charles James played a very important part in my life," Halston later admitted in a dry understatement. "He introduced me to a 'higher' element in fashion. I am a great admirer of his."

James grandly described Halston's interest in him as "one who much admired my creativity [and] envied my position in fashion." He would later claim credit for most of the important points in Halston's career, including bringing him to New York and getting him employed at Daché and later Bergdorf Goodman. By the time Halston and James became friends in New York, James was living in a rented studio apartment at the Chelsea Hotel with a Beagle dog he kept tied on a leash to the doorknob, and if he was drunk or stoned enough he might answer the door in his underwear. When he was sober and functioning, however, he was enormous fun, knowledgeable, and unpredictable. One night while having dinner together in a Greenwich Village restaurant that catered to gay men, James and Halston got roaring drunk. Through the restaurant window they noticed that out on the street there was a huge police horse with a policeman in full regalia sitting on it. Suddenly James snatched a china plate from the table and ran out into the street where he hit the horse hard on the ass. The horse reared up in the air and nearly threw the policeman to the ground. On another evening James lectured Halston on dressmaking while urinating in the street.

"Halston learned a great deal from Charles James about designing and the world of style and society," said Lilly Daché, "and probably other things too."

FOR THOSE "OTHER things" Daché was referring to, Halston didn't need Charles James to teach him—indeed, he didn't need anybody. He adapted quite well to the fast-lane sexual smorgasbord offered by a city as big and open as New York. He virtually fell in love with the beauty and freedom of the Fire Island Pines, a wealthy homosexual resort community where Arthur Williams first took him the summer of 1959. Fire Island is an attenuated thirty-mile wisp of sand down the southern coast of Long Island composed of several isolated communities, most only accessible by water ferry or seaplane. With no cars and only a network of narrow wooden boardwalks over the sand, Fire Island is a dreamily lush environment. Although there are several straight, family-oriented communities farther west, the Pines and its sister community, Cherry Grove, were all about sex. It motivated them like a power generator. The Pines and Cherry Grove were connected by a vast, shadowy pine barren known as the "meat rack." Said a friend who first met Halston on Fire Island, "He loved being in the Pines because it gave him the opportunity to be wildly promiscuous."

For the next six or seven years, from March to the end of September, Halston's weekends were spent mostly in the Fire Island Pines. It became a pressure release from all the formality and propriety of his weekdays with the ladies. Every Friday he would leave Manhattan by 6 P.M. in the Volkswagen bus of Don Ritchie, Arthur Williams's roommate, and head out in traffic on the Long Island Expressway to catch the ferry in Sayville. There was a mattress in the back of the bus and while they were stopped in traffic Halston would curl up and go to sleep, admonishing, "Don't wake me until we get to the boat."

Arthur Williams owned the house that he and Halston shared for the next eight or so summers (and would later own twenty more, buying, renovating, and selling them). "Our house in the Pines was like a commune," said Williams. "Halston chipped in with everybody, he cleaned, washed windows, and followed the rules." There was one house rule, which was that you could not invite people to stay over with you. "We didn't want a bunch of funny people waking up and have to make breakfast for them." That seemed all right with Halston, who stayed up till dawn each night in the meat rack and preferred to wake up alone.

It was also in the Pines that Halston first started regularly using marijuana. "He loved smoking grass," said Williams, "We had never heard of this and one weekend he brought out fifteen joints. That night he turned on all the guys in the house and you can imagine the catastrophe. They were wearing Chinese kimonos, acting crazy. They started to make chocolate cake and I hate to tell you what the house looked like the next morning. After that Halston was always smoking on the weekends, hot and heavy. One time he brought a pound of it out and sold it to everybody."

It was a tradition in the Pines to give elaborate theme parties, a "white" party or "black" party or "Heavenly Bodies" party and for these Halston went all out. He spent weeks of preparation for himself and his friends. Milton Buras, a successful hairstylist and friend of Halston's from the Pines, remembered, "He loved theme parties and he would go to any extreme. I remember that for a Cleopatra party we actually got some gal to crawl into a rug and be rolled up."

It was also in the Pines in 1964 that Halston met Joanne Crevelling, a business executive at Macy's with an astute eye for fashion. For the next several years, Crevelling became one of Halston's closest friends and business associates. "The one amazing thing was that Halston and I were both the same height, both tall and skinny, and we both had the same skin color. He looked at me when I met him on Fire Island and said, 'I'm going to like you very much, I think we should become friends.' And we did. We spent two or three summers together every weekend, and Halston had an incredible sense of humor, so all we did was laugh."

Crevelling remembered going with Halston to one party in the Pines where everyone dressed as a celebrity. *Life* magazine had just done a story on Siamese twins joined at the hip, Mascha and Dascha, and Halston decided to go as them. "He called up Beckstein, the shirt man, and Continental Tailors, the pant man, and he had clothes made up, big enough for two people, attached at the hip by a big Russian belt through both sets of belt loops."

But not everyone liked Halston as much as Joanne Crevelling. "He was piss-elegant," said an antique dealer who knew him on Fire Island during that period, "A pissy queen with these grand ideas." Arthur Williams agreed: "Glassware had to be crystal and it had to be Baccarat. At Christmas we had to give everybody things from Tiffany, there was no other way." Arthur Williams bought Halston his first Pekingese dog, named Keku, who sat on Halston's lap like a little baby. Williams remembers that on a long weekend car trip to Vermont in a snowstorm, Halston kept insisting that Williams stop the car every hour or so so he could get out in the swirling flakes and put a piece of newspaper in the snow in front of the headlights for Keku to take a tinkle on.

Halston's Fire Island acquaintance Milton Buras also remembered that everything to Halston was "amuuuusing," pronounced in a drawn-out and sarcastic manner. People he was attracted to were "amuuuusing . . ." as well as people he wanted to ridicule. And he didn't mind ridicule. He had a very wicked tongue and showed a cruel streak when he wanted to. He didn't like Jews very much (or blacks or Puerto Ricans, but especially not Jews). Arthur Williams says he remembers one time when he said to somebody very offhandedly, "The only thing wrong with you is you're Jewish!" Occasionally, the J.E. temper would flare up. One day on Fire Island, Williams was throwing a stick into the bay for his own dogs to catch and Keku ran in the water after it and nearly drowned. Halston went into a frenzy. "He accused me of luring his dog into the bay so it would drown," said Williams, and "slapped me in the face, leaving a red welt that remained for days."

FOR AN AMBITIOUS young man, a job with Lilly Daché, however prestigious, was still only a middle-level position in the millinery business, and also a dead end; nobody was going to get more important at Lilly Daché's than Lilly Daché herself. Even more so, life with Daché had its wild peaks and valleys, and sometimes things could turn very nasty. One major flap was over Halston's largesse in saying to some fashion-magazine editors "keep it" after they had borrowed hats from Daché for use in photo shoots. Although the editors loved him for it, Daché was incensed and warned him several times that her creations were not his to give away. During Halston's first Christmas at Lilly Daché's she tore up an envelope in front of his eyes that allegedly held his Christmas bonus and said, "That's what you get for giving away my hats!"

The following Easter brought the the differences between Halston and Daché to a head. Easter Sunday and the Easter Parade still constituted the biggest day of the year in terms of exposure for millinery. And for a long time, all the top hat designers had appeared on TV during the parade with girls modeling their hats. That Easter, Halston was with the Daché contingent, showing hats and chatting to passersby and the press, when a Daché house model named Debbie asked Halston if she could wear a hat he had designed because she had been "asked out by some john for tea at the Plaza." She promised to return the hat to the salon in the morning, and Halston told her it was okay. Later that afternoon, Lilly Daché and her husband were having tea themselves at the Plaza Hotel when they saw Debbie wearing the hat. Daché approached the girl in a rage, snatched the hat from her head, and caused a scene. Debbie explained that Halston had given her permission to wear it.

The next morning, two policemen arrived at Halston's door to tell him of the charges Daché had levied against him. He was not arrested, but to get Daché to drop the charges, Arthur Williams had to explain that the hat was only borrowed and would have been back on the racks that very morning. Halston was seething with anger and muttering threats, but by that afternoon he had relented and was persuaded to come back to work. From that moment on, however, he couldn't wait to leave Lilly Daché.

He didn't have to wait long. One day soon after, Halston was having lunch with with Charles James at La Côte Basque when Edwin Goodman, the president of Bergdorf Goodman, was seated next to them. Goodman was having lunch with his family and one of his favorite employees, Jessica Daubé, the co-head of the millinery department. Daubé had been anointed the "High Priestess of Millinery" by photographer Cecil Beaton. Daubé wasn't primarily a designer, but she was the millinery department's *premiere vendeuse*, credited with selling $2 million a year worth of hats. Of course, she already knew all about Halston. Bergdorf was doing all the bridal costumes for the John Mills wedding, one of the big society events of the year—all except for the bridal hairpiece, which the Mills family had decided to give to Halston at Lilly Daché. Halston had been back and forth to Bergdorf's, consulting with them on fabrics and style. Miss Daubé recognized instantly that he was clearly a brilliant milliner, and, according to Halston, "Miss Jessica felt I must be something special because I was doing this social plum."

Miss Jessica was also having problems with one of her top hat designers, a young Cuban-born man named Adolfo Sardina. Adolfo, as he later became known as a couturier for Nancy Reagan, among others, was at the time a talented milliner who wanted more than just to design hats. Adolfo asked to have his name put on the Bergdorf hat labels and was turned down. The owners and management of Bergdorf did not like to play up individual designers on their staff, the store itself was the calling card. This made the ambitious Adolfo Sardina very unhappy, and when push came to shove he left Bergdorf's employ with little notice, creating an unexpected opening on the staff.

On the fortuitous day at La Côte Basque when they sat near each other, Miss Jessica leaned across her table and said to Halston, "If you're ever going to make a change—come and talk to me."

Not long afterward, Halston had that talk with Jessica Daubé and in early 1959 gave Lilly Daché his notice. He had been in New York for little more than a year.

4

1959 TO 1967:
MR. HALSTON
OF BERGDORF'S

Lilly Daché may have taken him out of the backwater and into the mainstream of New York millinery, but Bergdorf Goodman was about to expose him to the very best in fashion and clientele in all the world.

"By Bergdorf" said the small beige label sewn inside every garment, and that was all it needed to say. Since the turn of the century when two master tailors first founded the firm, the name Bergdorf Goodman meant taste, elegance, and wealth. It was also, in 1959, when Halston joined their staff for a very ungrand $125 a week, the only American store to continue to have line-for-line copies of French couture gowns sewn in their own custom workrooms by a corps of legendary seamstresses. So trusted was the store for its impeccable taste and style that one society customer told *Life* magazine, "If Bergdorf's suggested a well-pressed fig leaf, I'd say okay."

But no need to sell fig leaves. The store's basic customer list of 1,700 women (although everyone was welcomed through their doors) spent close to $20 million a year on clothes. Fifty or so clients spent over $100,000 a year on their wardrobes (although in a year when a woman needed furs, the clothing budget could swell an additional $50,000). One woman ordered fifty suits at a clip, another thought nothing of ordering half a dozen suits at $1,000 a throw, or three or four ball gowns at $10,000 apiece, or a $50,000 sable coat for herself and a $750 Vicuna for her six-year-old daughter. "Bergdorf's exposed me to the very best," gloated Halston. "A suit was one thousand dollars and a blouse five hundred dollars, there was no question. Women bought four and five at a time."

Bergdorf's stands on the corner of Fifth Avenue and 58th Street in the former Vanderbilt Mansion, a handsome nine-story building of white marble flanked on one side by the jewelers Van Cleef & Arpels, and the other by the Pulitzer Memorial Fountain and the southern tip of Central Park. When a customer walked through the revolving glass doors she was transported into a hushed and sobering environment, a series of little shops on six different floors decorated with plush gray carpeting, French antique furniture, and cut-crystal vases of fresh flowers. On each floor there was a *directrice* to greet you, a *vendeuse* to help you with the merchandise, and private antechamber in which to view it. The store boasted constant attention from its 178 saleswomen and 11 salesmen. There were also 12 full-time mannequins to model clothes and two full-time lingerie models. Bergdorf's also stocked, like a great wine cellar, one quarter of a million yards of the finest fabrics available anywhere in the world.

It was here at Bergdorf Goodman that Halston honed the grand persona and exaggerated voice with rounded syllables and affected accent that were to become his personality trademarks. He was referred to, in the stuffy dictum of the store, as "Mr. Halston." Sometimes, in fact, in the midst of a jag on how clever or important he was, he would lapse into the third person himself: "Mr. Halston knows just the hat you need, Madam." "He learned to use that voice and that certain affectation," said Tom Fallon, who was Halston's assistant at Bergdorf's for several years. "He presented what I would describe as 'an appropriate package' at Bergdorf's. Bergdorf was full of 'attitude.' It was a dying carriage trade—and the grandest salon in New York at that point, so Halston's manner was very appropriate. He was also physically beautiful and full of fun, full of mischief in that rather controlled way of his. He was perfect for Bergdorf."

And Bergdorf was perfect for him. Halston was given office space on the mezzanine but he was more often to be found either on the first floor, in the ready-to-wear millinery department with its dark paneled walls and working fireplace, or on the second-floor custom department, with its individual French antique mirrored dressing tables lighted by small pink lamps, or in the tenth-floor custom workrooms, where he reigned over a staff of some 120 "girls," whose median age was sixty-two and whose total weekly output was 125 exquisitely handcrafted hats at a salary of $38 a week.

"You went to your milliner the way you would go to your hairdresser or your psychiatrist," said Leonard Hankin, the store's executive vice president for four decades. "The milliner had all the gossip—who was doing what to whom. After you had your lunch and after you had your two or three drinks, you would come in and you would spend a couple of hours with the salesgirls. It was a high old time, incidentally in the course of which you would buy a hat."

Said Halston, "The Who's Who of the world was always in and out of Bergdorf in those days. First of all, that gives you all the good contacts that one needs . . ." And Halston made contacts galore. It was at Bergdorf's, wrote Francesca Stanfil in *Women's Wear Daily,* that the "ladies began to listen to him." Barbara Hutton's chauffeur would carry the ailing heiress into the store and put her in a chair in front of Halston where she would spend hours. He was the only one in the store Greta Garbo would really talk to, and on a daily basis he sold hats and designed for Mrs. Chiang Kai-shek (after whose sister-in-law he named his Pekingese dog). There was Mrs. William (Babe) Paley, who came to adore him. Mrs. Vincent Astor, Mrs. Paul

Mellon, Mrs. Henry Kaiser. Elsa Maxwell. Fleur Cowles. Mrs. Henry Ford II, Mrs. Edsel Ford, Mrs. Benson Ford, Josephine Ford. Slim Keith. The Duchess of Marlborough. Mrs. Willie K. Vanderbilt. Mrs. Russell Grace, Mrs. Douglas Fairbanks, Jr. Joan Fontaine, Rita Hayworth, Jennifer Jones, Bea Lillie, Judy Holliday, Marlene Dietrich, Mrs. Harlow H. Curtis, Mrs. Agnes Meyer and Gisele MacKenzie.

"Almost from the very start," said Leonard Hankin, "he could take a customer's wish and express it in exactly the way she would want it done. He personalized his hat for the customer. A Halston hat became more than just something you just stuck on your head." His charm was potent, too. "In the beginning," said Hankin, "he was not too New York, not too slick, and he still retained some of the gentility of the Midwest. However, the other people in the store were wary of him, of their customers."

Once the Bergdorf customers discovered him, they couldn't get enough of him. "He could charm man, woman, and beast," said Joanne Crevelling. "He could talk to anyone. He knew just what to say, just what topic would interest you."

Halston had a lot to say about his ladies. Mrs. William S. Paley was "a designer's dream, the most beautiful hair, the most beautiful face." Mrs. Gary Cooper was "a marvelous type." Mrs. Winston Guest had her "own style, her own convictions." The Queen of Thailand came in "with her whole court." One winter he devised a babushka for Anita Loos: "She wanted something to keep her head warm. She wears a little chignon on the top of her head that pushes an ordinary hat out of shape." He made Carol Channing what became a trademark safari hat because she wanted something to cover her thinning hair. It was a design he originally came up with for Mrs. Henry Kaiser to help shield her from the Hawaiian sun on a vacation trip (Mrs. Kaiser ordered a dozen of them when she discovered the pink color matched the exterior of her house.) For Diana Vreeland he made several babushkas for a business trip she took to Bonn in February. He persuaded Mrs. Winston Guest, "who never changes her style," to buy her first cloche hat. "Now I can put it on twelve different women and it will look right," he said. Perle Mesta, another customer, was a role model; "[She has the look of] the average American matron," he said, claiming that if a hat looked good on Perle Mesta, he "could sell hundreds of it." Mrs. Willie Vanderbilt bought her hats by phone, and Halston sent them over to her mansion to try on.

"When I would go to Bergdorf's to look at hats," said Myrna Davis, then an accessories editor for *McCall's* who later became one of Halston's close friends, "I always thought he was beautiful looking, very handsome and very young. He used to dress ultraconservatively, in gray suits and big shoes with thick soles. They turned out to be Loeb shoes, from Paris, which cost several hundred dollars a pair. And I'd say to him, 'Don't you think you ought to wear moccasins?' and he'd say, 'Oh no, a big guy like me, you have to wear this kind of shoes.' He would suggest a hat and I'd say, 'Mr. Halston, I can *not* wear that hat,' and he'd put it on and it would look wonderful."

"Also," said Davis, "when Halston sold a woman a hat, within twenty minutes he could have her buying a chinchilla coat. That was his whole thing. He had a way about him. He talked me into buying a mink coat—'Oh, you should, you must . . .' He was very mischievous that way. He loved the idea of luxury."

The epitome of luxury, for Halston, was Paris. He made his first trip to Paris to see the collections for Bergdorf in 1961 with Ethel Frankau, who was in charge of Bergdorf's custom dress department and went to collections every year to buy up to 200 design models to copy in New York. Frankau was a small, quiet lady who was a former schoolteacher. It was said that Frankau's taste "defined" Bergdorf Goodman's taste. She'd been making the trip to Paris for thirty years and she knew everyone—every designer by first name, every special fabric shop and button store in the city. "I had the advantage of the terrific schooling of a young man sitting in the front row, being one of the young-est persons in the fashion business," Halston said. "Ethel Fran-kau taught me the conservative approach to fashion—what the conservative women wear, which is certainly different from what appears in the press. Ethel and I would go to seventeen complete couture collections plus five devoted solely to hats. Balenciaga was always the last. He was really the great one."

He also made the trip with Jessica Daubé, who "adopted" Halston, according to Hankin. "She really taught me the role of each of the couturiers," Halston said. "I knew Balenciaga, I've stayed with Hubert de Givenchy. I met Coco Chanel. I saw Yves Saint Laurent's first collection. I know things about the history of fashion, why it is the way it is." He not only saw the work of all the major designers, he also watched how they progressed from season to season, how much they had to change, how much they had to throw away. Sometimes he made the trip with Odna Brandeis, another Bergdorf millinery designer, who taught him the location of the secret shops at which to buy the finest silk ribbons or a hidden atelier where an old French woman made the most incredibly realistic silk flowers. He loved Paris and the collections so much that when occasionally Bergdorf did not pay for him to go, he paid his own way. The shows in Paris in those days were laughably stiff, with models smiling ambivalently as they walked woodenly down the runways holding cards with numbers so the buyers could scribble them down. Columnists and copyists were barred from most shows—it was absolutely forbidden to sketch, and strangers were charged a $3,000 admis-sion fee called a *caution*. This made Halston very popular, because with his phenomenal memory and ability to describe in detail what he had seen, entire ensembles and collections could be reconstructed from his words later at lunch or back at the hotel. Of the Paris collections Halston said, "I absorbed lines, proportion, and fabric. Such dedication and thought went into every stitch of those *haute couture* clothes."

After only two years at Bergdorf Goodman he asked that his

name be put on the label of the hats he designed—the same request that got Adolfo fired. Yet after some hesitation, Andrew Goodman agreed and Halston became the store's first name milliner. Without a doubt, he became the most important milliner in the world when in 1963 Jessica Daubé retired and Halston threw her a farewell dinner at the Bijou Restaurant.

Halston's name was soon everywhere. His hats were used almost exclusively as accessories by Norman Norell, then considered America's best designer. Halston became responsible for two millinery collections of fifty new models a season for custom millinery at Bergdorf, as well as designing hats for a dozen Seventh Avenue collections twice a year. A big sable beret sold over a hundred pieces at $1,000 each. He originated the scarf-hat for Bergdorf's, which became a sixties fashion rage, and introduced leather turbans and felt babushkas to the market. The hats proved so popular that Bergdorf began to stage "hat shows" to sell his hats wholesale, at which stores like Marshall Field's and I. Magnin bought about fifty styles of each. The buyers were required to purchase a minimum of six hats to sustain a franchise, but stores like Magnin bought more like eighty, for all its branches. His creative ideas seemed inexhaustible, his passion for his work prodigious; at age twenty-nine he was at the very top of his profession.

That is not to say that all was roses with Halston. He had a quick temper and was easily hurt. And there were moments when one caught a glimpse of a dark side of Halston. "I felt a lot of pain in that man, and I was very aware that this was a young man full of rage," said Tom Fallon. "And I could hear the mechanisms of his voice sharpen and his manners get more harsh when he sensed, I think, that he was being attacked. He would rise up into that Mr. Halston business." Fallon remembers that one day he and Halston went next door to Van Cleef & Arpels where they were greeted by a snooty woman with a French accent. "I am Mr. Halston," he announced to her very grandly, and the woman, to mock him, asked, "Did your secretary make an appointment, Mr. Hal-*stun*?"

Halston's eyes turned to daggers. "Listen, my darling *vendeuse,*" he said in acid tones, "I have the best *vendeuses* in the world working for me, so I don't need your act. Now fetch the manager out here *right now!*"

"It was one of the few times I ever saw him go after somebody like that," said Fallon.

Usually in matters of pride, Halston was exceptionally thin-skinned. In the summer of 1967, Bergdorf Goodman sponsored a fashion show to benefit the Southampton Association at the Meadow Club, one of the world's toniest beach and racquet clubs, and Halston went to Southampton for the weekend. He returned to the store from Long Island on Monday furious over some incident that had occurred while he was away. "That Southampton set," he said. "Who do they think they are?" Fallon asked him what was wrong and Halston said something that stunned him, "Remember this, Tommy—have no illusion about who we are. We are tradespeople to our customers, and we will *never* be socially accepted."

IT WAS ALSO while he was at Bergdorf that another, more subtle, talent emerged—one that would serve him brilliantly in his career: his ability to court and manipulate the press. Shortly after Halston arrived at Bergdorf he became not only the darling of the women who bought, but also of the women who wrote. These were a power crew of journalists and magazine editors with whom he would begin long-lasting and important friendships and who would champion his work for the rest of his career. "His great, great talent was his relationship with the editors and writers," said Leonard Hankin. "His charm, his poise, his looks far transcended any overweening or overriding talent that he had as a milliner. Oh, he was a good milliner, but he was a sensation with the press. They adored him. He made all the girls look smart with their editors. One of the girls on the staff of *Vogue* or *Bazaar* would call him at the store and say she desperately needed a hat for a photography shoot at nine o'clock the next morning. Halston would have all the girls assigned to him in the workroom sew through the night. Every few hours they would bring him a half-finished version and he would say, 'No, not this,' or 'Take this and take it up half an inch,' and when the editor showed up the next morning she'd have the most exquisite hat. Of course, Halston would get editorial credit, and the girl would get all kinds of Brownie points with her editors. So the relationship grew with Halston and the press."

Vogue editor Polly Mellen remembered when she was at *Harper's Bazaar* doing a sitting with the great Russian ballerina Maya Plisetskaya, who was being photographed by top fashion photographer Dick Avedon at his studio. They needed a hat or a headpiece at the last minute and Mellen called Halston. He showed up at Avedon's studio with a box from which he took "incredibly long feathers and burnt ostrich and that wonderful glycerin feather that's black-green" and began to fashion a hat for Plisetskaya. Avedon, who was impatient and nervous about the time, said, "We only have Madame Plisetskaya for the day and the Russian interpreters are waiting."

Mellen remembered Halston saying, "Don't worry, Dick," and in five minutes he produced the most remarkable feathered headpiece.

Halston also became the favorite milliner of Eugenia Sheppard, whose "Inside Fashion" column was the most widely syndicated of all. "Within a few years," said Coty Award–winning designer Clovis Ruffin, who first met Halston when he was at Bergdorf, "Halston had been lunching with everybody who was an editor. He was only a hat designer at the time, but he knew people who were going to be big. Every day at lunch, every night at dinner, he wined them and dined them and people knew him. He just didn't invent himself."

Most importantly he became a chum of John Fairchild, the mercurial and powerful publisher of *Women's Wear Daily*. Fairchild, not easily won over by people, was taken with him. "I met him when he was going to Paris to copy hats," said Fairchild. "He was such a nice guy . . . I don't think I met anybody as decent and kind as he was." *Women's Wear Daily* had been known for years as one of the nine boring trade newspapers owned by the Fairchild family, but since 1960, when John Fairchild was brought back from the Paris office by his father to take over, the paper's tone and importance had been changing quickly. Fairchild was moving the focus of the coverage away from manufacturing news and retail figures to the people who wore the clothes and their life-styles, as well as to the personal tastes and lives of the designers. Slowly, as he merged fashion with gossip, Fairchild began to redefine fashion's role in society. There was no attempt to pretend that the newspaper had an impartial or balanced view, and throughout the sixties *Women's Wear* developed a taste for scandal and gossip as Fairchild hired more and more paparazzi and columnists. Because Fairchild frequently feuded with designers and socialites—and banned their names and photos from his newspapers—one manufacturer called *Women's Wear* "the terror tabloid of the fashion world." Yet as capricious as it could sometimes seem in the beginning, over the years *Women's Wear* became perhaps the single most powerful trade newspaper of any American business. Its editorial positions and reviews had the same kind of clout on Seventh Avenue that the drama critic of the *New York Times* had on Broadway: the absolute ability to destroy or make a show or a designer's collection with a single notice.

Halston's becoming one of Fairchild's fair-haired boys had much to do with his close friendship with the most widely read of Fairchild's columnists, Carol Bjorkman, a beautiful young woman who wrote a column called "Carol Says." Bjorkman was one of many young women in Halston's life who were so captivated by him that she couldn't get enough of him. He became her favorite party escort. Halston was quite mad for Bjorkman as well. She had an upbeat, pixilated personality— a touch of Holly Golightly mixed with a dash of Dorothy

Parker—and she wrote her columns listening to jazz as she burned a scented candle at her side (very chi-chi for the time). Bjorkman was also known for her stylish Balenciaga suits, a white poodle named Sheba that she often carried around tucked under her arm, and for being the well-kept mistress of Seventh Avenue fashion magnate Seymour Fox. She was also a former assistant to Valentina, Greta Garbo's dressmaker, and a liaison for Yves Saint Laurent in America. She also knew many of the great ladies of the time and introduced them to Halston, including Babe Paley and Mrs. Charles Wrightsman. Bjorkman also had the full-time services of a limousine that was paid for by her wealthy lover, and she and Halston put it to good use. For a time they were inseparable: lunches at La Côte Basque and Pavillon, fashion shows and cocktail parties, and all the finest restaurants before a peck on the cheek goodnight when Bjorkman would go off to Seymour Fox and Halston to his own diversions.

Carol's columns were unabashed advertisements for him. "Halston of BG is the Young Elegant responsible for many of the beautiful animals riding atop heads," she wrote, "both on celebrities and Social Registerites. He has helped create the Anna Karenina look, starting with Mrs. JFK's big black mink beret, Mrs. Basil Goulandris' black mink Nefertiti model, the new Mrs. Huntington Hartford's chinchilla stocking cap, Mrs. Henry Ford's sable, Mrs. Michael Phipps's mink and all of Rocky Cooper's fur hats. Now with hair coming down and the smaller head look, hats are back, and Halston has made this come true."

"Halston spoke to Carol two or three times a day," said Myrna Davis. "They had a very special thing going for years and years. And then one night, in 1966, we were all out someplace, some sort of club or disco, and there was a swimming pool in the middle, and Carol said, 'Halston, look, I keep getting black-and-blue marks all over my legs.' Within a week or two, she was in the hospital. She had leukemia, and in a few months she was dead." Halston took it very badly. He was so devastated, he was never able to mention her name again. It helped him to keep his grief private, an emotion he saw as undignified to exhibit in public.

Halston was also blessed with the admiration of perhaps the single most powerful press person in the world: Diana Vreeland, the legendary editor of *Harper's Bazaar* and *Vogue* and a woman with such absolute power that she was sometimes called a "fashion dictator." Mrs. Vreeland, as she was always referred to, was a major oddball and original, a lady with such distinct style and flair she became the inspiration for the Kay Thompson magazine editor in the Fred Astaire–Audrey Hepburn film *Funny Face*. Indeed, reportedly in 1959 Vreeland declared that next year's big color would be "billiard green," and sure enough, designers and manufacturers were so swayed by her proclamation that the next season's big color was green. She had a remarkable-looking craggy face with a hook nose, big slash of red lipstick on her lips, and rouged ears. From behind the desk in her famed blood-red office she invented—because she said they were important or good or in—people, like Twiggy, Suzy Parker, and Penelope Tree; phrases, like "Beautiful People" and "pizzazz,"; and kooky fads, like vinyl hairpieces in neon colors, ethnic clothing, and plastic jewelry. Vreeland was also a mercurial and difficult taskmaster, but if she was pleased by a designer or photographer or stylist, few editors could be more influential than she.

Mrs. Vreeland reportedly discovered Halston through Frances Stein, a brilliantly talented, hot-tempered accessories editor at *Harper's Bazaar,* who was later to become a short-lived business partner of Halston's. After only two weeks on the job, Stein was working on a layout in the studios of fashion photographer Melvin Sokolsky when she got a call from Vreeland saying that she wanted all the hats in the photo shoot to "look like Thanksgiving dinner." These kind of requests were not unusual from Mrs. Vreeland, who often used metaphor in her descriptions. Indeed, she spoke in a cadence and used imagery that pretty much amounted to her own *patois*. Stein, eager to please her boss, called Halston at Bergdorf and implored him to help her. Legend has it that Halston rushed right over to Sokolsky's studio and together he and Stein made the "Thanksgiving dinner" hats in Sokolsky's darkroom. "Frances fell in love with him," said Arthur Williams, "literally in love with him. She was his disciple and his word was God."

"If a tweed turban was needed to go with a tweed suit that was going to be photographed at Avedon's at 11 A.M., Halston would get it there by 11 A.M. and it would be perfection," Stein said.

Even Mrs. Vreeland was impressed. After one look at Halston's interpretation of her idea, Mrs. Vreeland herself began to depend on the creative milliner. "I would say to him, 'I had a dream about a hat last night,'" said Vreeland, "and I'd go about describing it," and Halston would produce it. Or she would say to him, "'Give me a bread.' I didn't really know what I meant by that, you see. But by God, he'd give it to me line for line. Once he made twelve snoods in the twinkling of an eye. He was probably the greatest hatmaker in the world and an absolute magician with his hands."

Halston had a stormy, intense relationship with Vreeland. Polly Mellen remembered some conversations when they would scream at each other and "yell and throw bolts of fabric across the room, and Vreeland would say 'fantastic,' and Halston would throw it at her feet and she would pick it up and wind it around herself."

YET WITH ALL his influential friends and good press, it took Jacqueline Kennedy and the pillbox hat to make him into an international star.

When Halston first met Jacqueline Kennedy she was still the unknown but terribly fashionable wife of an up-and-coming senator from Massachusetts. No one could have known that the Kennedys were on the verge of becoming the biggest media couple in the world since the the Duke and Duchess of Windsor. More important for Halston, Jacqueline Kennedy was destined to have the greatest single influence on the fashion world of any woman in American history—and she would have a Halston hat on her head while doing so.

It all started when she was on the campaign trail with John Kennedy and she needed literally dozens of hats for her sundry campaign appearances. This was the tail end of an era of propriety in America when all respectable women were expected to wear hats, particularly the wives of presidential candidates—particularly the wife of a presidential candidate who did not like to wear hats himself, a fact that had much distressed the American millinery industry. And so hats Jackie Kennedy wore, by the dozens. Mrs. Kennedy had long been a patron and valued client of Bergdorf Goodman, and she ordered her hats from them on consignment—most of which Halston designed for her as head of millinery.

The future First Lady, however, was not particularly fond of hats. First, at the time she wore her hair in a big bouffant, which did not lend itself to hats, and second, she had an extremely large head and felt that hats weren't becoming to her. In fact, it was because her head was so large that Halston became invaluable to her: Halston and Jacqueline Kennedy had the same head size. "He was the only one who could do her hats because of her strange head size," remembered Tom Fallon. "This was very important, certainly in custom millinery. Before the hats were sent to her, Halston would put her hats on his head and sit there and look at them with two mirrors, one behind him one in front, turning his head at different angles to make sure they looked right. It was funny, this wonderful big palooka of a guy with these ladies' hats on."

Marita O'Connor, a top saleswoman in the millinery department, became a "personal shopper" for Mrs. Kennedy. Often

Jackie would send sketches of hat styles she drew herself on her own stationery and the Bergdorf millinery department would then execute them for her. The next time she passed though town, O'Connor, and sometimes Halston, would bring the finished hats to her suite at the Carlyle Hotel for a fitting. Halston adored the pretty and fashionable young wife of the future president; he remembered going up to her hotel suite and finding her listening to Frank Sinatra records on the stereo. In mid-November of 1960, pregnant with her second child, Mrs. Kennedy wrote to Marita O'Connor to say that she had decided to buy all her clothes from Bergdorf Goodman while she was First Lady and that she intended to name them her official clothier. In the same letter she included an order for over a dozen hats. "Oh dear, it was so pleasant when I didn't have to wear hats," she wrote. "They will pauperize me and I still feel absurd in them." Mrs. Kennedy added that she wanted her Inaugural wardrobes fitted and finished by December 10, when she would enter the hospital to give birth. The staff at Bergdorf launched into preparations for three outfits: a suit for the Inauguration, a gown for the Governor's Ball, and a gown for the Inaugural balls.

"I remember the day Halston brought the pillbox to Mrs. Kennedy at the Carlyle," said Andrew Goodman. " 'You're so young to be so successful,' she said to him."

Everything had been approved, designed, and executed when Mrs. Kennedy was informed by her husband that she could *not* name Bergdorf her official clothier and that she was going to "appoint" the designer Oleg Cassini as her official designer. Cassini was primarily famous as the chief costume designer for 20th Century–Fox in the forties and for his glamorous cocktail dresses on Seventh Avenue. He was hardly a world-class designer, and not even American born; he had been born in France of Russian parents.

Reportedly, the Kennedy clan was arranging for Oleg Cassini to design Jackie's wardrobe in appreciation for the years of friendship to the family as well as the goodwill of his brother, Igor Cassini, a powerful newspaper columnist known professionally as Cholly Knickerbocker. Joseph Kennedy had met Igor Cassini in Palm Beach shortly after the war, and the two brothers became his good chums. Oleg Cassini wrote about his friendship with Joe Kennedy, "We shared an intense appreciation of beautiful women," and for a time, every Tuesday night at eight o'clock, Oleg would show up at La Caravelle with a few pretty models or young starlets for Joe to meet. Also, in Oleg Cassini's travels as a desirable single man, he, too, knew Jackie Bouvier as a young debutante and had been her "dancing partner" on occasion in Palm Beach.

According to Mrs. Kennedy, the change in plans caused "turmoil" in her life. "Mrs. Kennedy informed us, somewhat tearfully," said Andrew Goodman, "that she couldn't wear our gown at the Inaugural Ball because her husband had a relationship with Igor Cassini and that he had promised that Oleg Cassini could do her wardrobe."

According to Oleg Cassini, he had merely sent a letter to Mrs. Kennedy, "modestly worded," suggesting that she include him in her considerations as a designer. Cassini was given two days' notice to bring sketches of his work to Mrs. Kennedy's bedside at the Washington hospital where she had just given birth to John Jr. Included in the sketches was a suit for her to wear to the Inauguration ceremony, a wool, Chanel-like, two-piece, three-quarter-length loosely fitted coat with a removable collar of Russian sable.

Cassini insists that the idea for a pillbox hat was his idea and that the original sketch shown to Mrs. Kennedy had one pictured. Leonard Hankin and Andrew Goodman remember that the pillbox hat was part of *their* original Inaugural outfit, designed by Halston, oversized with some extra height, to be worn at the back of her head to accommodate her hairdo.

Neither Halston nor Oleg Cassini invented the design. Like almost everything in fashion, it was an idea borrowed, some say from Balenciaga, others from Christian Dior, who had shown dozens of pillbox-shaped hats in collections that hundreds of designers had witnessed over the years. Also, the designer Adrian had helped popularize the pillbox with a hat that Greta Garbo wore in the movie *As You Desire Me* in 1932. The pillbox is simply any oval hat with a flat top and straight sides, usually worn at a jaunty angle.

The design for Mrs. Kennedy's hat, claimed Cassini, evolved from a suggestion made to him by Diana Vreeland, to whom he had gone for inspirational advice on how to dress Mrs. Kennedy. Cassini says that it was Mrs. Vreeland who suggested to him that a pillbox hat would be best because it could accommodate her bouffant hairdo. Cassini wrote that "the actual execution of the hat was done by Marita at Bergdorf Goodman, Mrs. Kennedy's preferred hatmaker." This is highly unlikely, since Marita was a saleswoman, not an "executor" of hats.

"It was rather surprising," Cassini wrote many years later, to read in the *New York Times* that Halston had created the pillbox. "An outright lie . . ." he wrote. He says that Halston very well might have been the one who made the hat itself in the workrooms at Bergdorf. "But," he asked plaintively, "who is the author of a book? The one who wrote it or the one who types it? Who painted the painting? The artist or the man who made the frame?"

"That's full of shit," said Hankin. "Halston designed it."

"A pillbox hat may not be important, but the truth is," Cassini implored passionately.

When the author of this book asked Jacqueline Kennedy Onassis to once and for all end the debate over who designed the famous pillbox Inaugural hat, her answer was one word: "Halston."

THE PILLBOX BECAME a brief fashion sensation, Oleg Cassini received international prestige, and the world sat up and took notice of Halston. That year the *New York Times* noted that Halston had become so famous, "that's the way he is known to almost everyone but the United States Passport Agency," and called him "a fashion force to be reckoned with . . ."

The summer of 1962, shortly after Halston's thirtieth birthday, it was announced that at the next Coty Fashion Critics Awards, fashion's equivalent of an Oscar, a special award would be given to Halston for his millinery designs for the custom-order salon of Bergdorf Goodman. Donald Brooks, the dress designer, was the year's main recipient of a "Winnie." On a balmy evening in late September of 1962, 700 beautifully dressed people from all over the world began to arrive in a long line of limousines at the Metropolitan Museum of Art. Later that night the elite of the fashion industry watched as Halston, eyes sparkling, the color high in his cheeks, rose to receive his award. On that occasion Halston told the *Times* that "fashion is never made by designers. Fashion is made by fashionable people. If Mrs. William Paley wears my hat, it becomes fashion. If it hangs in the stockroom, it's nothing."

THE SWINGING SIXTIES

O ne night at 4 A.M., Arthur Williams was awakened from his sleep by a phone call from a man identifying himself as a police lieutenant from the New York Police Department who said that they were holding a friend of Williams's named Roy Frowick in the Tombs, the notorious downtown holding tank. He said that Frowick was frantic about having a police record, and that if somebody rushed down there with a thousand dollars, it could be arranged that Roy Frowick wouldn't get booked.

Williams tried to clear the sleep from his head. "But what did he do? What are the charges?" Williams asked.

"We picked him up in Central Park blowing somebody," the lieutenant said.

"I only had four hundred dollars," Williams remembered, "and I called everyone I knew in the middle of the night, woke them out of bed and begged them for money and couldn't tell anyone why. I took a cab downtown to the Tombs. The whole thing was scary as hell. There was Halston in a cell. He was furious. I went into some dirty little corner and handed the cop nine hundred dollars and they let him out. By this time it was morning and the sun was up and we were in a taxi and Halston was crying and shaking and furious, in a rage. I never knew about his explorations in Central Park. I would never have suspected that was the other part of Halston, because it didn't fit with the grandeur. To be one thing during the day, and to switch to some sort of hooded nightmare at night . . ." Williams's voice trailed off in frustration. "This was really astonishing, because the way we lived our lives was totally correct."

But Halston loved adventure and living on the edge, and he got into all sorts of mischief with Arthur Williams. One of their greatest adventures was a sort of a harmless "sting" operation perpetrated on one of the wealthiest women of Portugal, Paula Mundette.

Paula Mundette's husband exported Portuguese cork all over the world, and they were enormously wealthy. Only five feet tall at best, she was a sad figure who sat on pillows in restaurants to reach a respectable height at the table. She desperately wanted to be accepted into New York society, and she even took a course at a modeling-cum-polishing school where she was taught colloquial English and American manners. She also spent a great deal of money at Bergdorf Goodman, especially in the millinery department, where she was forever searching for a hat that would make her look taller.

One day she took Halston and one of the saleswomen, Marti, to lunch. During lunch she mentioned that she was thinking about renting three separate floors in a building off Madison Avenue in the sixties and combining them into a triplex apartment pied à terre for herself in New York. She would be paying nearly $10,000 a month rent, a staggering amount for that time. She wondered aloud how she would decorate such a big place, and Halston suddenly had a plan. He said he knew a wonderful decorator for her, one of the most important interior decorators in New York: Arthur Williams.

Now Arthur Williams, by then a rising star in the packaging department at the French cosmetics house of Monteil, did in fact have excellent taste in interior design, but he was hardly a designer by trade. In any event, Halston didn't even tell Arthur Williams he had represented him as a decorator when he invited Williams to lunch with Paula Mundette at L'Ermitage. During the meal several of Halston's clients from Bergdorf passed his table and stopped to say hello or waved across the room, and Mundette was suitably impressed. Williams was astonished to hear himself introduced as a world-famous decorator, but he didn't miss a beat. He agreed that he was, and after lunch Paula Mundette took them to see the three floors. Halston and Arthur walked around talking color and design, and she gave Arthur the job.

"We pulled the place apart, from top to bottom," Williams said. "We tore the walls out. Twice a week Halston and I would have lunch with Paula Mundette at L'Ermitage and she would hand him rolls of one-thousand-dollar bills tied with rubber bands, sometimes ten thousand dollars a week. We kept it going for a year and half. When it was finished the apartment was superb, except for one thing: Halston liked stripes, and every time Paula Mundette walked into the dining room the striped wallpaper made her so dizzy she fainted." Also, Williams and Halston had forgotten about putting in a kitchen until the work was nearly finished, and Mundette wound up with a kitchen "the size of a Pullman," said Williams.

Nevertheless, Mundette was happy with her new apartment, and Halston and Williams were happy with all the money they had made. They decided on a very special way to spend it. They both took six-week sabbaticals from work, using various excuses, and then went off on a lavish vacation—first to London to visit Nanita Kalachnikoff, where they stayed at the Claridge Hotel. "Our first day in London Halston bought three thousand dollars' worth of beaded pillows, four thousand dollars' worth of tortoise shell boxes and six Savile Row suits." Then the two went off to Morocco and took suites at the Mamounia Hotel.

"Halston loved Morocco because the boys were so cheap to buy," said Williams, "Only four dollars each, and he'd have three a day." While in Morocco they paid a visit to the "Street of Steam," a red-light district where there were several steam baths that featured live sex shows. "We were tipped off about this place," said Williams. "The show involved a man and two women and some dildos and bestiality. Halston was loving it when the steam pipe near his head burst and he was scalded on his face. We had to rush him to the American hospital where they treated him for burns."

Arthur Williams developed his own problems. He contracted Ménière's disease, a disorder of the inner ear, in Tangier, and could hardly stand up or walk straight. He expected a sympathetic friend in Halston, who only seemed to feel inconvenienced because they were expected to join Kalachnikoff and Dali in Barcelona, where Dali was throwing a party. Halston at first suggested that he leave Williams in Tangier, but Williams insisted that Halston help him travel to a better hospital in Madrid. Once in Spain, according to Williams, Halston ditched him at the hospital and rushed on to Dali's party, taking with him Williams's luggage and all his clothes.

Williams was furious. "After the incident in Spain," said Williams, "I went back to New York, went out to my house in Fire Island, put all of Halston's clothing into bags, and dumped them in the bay."

FOR ALL THE success and good fortune in Halston's life, there seemed to be one aspect of it that was totally absent: romance. Halston had an emotional rigidity to him that lay not far below the surface, and despite a warm and loving manner he didn't seem able to drop his shell and connect with other people. Only rarely did he appear to be vulnerable. As far as romance was concerned, friends do remember his having a *petite affaire* with a French boy he met one spring in Paris in the Bois de Boulogne at 4:30 in the morning. But when he brought the boy back to the U.S. for an extended visit, it turned out that his friend had passport and visa problems. The romance fizzled, and the boy went home via Canada.

Although while Carol Bjorkman was alive he made the club scene for a while, and he occasionally attended a dinner party thrown by an aquaintance in the design world, Halston was very much of a homebody for the most part. "He was a very private person at that time," said artist Ron Ferri, who with his wife, Monique, was in Halston's circle of friends at the time. "He would never go out anywhere, to a club, to a bar, to anything where there was a lot of people, because Halston was a very, very, shy person and he would never go out. I would try to get him to go out and he would say, 'No, no, you guys go out, I'm staying home.' "

He told the press that "there are no nightclubs in New York that I enjoy. The only place left to go is El Morocco. Trude Hellers was fun once—about a year ago—but of course now it's out. Ondine is a wicked place. Carol Bjorkman and I went there. She even let her hair down and wore black stockings. I just had to see what a discotheque looked like. They prove there is still a lot of tough chic around."

As for his personal life, "Mostly I stay home. New York is a city where you cannot have any privacy unless you fight for it. Two nights a week I dial my own number and leave the phone off the hook so I can be home alone without being bothered. I don't even have an answering service—if you have one, then you leave no excuse—you have to call back."

What he was doing those nights with the phone off the hook was entertaining call boys. "He was one of those people," said Clovis Ruffin, "for whom having sex is like baking brownies; you mix it, you bake it, you time it, you're done. Halston had no time to sit around staring at boys across restaurants, trying to get friendly and sending drinks and everything. He knew exactly what he wanted."

Said a close friend from the time, "Each night at exactly eleven o'clock Halston excused himself and went home because he had a date coming over at eleven-thirty. People saw Halston at the showroom or at parties; nobody really ever went to his apartment except for sex dates and the maid."

He did, however, after his falling out with Arthur Williams, establish perhaps the closest platonic relationship of his life with interior designer Angelo Donghia, whom he met in the Fire Island Pines at the Cleopatra party. They became such fast friends that "they called each other Tarzan and Jane," Clovis Ruffin said, "I don't remember which was which." Donghia, like Halston, was a man on his way up to the very top of his field. The grandson of Italian immigrants, he was born in Van-dergrift, Pennsylvania, and graduated from the Parsons School of Design. Handsome, suave, and sophisticated, at the time Donghia was just starting out with the firm of Yale Burge. He shared with Halston impeccable style and taste. While Halston's forte was clothing, Donghia had a brilliant eye for space and environment, for *objets d'art* and the combination (or absence) of colors. At the height of his career he would reign over a business grossing $135 million a year, not only in design, but in clothing and home-entertainment products as well. He was so esteemed in his field that Ralph Lauren even got him to decorate his New York apartment for him. In every sense, Donghia was Halston's match.

On a personal level, Donghia was the perfect counterpoint for Halston. Donghia loved to shop and cook for friends and make a home. Halston preferred restaurants and rarely had company in. Halston was cool to the touch and reserved in public, Donghia was warm and emotional. After Arthur Williams threw Halston's clothes in the bay, Halston shared a house in Fire Island Pines with Donghia for six or seven seasons. There they whiled away many hours sitting around the pool doing needlepoint and gossiping. The two became such close friends that even their widowed mothers got to be close and went off on vacations together, which their sons financed. When their mothers visited New York together, they would throw big dinner parties at Angelo's apartment for all their friends, and after dinner the two mothers would put on a fashion show in duds supplied by Halston.

It was also Angelo Donghia who helped Halston move to a rent-controlled apartment in the building in which Donghia already lived at 360 East Fifty-fifth Street, around the corner from Sutton Place. Donghia had heard of an apartment that was becoming available in the building, and he and Halston went to the superintendent and tore a five-hundred-dollar bill in half in front of him. They gave one half to the superintendent and promised him the rest if Halston got the next apartment. Halston first moved into a small apartment on the eighth floor and later to a one-bedroom penthouse with a small terrace on the seventeenth floor. Angelo decorated the apartment for him, in a "chi-chi" look with a big overstuffed white sofa, white-and-brown cotton throw pillows, potted plants, a Zebra throw rug, and a white Parsons dining room table, which was rarely used. There was also a beautiful collection of blue-and-white Chinese porcelains, and a glass coffee table with a stuffed white snowy owl on white pebbles in its base. "The maid came in to that apartment every single day," said a close friend at the time. "He had clean sheets, pressed and starched every single day."

Clovis Ruffin, later to become a Coty Award–winning designer himself, grew up in that building and remembered Halston when he first moved in. "I always saw him. I used to have this image of Halston storming through the lobby looking very grand with something thrown over his shoulders, and he was always racing into a car, so I always sort of knew who he was."

After Halston moved to East Fifty-fifth Street he began to develop a circle of young professional friends who were on their way up in the glamour industries of New York. These included a young window dresser from Henri Bendel named Joel Schumacher whom he met at Fire Island; artist Ron Ferri and his wife, model Monique Dutou, who lived 360 East Sixty-fifth Street as well; choreographer John Butler; Mel Dwork, a decorator; and Myrna Davis.

This small circle socialized together several nights a week, and even held birthday parties for their dogs. Halston's friends universally adored him for his generosity of spirit and personal kindnesses. Myrna Davis remembers going to Paris to meet him in 1967 around the time of the Paris collections. She had mentioned to him that she had always wanted to buy a certain Cartier watch, which at the time was being made only in a limited edition in Paris. Halston encouraged Myrna to join them in Paris, but she demurred. One day not long afterwards Myrna was walking down East Fifty-seventh Street when she heard her name being shouted. She looked up and there, going over the lower roadway of the Fifty-ninth Street Bridge, were Angelo Donghia and Halston in a big black limousine on their way to the airport, hanging out of the windows screaming, *"Myrna! Myrna! Come to Paris!"*

Myrna said to herself, "You know what, I'm going to Paris."

The following week in Paris with Halston was one of the best times of her life. "It was wonderful to be with him," she said, "He made every moment of that trip glorious. He knew everything about Paris, every shop, every special place. I remember that he took us to a seafood restaurant named La Marie somewhere around the Odéon and later we took a walk and he found a shop open late at night where he bought us a box of chocolate in a black satin box."

On the day they arrived at Cartier to buy Myrna her watch, the store was out of the style that she wanted. Halston had a word with the manager of the shop, explaining that he was "Mr. Halston" of Bergdorf Goodman, and that a watch would make his lady friend happy. Later that afternoon there was a call at Myrna's hotel from Cartier; her watch had arrived.

There were also moments with him, like one night sitting on a bench outside place de l'Alma, when Myrna might have thought that he was romantically inclined. "Certainly he wasn't," she said, "but he had a way about him—he could be sweetness and charm. I remember sitting and talking with him and thinking that this is one of the most beautiful evenings of my life. It was so lovely and he was so romantic in just his way."

AND THEN, IN the summer of 1964, Halston did find romance, of a sort.

Halston was at Tea Dance, the so-called late afternoon Fire Island ritual when many residents gathered at the bayfront Boatel, a beautiful, multileveled complex of disco, restaurant, motel, and yacht-docking facilities, for dancing and cocktails, posing and staring. One Saturday afternoon Halston and Angelo were sitting at a table watching the crowd when Halston saw a handsome, well-built young black man talking with his friends. Halston liked minority types—there was something forbidden and sexually charged to him about blacks and Latinos—and after studying the boy for a few minutes from afar, he sent the waiter to say that an admirer wanted to buy him a drink. Halston watched as the black boy coolly declined.

"I don't accept drinks from strangers," twenty-four-year-old Edward J. Austin, Jr., told the waiter grandly. Ed Austin had almost as grand an air about him as Halston. But not to seem totally unfriendly he added, "Send a drink back from me to whoever sent it."

Later, when Tea Dance was over and Austin was headed back to his friend's house, he noticed a tall, handsome man waiting at the end of the dock under a lamppost, smoking a cigarette. The man smiled and motioned Austin over. The two of them chatted for a while. "I still didn't know who he was," said Austin. "He gave me a fake name—he told me his name was Eric. In the meantime, he had invited me to his house that Monday night. I met him on a Saturday and he invited me to his house on Monday. Later I saw my friends and they said,

'His name isn't Eric, it's Halston, you know, the designer, Halston, from Bergdorf Goodman.' That started the relationship."

At the time Ed Austin was an assistant buyer in the menswear department of Alexander's department store. Born in Union City, New Jersey, in 1940, he was brought up in Newark. He began working at age fourteen selling men's shoes. At the time when he met Halston he was living in a small apartment on Third Avenue and East Twenty-seventh Street. For the next five or six years, he would become Halston's weekly sex partner. On that first Monday night when Austin went to Halston's penthouse on East Fifty-fifth Street, Halston cooked dinner and they stayed in. There would be a lot of eating in. "He kept me hidden away from his friends," said Austin. "He wouldn't take me out to dinner publicly. I still don't know the reason for that, unless he was trying to protect his own image." In the ensuing six years of weekly sexual encounters with Austin, only Halston's closest friends even knew such a person existed. "He would never, never, never let anyone see us together. I didn't question him about it because it wasn't important to me." Austin did get to meet Angelo Donghia when Halston brought him into the Alexander's men's department and Donghia bought a coat. On the rare occasion when Austin was asked to join Halston with a friend, he got no more of an introduction than "This is my friend Ed."

For the next five years their relationship followed almost exactly that pattern. They had dinner at Halston's house two or three nights a week and then to bed. The doormen would occasionally stop Austin and ask him to use the service entrance, but Halston soon put that situation right. Only infrequently would Austin sleep over. "The house was as neat as a pin," said Austin. As for romance: "He didn't like to hold hands and coo," said Austin. "My love for him was strong, but it was a mature love. Before Halston, when I fell in love I was like a kid, it just knocks you out. It wasn't like that with him. I respected him. I loved him for what he was and how he treated me and what he did for me. I could have spent the rest of my life in love with Halston. I was comfortable in my relationship. But he had his other personal life, which I was not included in. He never met my friends, by choice.

"Everybody put him down because he was grand, but Halston was a real, real nice guy. If there was one person in my life that absolutely turned me around and let me see what life can be, it was Halston. He wanted the best of everything that he could afford. He wanted everything to be the best, that's what he gave me. 'Don't go cheap, go with the best. If you can't go with the best, don't bother,' he would say."

Austin said that in his five years or so of sexual relations with Halston he never once cheated on him, but that he knew Halston saw other people. "I only know about one for sure," he said, "because he got caught. I guess I got caught, too, because I got gonorrhea, and it could have only come from Halston. I confronted him about it and he said, 'Don't worry, take two pills.' Well, I went to see the doctor and he paid for it. Then I kind of chilled out, too, because I'm very monogamous.

"Halston was a spiritual person," said Austin, "but he was always very private, very private. That's why it amuses me when I hear people talk about how grand he was. They didn't know Halston. That was him on the outside. There's a reason why people do that and that's to protect the inside. He became a grand object in people's fantasies, and the best thing was to keep quiet and let them fantasize all they wanted. He let very few people really know him. People said that Halston changed. Well, Halston didn't change, the circumstances began to change."

IN LATE 1964 Bergdorf Goodman agreed to allow CBS TV to use the first floor of the store as a fantasy setting in the first TV special of a budding new star, Barbra Streisand. The nine-minute segment would include many lavish costume changes, including several million dollars' worth of Bergdorf furs topped by Halston hats. Barbra Streisand adored the hats he made for her—particularly a riding hat with streaming chiffon ribbons—and she became a Halston fan. As a thank-you she had arranged for Halston to have four tickets to the taping of another segment of the show where she would sing to an audience accompanied by a full orchestra. "Halston invited his mother to the taping with us. She was going to fly in for it as a treat, but just a few days before the taping his father died."

Halston was deeply upset and torn by conflicting emotions. All these years he had had "absolutely no use for his father," as one associate put it, and now he was gone. "Halston seemed frantic. He kept saying, 'I've got to go home and bury my father. I've got to bury my father.' He jumped into a taxi and rushed out to the airport." The funeral was one of the most difficult times in Halston's life. He had always handled death by distancing himself from it; now he was confronted with the irrevocable fact that Ed Jr. had finally stopped being so miserable, and he had done it at the pitifully young age of fifty-nine, worn out from his own excesses.

Afterwards, Halston rarely talked about his father, and when he did his words were always tinged with bitterness. But he had great allegiance to his mother. He called Arthur Williams from the airport on his way to Gainesville and said he had decided that after the funeral he was going to bring his mother back with him, that perhaps New York would be the perfect tonic for her. Halston asked Williams to go to his apartment and look around carefully and hide or remove anything of Halston's that might prove embarrassing—an errant dildoe or a gouache of a cock near his bed.

Halston returned a few days later with his mother in tow. A generally upbeat woman, she was at this point understandably quiet and glum. "The night we went to the taping of the Streisand special," said Williams, "Mrs. Frowick didn't say a word all night. Later, after the show, I was praising Halston to her and how much he had accomplished when she suddenly lashed out at me, things like, 'He's not my only child, you know. I've got a son in the State Department.' " Williams chalked it up to stress. Mrs. Frowick went back to her home in Gainesville.

Halston called his mother almost every Monday night of his life until her death in 1982. Although he offered her anything she wanted, from furs to diamonds to big houses, she was a modest women content with very little. When Ed Jr. died, Bob Frowick, who was with the Foreign Service in Romania at the time, began to send her $50 a month to help her out, but after just a few months Halston called his brother and said that he would take care of her. "She lived in a nice little three-bedroom house in Gainesville," remembered Bob. "It was a nice house with a pleasant yard, and she never wanted to leave, even though Halston offered her the moon." But eventually the neighborhood started to get rundown and Hallie May agreed to move. With Halston's help, his younger brother, Don, built a new home with a swimming pool, and on the other side of the pool was a guest cottage where Hallie May lived the last years of her life. She lay down to watch TV one day and didn't wake up. She died of natural causes.

Bob Frowick was in Belgium at the time, and all the children flew to Gainseville for the funeral. "The reunion was so profound for Halston and all of us, both in sharing our grief and enjoying each other, that it caused Halston and me to rediscover each other. After that Halston started to have family reunions and we drew closer."

THE SIXTIES WERE a turbulent time for the fashion world. After years of traditional growth and relatively slow change in taste and styles, a revolution had swept the clothing industry, and nobody was on safe ground anymore. A kooky, costumey phase had come to the fore, ethnic clothing or avant garde. There were spurts of modern minimalism, topless bathing suits, and see-thru blouses. Suddenly, designers with recognizable names were beginning to emerge from behind the anonymity of the mass manufacturers label, and the center of creativity for the ready-to-wear industry had suddenly shifted from Seventh Avenue to London. "Swinging London," as *Time* magazine had dubbed it in 1967. If American manufacturers were disturbed by this sudden shift of the creative center and the explosive changes in style, they were even more disturbed by the fashion trend emanating from the grass roots of America. While at least the Brits were in the grip of an affluent, young group of swingers that spent lots of money on clothes, in the U.S. the trend was toward dressing down, especially for the vast numbers of hippies, who wore mostly blue jeans and tie-dyed T-shirts.

As for the older, more dignified customer to whom Bergdorf catered, well, they still existed, to be sure, but even their interest in millinery was becoming a rarefied thing. Woman felt that they didn't have to wear hats anymore, not even proper women at church. Only about 150 millinery firms still existed by then, fewer than half the number of a decade ago, and most of them were family owned and grossed less than $2 million a year. The time had arrived for Halston to make his move—to get out of millinery before it became altogether obsolete. But whenever he mentioned wanting to go further than millinery, he would be reminded that he was only a hatmaker. To this he had a set response: "So was Chanel."

By 1966 Halston's name had became synonymous with Bergdorf Goodman, and neither Halston nor Bergdorf's was thrilled with the situation. This was still an age when not many designers were as well known as manufacturers, and as Halston's fame grew, so did the tension between him, Leonard Hankin, and Andrew Goodman. Not a week passed when there wasn't some foot-stomping or tantrum-throwing over a real or imagined slight. "He was petulant and temperamental," Goodman said. "He was always threatening to quit. And he was full of himself." They didn't want to lose Halston as an employee, but he was becoming more difficult than he was worth. As for Halston, Hankin and Goodman were at heart "Jews." Arthur Williams remembered Halston calling Hankin "a numbers man." "Finances irritated Halston," said Williams. "You couldn't run things the way Halston wanted to run things with his sense of extravagance and remind him of numbers. You had to let him be."

Indeed, Halston told a trade paper that at Bergdorf "I can cut into a five-hundred-dollar piece of sable without a qualm. If I had my own shop I might hesitate and then the designing urge would be gone." Leonard Hankin wanted Halston to control that "designing urge" and have more qualms about costs, but Hankin was only the first in a long series of financial people who unsuccessfully tried to curb Halston's prodigious spending. The best of everything was Halston's rule—for me *and* for you.

Goodman remembers one particularly irksome example of Halston's extravagance when he and his wife, Nena, were in Paris having dinner at Maxim's. Goodman suggested to Nena that they order some caviar. Mrs. Goodman said no, that caviar was too expensive. "A few minutes later Halston came in and he was with Carol Bjorkman," Goodman said, "and Nena nudged me and said, 'Look at that, Carol and Halston are having caviar and champagne and you're the boss and you can't afford it.' "

In 1966 Halston approached Goodman and Hankin about designing his own ready-to-wear line. He envisioned the line being sold in a Halston boutique, which they would build for him in the store. Both Hankin and Goodman were very doubtful that the idea would work, and reluctant to expand Halston's role in the store. "Andrew and I talked about this at length," Hankin said. "We recognized that he had superb press ties and superb relationships with customers." But the cost of backing him in a brand-new line and spending the money to design and open a shop was a great risk. While they deliberated, Halston had some samples made with an outside tailor. "They weren't terribly impressive one way or the other," said Hankin, "but sufficiently so to allow us to go ahead with this venture." Arthur Williams remembers that a few good words from John Fairchild also helped to encourage Goodman and Hankin. "So we let him spread his wings," Hankin said. "It was a gamble for us based more on his personality and on his relationship with the press rather than any demonstrated talent."

"Making hats is tremendously good training for being a dress designer," Halston reasoned. "You learn to think in three dimensions, so your dresses have a sculptural quality. Also, you think in terms of small details."

Halston was given a larger workroom and assigned several fitters and seamstresses to create the line. They also gave him access to the Delman shoe salon so that he could design the shoes for his collection, as well as the hats. Noted interior designer Joe Braswell designed the elegant new Halston boutique, located on the second floor, and on June 28, 1966, Halston showed his first collection: an eighteen-piece interchangeable wardrobe for fall, priced from $395 to nearly $600 an outfit. Halston's coming of age as a clothing designer infuriated his longtime fan Norman Norell, who proclaimed that he would no longer allow his models to wear Halston hats at his shows. "Maybe he thinks I'm competition now that I'm designing clothes." Halston laughed. "But I still love Norman."

Halston's first collection generated the most excitement that the store had seen in years. Fashion shows at that time were still stiff affairs, with runway models taking a controlled stroll up and down the runway with hesitant smiles on their faces. But not Halston's show. His girls seemed to swing down the runway as if they were having fun. At one of his shows he gave a model a copy of Jackie Susann's *Valley of the Dolls* to hold as she strutted down the runway, and he used music in the show— "something that seemed quite startling at the time," said Tom

Fallon. He found the model for his wedding dress on the first floor, selling cosmetics. Her name was Berkley Johnson, and she later wound up on the cover of *Vogue*. Although the summer season was on, "Everyone's come back into town to see it," said Betsy Theodoracopulos, who sat in the front row with Charlotte Ford, Linda Hackett, Mrs. John Converse, and the Goodmans. After the show, champagne and strawberries were served.

The next day in *Women's Wear* Carol Bjorkman raved, "Every once in a while the fashion pendulum swings a certain way and out comes a star . . . At this point the world of fashion is ready to envelop with hungry open arms anyone who comes out and says *I'm for something else.* Halston of Bergdorf Goodman came out yesterday and said, *'I'm all for women—I'm all for women looking prettier and sexier, I'm for a neater and more put together look.'*" Bjorkman went on to say that he was the best designer since Givenchy.

Yet elsewhere in the issue two other reporters identified only by their initials saw a very different show. In a two-page spread, the review noted that while many important society ladies attended the collection, "Halston is a great milliner who is not yet a great designer of women's wear. The day things are pretty and always in taste and they look today. The evening numbers are not extraordinary." In contrast to Bjorkman's review, these two other reporters saw "a regulation black dress," and a "zoot suit," and a "Nehru jacket with a long stiffened coat" and "a red hat, many sided–solid, reminiscent of those *Life* magazine globes you used to cut out and past together and they were always getting crushed."

Hankin's assessment of the line: "It had no real personality. It was bits and pieces."

"It was a disaster," remembered Williams. "One dress looked like it had one hundred and eleven buttons."

"The clothes looked like they were made out of concrete," was the assessment of his friend Joanne Crevelling.

"You can sum this all up," said the numbers man, Hankin:

"There was a tremendous amount of brouhaha, and a great deal of interest, and nothing really happened with it . . . No business and no direction. But he had so much faith in himself and his ability to sell himself that I think he came up with all kinds of excuses of why this particular thing had not worked."

Halston's next shows—on October 13, of informal ready-to-wear, and in January 1967, a spring-summer collection, which CBS TV covered—fared not much better. By then he had picked up a considerable following among the Bergdorf women; his shows were considered an "event." Carol Bjorkman reported that 350 women attended the show that Halston designed for "all the young ladies of means who like to look young without looking coo-coo." This included a short white strapless dress with 500,000 feathers, which Mrs. Alfred Vanderbilt bought, and a long black dress with 700,000 feathers, which Mrs. Charles Engelhard purchased. Then on June 15 he showed a dark, medieval collection.

Despite the shows, and despite the fact that his ladies bought an occasional piece here and there, the volume was not great enough to justify the huge investment and the great cost of making each piece. Above all, Halston was still considered mainly a milliner, and *Women's Wear* continued to refer to him as "New York's top milliner." Nevertheless, Halston might have stayed longer at Bergdorf if, one day in late 1967, Leonard Hankin hadn't called him into the office and told him that they planned to close the custom millinery workrooms and that his line of clothing and boutique were not enough of a financial success to warrant continuing them.

"I think he was quite shocked," said Andrew Goodman, "when we closed the millinery."

Leonard Hankin said, "We had just about had it with Halston. He said he wanted to move on and I don't believe that anybody made any serious attempts to stop him." The next time he walked into Hankin's office and threatened to resign, Hankin said, "Then resign."

On November 24, 1967, Halston formally announced to the

press that he had resigned after completing the spring-summer collections for 1968 and would take a few months off to reflect. On January 9, 1968, four days before he officially parted company with Bergdorf, *Women's Wear* gave him a lavish two-page spread with photos, a treatment usually reserved for the biggest names in the business. The article was *Women's Wear*'s affirmation that Halston's departure from Bergdorf was not an ending, but a beginning. Entitled "Halston on Record," for the first time in print, a truncated, edited, and rearranged version of Halston's past appeared and a convenient story emerged that would be embroidered throughout the years. In this version he was the son of an accountant and was two years younger than the date on his birth certificate; he had attended the University of Indiana for two years, not just for one semester; and his education at the Chicago Art Institute was made to sound much more elaborate than just the one course he had taken. No mention of Basil was made at all (no wonder) just that he had sold hats at the Ambassador Hotel, that "business boomed," and that he moved on to his own shop on Michigan Avenue, before deciding to come to New York, he claimed—without a job. "Just like I'm doing now," he told *Women's Wear*'s June Weir.

"I'm thirty-five years old," Halston said (actually he was just a few months short of thirty-seven), "at thirty-five to do what I've done—give up a very special job without something definite ahead—might seem crazy . . ."

Crazy it wasn't. First he took time off to visit his brother Bob, then a senior attaché at the State Department in Washington, D.C., before a trip to Paris "to see my friends and a few couture collections." In Paris he was spotted by *Women's Wear Daily* at the opening of a Nino Cerutti boutique in Paris, his companion for the evening no less than Hubert de Givenchy. And a week later, he was seen lunching at the Colony with Alixandre, the furrier.

As the rumors increased about his future, Halston told

Women's Wear, "There's a rumor that I'm going to Bonwit's to do hats. Another that I'm going to Paris to work at Dior. I've heard I'm going down to S.A. [Seventh Avenue] to become one of [financial Kingpin] Ben Shaw's boys. Someone told me I'm going to Bendel's to be Gerry Stutz's assistant. Another person heard I was going to run Saint Laurent's Rive Gauche when it opens in New York. Oh, yes, I also heard that I was fired. Needless to say, none of these rumors is true."

On April 25, 1968, just three months after leaving Bergdorf as a salaried employee, Halston incorporated his own business as Halston Limited and set up temporary headquarters at 13 West Fifty-seventh Street, where he announced his first solo business ventures: several collections of hats in different price ranges. First there was a lower-priced, mass-market line called Halston U.S.A., to be manufactured by Lin-Mac, one of the industry leaders, that was targeted for hat bars in better department stores and priced between $18 and $95 retail. Then there was also a higher-priced collection called Halston Ltd. to be made in his own custom workrooms, for stores like Bonwit Teller and Neiman-Marcus, with hats starting at $70 and soaring as high as $1,200 for Russian sable. He also licensed a line of fur hats and fur collars with the Hat Corporation of America, which sold for up to $700 each. Bonwit Teller and Bloomingdale's each signed up to carry his men's fur hats. "I'd been making them for a number of years for men like Onassis and Henry Kaiser, but now they'll be for popular consumption," Halston said magnanimously. And of his cheaper hats, "This will give a further extension of myself to the general public," adding, "uptown in Russian sable, downtown in raccoon." He also pointed out, characteristically, "Most designers just lend their names to their junior label collections and don't have much to do with the design. But I will design and I will oversee making duplicates. I'll have control." His first order from Bonwit's, he boasted, "was the largest order I've ever had since I started in the hat business." Halston U.S.A. sold over $200,000 in 1968 dollars wholesale in its first six weeks alone. "And when you consider that the millinery market is dying on the vine," Halston said, "this said something to me."

What it said was that there's big money in mass market, and in September Halston announced the formation of his own ready-to-wear dress business, with dresses priced at about $150, coats and suits, $200. His first collection of thirty pieces was scheduled for a showing in the fall. His plan was to keep the line exclusive by restricting his sales to only one store in each major city, and to keep it current in the fast-changing market by getting new merchandise into the stores fast. "By golly," he said, "that's the way we do it in the hat business, in and out fast. Why not with clothes? We're doing amusing, not kooky, clothes for fast delivery and selling." He would implement this fast-paced line by retailing a new group of about a dozen articles of apparel every six to eight weeks. It was an ambitious starting schedule.

But all this hustling was just for the money. His real dream, the great love of his life, was to open his own "house," like the great couture houses of Paris, his own domain in which he would be surrounded by his loyal staff and his "muse," a beautiful young girl who would inspire him in his designs, and he would become the Sun King in a universe of his own creation. "The dream of every American designer," said Halston, "is to remove yourself from the marketplace, have a made-to-order business, have your own building, have the fame, fortune and notoriety, a good clientele and so forth." The dream was to become an *haut couturier.*

THE KINGDOM
OF HALSTONIA

Not just anybody can call himself an *haut couturier* and really be one. The term *haute couture*—which literally means "high needlework" and implies the utmost in hand-crafted quality—was officially defined in 1868 by an organization of dress designers called the *Chambre Syndicale de la Couture Parisienne*, a definition that to this day is still adhered to. The *Chambre Syndicale* decreed that to receive the appellation *haut couturier* a house must, among other qualifications, establish workrooms in Paris; present a collection twice a year which is then duplicated for private customers; create seventy-five or more garments a year; employ a minimum of three models; and produce handmade, one-of-a-kind confections. By the early nineteenth century *haute couture* had become a sort of stylized art form, in which the design and fitting of a garment could take months and the customer was expected to come back a dozen or so times for consultations at which the *couturière* or *couturier* would preside. "The subtleties of French *haute couture*," said Diana Vreeland, "were in the actual completion of an outfit, in the delicate pressing and steaming of a skirt, in the tiny *spécialités* a customer could demand . . . the size of a button, the width of a collar . . ."

Until the mid-nineteenth century there were no big-name dress designers, only talented dressmakers who usually took directions from their clients. Curiously, the founder of French *haute couture* was born an Englishman, Charles Frederick Worth, who in the 1850s became the first designer with a name recognized by society women because of the skirts he made for the czarina of Russia. With the invention of the sewing machine in 1860, there came a proliferation of manufacturers and a sudden interest in designers. Recognition as an *haut couturier*, however, was accorded to only a rarefied few. Their names are still synonymous with glamour and impeccable taste: Chanel, Lanvin, Poiret.

At any one time only about two dozen *haute couture* houses have existed. And although there have been a few American-born *couturiers*—most notably Mainbocher, who was born in Chicago but moved to Paris in his twenties—there were no internationally recognized American designers on a par with, say, Givenchy or Dior. The Paris residency qualification alone was enough to prohibit Halston from officially being named an *haut couturier*. But Halston knew what he wanted. "He wanted to be recognized as the Balenciaga of America," said writer R. Couri Hay, who knew him well at the time, and that's what he set out to achieve.

Halston had long been toying with the idea of opening his own fashion house. In July of 1967, when he was in Paris with Tom Fallon to see the collections, he told Fallon that he had been talking to Givenchy about going into business with him. "Halston said that he was going to open a very grand house in New York where he would make custom clothes and have a ready-to-wear line and that he would also carry Givenchy's clothes." Back in New York, during long lunch breaks from the slow trickle of clients at the Bergdorf boutique, Halston and Fallon went to look at various real estate parcels for his "house." One of them was the Florence Lustig building on East Fifty-seventh Street, which had a rather ornate stone French facade that housed a jewelry shop. Halston also looked at a property on East Fifty-second Street where Paley Park would later be built. But the rents were exorbitant and the purchase prices prohibitive. The cost of doing it right might go as high as a million dollars.

Halston asked Joanne Crevelling to write a business prospectus for him, assuming he could get four or five of the millionaire husbands of his clients to stake him. He was surprised and a little hurt when, after the wealthy women on whom he thought he could depend showed the twenty-five-page prospectus to their rich hubbies, he was turned down flat, according to Joanne Crevelling. "About three months later," Fallon said, "Halston told me that the backing for his business was not going to work. He said he didn't know how long it was going to take him to get his business open and that he was rethinking his whole concept."

His new conception was not couture, but ready-to-wear, and he finally found his money—not a million, but $125,000 from Mrs. Estelle Marsh of Amarillo and San Antonio, Texas, "a close personal friend," Halston claimed. Actually, he knew Mrs. Marsh, whose husband had made a Texas-sized fortune, from Bergdorf's where he had made an extremely positive impression on her by having four Mainbocher shirts she brought in to the store duplicated for her in the Bergdorf workrooms. Because her husband's fortune was based in part on investments in natural gas, Halston frequently joked that his new business venture was "built on hot air." When Mrs. Marsh wasn't around, "Halston used to call her Mrs. Marshmallow," said Clovis Ruffin.

But $125,000 didn't buy much in Manhattan, and Halston's first showroom did not turn out to be a grand edifice or have a swanky address. Instead, for $125,000 he settled for the third floor of 33 East Sixty-eighth Street, above a restaurant called

Phoebe's Whamburger, in what had once been an elegant six-story town house where Franklin Delano Roosevelt reportedly spent some of his childhood. It was an unlikely location for a fashion house. By then the building was in general disrepair and the two-person elevator was old and lurched creakily. The tan paint on the stairwell was peeling, there was a rock promoter's office on the second floor, and Phoebe's Whamburger turned out to be a local meeting place for mothers and kids from the private schools in the neighborhood. The result was that at 3 P.M. every school day the building became besieged by children in pleated jumpers and blue blazers.

Halston signed the lease on September 1, 1968, and set to work on fixing up the interior for the next three months. It would be no mean trick to turn the dilapidated floor-through of the brownstone into a chic and elegant space. Yet with its warren of rooms, high tin ceilings, and elongated windows overlooking the buzz of Madison Avenue, the place did have a certain innate style. Perhaps with money and time, a good architect and a contractor, it could be transformed into something smart. But all that Halston had was the brilliance of his friend Angelo Donghia. Clovis Ruffin remembered, "When Halston really didn't have enough money to finish off the space, he went to Angelo for help." Donghia agreed to design the salon for him—gratis—on the condition that every time the salon was photographed or discussed—as they hoped it would be—Donghia's name would be mentioned. Even with Donghia's gratis help, "He ran out of money in three months time," remembered Joanne Crevelling. "He spent $80,000 fixing the third floor alone."

Donghia decided that the simplest and cheapest thing to do was cover everything, including the walls, with fabric. Along with Seymour Avigdor, a promising young designer and apprentice to Donghia, the two spent days scouring the fabric market and discount houses for interesting prints. They bought thousands of yards of Indian batik, many from the Far East, and then literally covered everything with a different pattern; the walls were shirred in one pattern and the borders along the ceiling and floors were shirred in another; there were buffalo-horn chairs with batik cushions in another pattern and an over-stuffed print sofa and pillows in yet another print. There were portieres and occasional tables, draped fabric over fabric, pattern on pattern. In every corner and cranny he stuck palm trees and palm fronds in terra-cotta pots. They put diving-board matting called "sisal" on the floors and on almost every table there was a pot of white orchids, Halston's "sexy" flower; not long after Halston opened his doors, *Women's Wear* dubbed the salon the "Orchid Palace." The total effect was brilliant. It was an overwhelming, lush, and tropical-looking environment. "There's something magic about these rooms," Halston said. "Women love it, the comfort of it." (Comfort or no, for the first several months there was no dressing room and the ladies had to change in the toilet.)

"There was never anything like it before in New York," said Joanne Crevelling. "Before you even saw the clothes you were presold. It was so different from the Seventh Avenue look of pipe racks and solid-color furniture with overflowing ashtrays. The decorating was very clever because Halston's clothes were so minimal in design, they would have looked shockingly plain in a more simple atmosphere."

As for Halston's promise that Angelo Donghia would be given credit for the interior design, two weeks before the grand opening *Women's Wear* noted, "Through Monday's mail comes a two-page release on the East Indian interiors Angelo Donghia of Burge Donghia is designing for Halston's new quarters, which open in December. But almost on top of the release comes a frantic phone call. 'The release is only for your information'—even though it's marked for immediate release. 'Mr. Halston feels it would detract from his opening if you ran anything at this time.' "

When the salon did open and the interior got smash reviews,

Angelo Donghia was only rarely credited. In one article about the decor, Halston told *Women's Wear*, "I never understood gold chairs and white walls," without ever mentioning Donghia's name. "It became a bone of contention between them," said Clovis Ruffin. "They were still friendly after that, but it was more formal, not as friendly. It was also at that point that Halston began to eclipse all his friends in fame and accomplishment. Angelo and Halston got into a competition. Halston looked like he was really going someplace and Angelo was just a decorator. The next thing you know Angelo invented chic and they got competitive from there on."

During the three months of renovation, Halston began to build the rudiments of a business structure. He took three other people into the operation with him. Although each of the trio had some remarkable talent, none of them seemed particularly qualified for the jobs for which Halston chose them. First, there was his long, tall, stylish pal from Fire Island, Joanne Crevelling, whom he named vice president of business affairs. Although she would later go on to run her own well-known public-relations company, at the time Crevelling was a twenty-eight-year-old assistant buyer at Macy's and hardly a savvy business person. His next choice, and the most sensible of the three, was Frances Stein, the *Glamour* magazine editor. "Frances was a true genius," said Crevelling, echoing the general consensus, "and she was hired to interpret the shapes." Stein would become a great influence not only on Halston, but also later on to Calvin Klein, before becoming a top jewelry designer on her own. There was also Joel Schumacher, then twenty-eight years old, a former window dresser and pal of Halston's whom he had met in 1963 on Fire Island. Schumacher had already made his mark as one of the designers of the successful Paraphernalia Youthquake lines. "Joel was in charge of knitwear," said Crevelling. Schumacher would also go on to become a successful and talented film director, with credits that include *St. Elmo's Fire, The Lost Boys, Flatliners,* and

Cousins. Halston gave each of his team, rather generously, a substantial percentage of the ownership. "There were four partners in the business," said Crevelling. "Halston had half, and Frances Stein and Joel Schumacher and I each had a third of the remaining half. We all had papers, drawn and signed from the Bank of New York."

"We like to call ourselves a Think Tank," Halston said. "Each one of us represents a very specific point of view. Take Frances. She looks at clothes with an editor's eye. Joel, of course, has the young outlook. I represent the high end of fashion. Naturally Joanne will handle everything to do with the business." He added, "Most importantly, we're all stars."

Yet there was really only room for one star in the Halston solar system, and within two years, Crevelling, Stein, and Schumacher would be gone, fired, have quit, or been worn out, until only Halston was running the show.

ON DECEMBER 2, 1968, the doors to the salon opened for the first time with an invitational showing of a small men and women's ready-to-wear collection that Halston had arranged for various manufacturers to produce on consignment. Sitting on the thirty little gold chairs that lined a makeshift runway were top buyers and influential journalists and tastemakers from across the country, including Bonwit's Mildred Custin, Bloomingdale's Joseph Schnee, Rose Wells from Federated Department Stores, and representatives of J. L. Hudson, A&S, Sakowitz, AMC, Neiman-Marcus, and Carson Pirie Scott. Only representatives from Bergdorf Goodman were conspicuous by their absence.

That day of his first collection turned out to be a momentous one for Halston. It wasn't so much the show itself—there were only twenty-five pieces—and the collection wasn't staged like the usual extravaganza with models wearing cocktail dress after cocktail dress sailing down the runway. But it was at this show that he first began to define his prominent role in American fashion. This was the seminal statement of the classic Halston look and the real genesis of his fashion message: "No cuckoo, no ko-ko," as Halston described it. Clean, elegant, simple, and spare. Luxurious and rich.

In that first show, and the next few after it, very little clothing actually appeared. Sometimes it seemed as if the models wore variations on a single pajama skirt or a simple wrap dress. The same thing seemed to come out of the dressing room again and again—a little pajama skirt, a little wrap dress—and each time everything looked more beautiful, more perfect. The way fashion guru and editor Polly Mellen later described it, "He would design a perfect jacket. First he would make it in black and double-faced wool. Then he would make it in a colored satin or velvet, or make it in a colored wool or matte and my eye would say, wait a minute. What's going on here. I want that jacket and I want it twice." At that first show appeared a caramel-colored, long jersey sweater-jacket and a tweedy, belted sweater worn with a simple white shirt. There was a burgundy-colored stitched-jersey jacket with matching pants and a white knit tunic. There were hardly any zippers or buttons, and the clothing was so simple and unconstructed that only the perfection of the proportions made the garment seem to hang so naturally. The collection made the front pages of both *Women's Wear Daily* and the *Daily News Record,* which lauded the collection for its "precise shapes, clean lines, confidence" and his men's clothing as "well thought out . . . all with plenty of savvy."

But it wasn't so much the reviews as the reaction of his customers that started the Halston legend snowballing. The very day after his show, Halston discovered Babe Paley, the greatest trendsetter of all the fashionable women, waiting at his front door at 9:30 in the morning to order an argyle pantsuit made to order. "It wasn't my intention to go into a made-to-order business," Halston said. "I wasn't prepared to make clothes for private people because I didn't have that kind of staff, you know, but of course, Mrs. Paley is probably the number-one client you could possibly want as a designer. So, I started, and because of Mrs. Paley I think I started making (made-to-order) clothes. My second client was Jane Engelhard (the wife of a platinum magnate), who is one of the loveliest, nicest ladies I have ever met in my life, who came to me with a whole Christmas list of things . . . took me over in the corner and asked me if I needed some money. Thank God, I didn't, but I'll never forget it. All of a sudden, I was in the made-to-order business." Just as he had hoped, the fashionable ladies he knew from Bergdorf began to pour through his doors. Catherine Deneuve, Alexis Smith, Bianca Jagger, Ali MacGraw, Liza Minnelli, Raquel Welch, Lauren Bacall, Anne Ford, Jackie Onassis, the Baroness de Rothschild, Mrs. Averell Harriman, Mrs. Gianni Agnelli, Amanda Burden, Doris Duke, all became private customers. Even the new First Lady, Mrs. Richard Nixon, had begun to shop at his salon.

Just like the grand European houses, Halston closed his doors during lunch. From around 12:30 to 2 P.M., not even the phone was answered, for that was when "amusing" things began to happen. Soon the chicest spot to have lunch in *tout* New York was Halston's salon, where an invitation was harder to come by than a reservation at La Côte Basque or Grenouille. "Come up and we'll have one of my famous lunches," he would coo on the phone to Lauren Bacall or Barbara Walters. "We always stop for a proper lunch" he explained. "Wine, salad, sometimes a quiche." This minimal and slimming lunch was served by Viola, his newly employed black maid, who wore a starched black uniform with white apron as she dispensed the quiche and salad and poured white wine into Baccarat goblets. (When Mrs. Vreeland came to lunch she always requested, and got, a peanut-butter sandwich with mocha ice cream for dessert.) With the air pungent with a mixture of Rigeaux candles and freshly brewed espresso, the sounds of Aretha Franklin or cool jazz on the stereo, Halston would recline on a faux-zebra-striped banquette and stroke his Pekingese dog as he charmed his lunch guests and traded harmless bits of society and show business gossip. Then after lunch, very casually, two or three house models would appear in clothing Halston felt was appropriate for his lunch guests, and more frequently than not a sale or two or three was made.

"There is never a hurried feeling when you go into Halston's," Barbara Walters said. "It's always, 'Sit down, have a cup of tea. What's your problem? You're going on a trip? Well, let's see.' You come away soothed by him and by the clothes you've bought." There was also never a sales pitch. Halston never sold, he suggested. He even unsold. He would say to a customer, "Darling, you don't need that, you have enough already," and the customer would swoon even more because he wasn't after them for their bucks. When Lauren Bacall went on a tour of the United States in the stage musical *Applause,* she bought some Halston clothes to take on the road with her and then called up for more. "No, you have enough," Halston told her.

Once, when a customer asked Halston to design something specific for her, he said, "Oh, you don't need anything; anyhow, I don't have anything." Then he started talking aimlessly for a few minutes and when the customer stood up to leave he quickly doodled a sketch on a pad and within a few seconds presented her with the perfect outfit. Eleanor Lambert, the doyenne of all fashion business publicists, was working for Halston at the time and she remembered that Halston had another ploy to please his ladies: he mislabeled the sizes on his dresses. "I was so proud that I wore an eight at Halston," said Lambert, "but I think it was a twelve marked eight."

This most fashionable salon had another side to it after dark, when all the rich women were at home having cocktails with their husbands. At night Halston would have a cocktail himself or two or three and perhaps fire up a marijuana cigarette. Often the after-hours salon became the setting for small private parties, an art exhibit by a friend, a poetry reading or small happening for a model's birthday. As time passed, Halston's East Sixty-eighth Street salon became not just a fashion house, but a real salon and meeting place for upcoming personalities of the time. Said Loulou Klossowski, a fashion assistant and former muse of Yves Saint Laurent, "Before any of us became famous in the fashion business he would give these mad, wild, crazy parties in his showroom, which was then done like a Persian tent. It was divine . . .''

A whole assortment of characters flowed in and out of the salon in slightly overlapping, offbeat groups. "Halston would invite a countess and a prizefighter together," remembered Clovis Ruffin, "Babe Paley and a Puerto Rican drag queen."

It also became slyly rumored among the in-crowd that marijuana was sometimes smoked after-hours at Halston's salon. Eleanor Lambert remembered, "They served apple juice because that's what people who smoked marijuana liked."

At one of his parties a well-known lesbian designer tried to appropriate a fedora from the showroom merchandise as she left. The woman was about to get into the decrepit elevator with the hat on her head when Halston stopped the party dead by roaring in his grandest round tones, *"Excuse me!* That is *my* hat."

The woman wasn't about to be intimidated and she snapped right back, "Oh, no it's *not.* I wore this hat here."

Halston's eyes glazed over as he snarled, "This is my house and that is *my* hat," and he plucked it right off her head. The elevator arrived and the woman got in before a fistfight erupted.

Halston and his salon were a sensation, the big success story of the year. Then on October 13, 1969, after less then one year in business, Halston was awarded his second Coty Award—a "Special Award" this time, for the "total look" of his first solo collection. As he mounted the stage at Lincoln Center's Alice

Tully Hall to receive his award from presenter and Halston customer Dina Merrill, a black-tie audience cheered for him. As he stood at the microphone holding the award and flashing his beautiful smile, he looked very young and handsome, on top of the world, full of modesty and light. On the occasion of this Coty, Halston said, "Fashion starts with fashionable people. The fact that they're wearing it makes it a fashion." This time he didn't bother to add, "and you're only as good as the people you dress."

IT WAS IN those early, heady days of Halston's East Sixty-eighth Street salon that "the membranes of the empire were in embryonic stages" as Francesca Stanfill wrote in *Women's Wear*. In a way, it was very much like an empire, with Halston as the emperor (as *Life* magazine would later call him), attended by courtiers, a queen mother, a court magician, jesters, and ladies- and gentleman-in-waiting. It wasn't unusual at all to have an attending staff in the fashion business; all the great French *couturiers* had a clique of models and various sycophants surrounding them. Now, with Halston's growing gravitational pull, the same sort of people nebula began to form around him.

At the innermost circle of Halston's new band of stalwart loyalists was his assistant and majordomo, Bill Dugan. Originally from Albany, New York, Dugan was a balding young man with a small, clipped moustache who remained with Halston for the rest of Halston's career. A 1968 graduate of the Pratt Institute of Design, Dugan was in his own right a talented designer. Unfortunately, as a backup to Halston, he had little opportunity to express himself and was perceived by many to be Halston's ultimate "yes" man. He was, indeed, never farther away than the snap of Halston's fingers. The longevity of his career can be attributed not only to Dugan and Halston's shared sensibilities about fashion, people, and diversions, but also to Dugan's fierce and unwavering allegiance to Halston.

Also as determinedly dedicated to Halston was D. D. Ryan, the former *Harper's Bazaar* fashion editor and wife of investment banker John Barry Ryan III. Dorinda Dixon Ryan was a constant fixture in Halston's entourage and in some ways the most enigmatic member of his private crew. Gregarious and charming, D. D. Ryan thought that everything was "divine, simply divine." She had come to her own special prominence by designing the costumes for the Broadway production of Stephen Sondheim's hit show *Company,* and was also an editor at *Harper's Bazaar* where she worked with Diana Vreeland. After her marriage to the wealthy and equally gregarious John Ryan, she left the magazine business and began to lead a glamorous and fashionable jet-set life, moving into the same building on East Fifty-second Street as Greta Garbo. Ryan had a strikingly distinct style of dressing and putting on makeup. Her shiny black hair was always worn with a severe part down the middle and pulled back tightly into a chignon. Her makeup was very stylized, with little peaked eyebrows, and she had a distinctive affected speaking voice. She was best known for her simple yet chic pajama-type outfits that many credit as being the genesis of some of Halston's earliest inspirations. After her difficult divorce from Ryan, D.D. would be at Halston's side for the rest of his career. Halston was famous for alternately treating D.D. generously and mistreating her in the office, when she would break into tears. Through the years she worked in many different capacities for Halston, including as a saleswoman in the couture department and as liaison with the design room.

Halston's sense of the outrageous was evident in the presence of 200-pound actress-singer Pat Ast as a salesgirl for the salon and boutique. Ast, whom he met in the Fire Island Pines, *amuuused* Halston. She was a raucous personality with wild, frizzy hair, rubbery facial expressions, and a voice like a wood chipper. Surprisingly, she was an excellent saleswoman, sincere and devoted. And it didn't hurt business when even a woman of her proportions looked fashionable and neat in her specially made-to-order Halston outfits. Her presence at Halston's was "a stroke of genius," according to one friend. But even Halston admitted, "Certain clients loved her, other clients found her offensive."

If Halston's court had a Merlin, it was no doubt Joe Eula, the illustrator and pundit who sat by Halston's right hand, literally, for almost a decade. Eula was a cherubic, bespectacled graphic designer who would execute most of Halston's sketches for him and serve as his most influential interpretive source. Eula was not only a brilliant illustrator in his own right, but he had the uncanny ability to transform Halston's verbal descriptions of clothing into beautiful sketches—works of art in themselves, executed in Eula's distinctive, sweeping brushstroke style. But Eula was even more in Halston's life than a creative spark. He was also a witty foil and good friend, a trusted advisor, but one with a tongue so sharp it could easily deflate any egos expanding in his direction—including Halston's. Eula was a devil on the side of the angels, lovable but unpredictable, and if he and Halston got into a spat, as they frequently did, there was nowhere to hide. "I didn't have an office," said Joe Eula. "My office was the edge of Halston's desk."

Born in Norwalk, Connecticut, in 1925, Eula was already a celebrated illustrator when he joined Halston's circle. They had "first met in passing years ago," said Eula, "many times, always in Europe when he would go for Bergdorf's and I'd go with Eugenia Sheppard for the *Herald Tribune*. But our official meeting was under a white organza kerchief when he did his first collection under the Halston name and we photographed it with Sally Kirkland for *Life* and I did the painted backdrops. We became close friends at that time." Eula also had great respect for Halston's talent. "The man's taste was on a par with Balenciaga, Givenchy, and Saint Laurent," said Eula.

Eula also had something of a reputation as a sort of Pied Piper of fashionable young people; he made Auntie Mame look like an old maid. In two seconds, Eula could solve your problems—or create new ones. He could look at the face of a young woman and say, "Baby, tweeze your eyebrows, you need more height, and wear lighter pink lipstick, it'll bring out your complexion." Or, he could whip out a pair of scissors, correct a bad haircut, and dry the tears of a young model. An entire coterie of fans populated his world and his frequent parties at his all-white, West Fifty-fifth Street floor-through apartment. This apartment became the melting pot of an international set, Eula's acolytes, the beautiful young heiresses and models who hung on his every word as though he were the Guru of Chic. Soon, Eula's crowd and Halston's mixed, and the scene spilled over into the salon, terribly chic and hip, populated by an assortment of glamorous but dissolute young men in cowboy boots whose fathers had European titles; gorgeous young heiresses on the verge of nervous breakdowns; up-and-coming fashion designers, including Giorgio di Sant' Angelo, Scott Barrie, and Fernando Sanchez; models Verushka, Pat Cleveland, Heidi Gold, and Karen Bjornson; Saint Laurent's stylist and muse, Loulou de la Falaise; and illustrators Antonio Lopez and David Croland.

Perhaps the jewels in the crown of this crowd were Marisa Berenson and her younger sister Berry. These two beautiful girls just in their early twenties were triply blessed; they were the granddaughters of fashion designer Elsa Schiaparelli, the nieces of esteemed art critic Bernard Berenson, and they were adorable and charming. Marisa was the delicate older sister, an aspiring actress who later went on to costar in the movie *Cabaret* with Liza Minnelli, as well as star opposite Ryan O'Neal in the Stanley Kubrick film *Barry Lyndon*. Marisa's younger sister, Berry, a warmer, more down-to-earth girl, was at the time dating illustrator Richard Bernstein. On assignment to photograph actor Tony Perkins for *Interview* magazine, she fell in love with him and they later married. Both girls adored Halston, as did many pretty young things looking for advice and direction, and Halston took them under his wing. When Marisa married attorney Richard Golub, Halston threw the wedding for them, and when Berry married Tony Perkins, Halston was asked to be godfather of their first child.

Eula was also the glue between Halston and young Liza Minnelli, although they had already met in 1966, when Halston was still at Bergdorf's and she was just thought of as Judy Garland's daughter. By the time she visited him at his own salon a few years later she had already been nominated for an Academy Award for her role in *The Sterile Cuckoo*. Eula claimed that Minnelli just walked in the door one day. "She was a shopper," Eula remembered, "and she was always looking for somebody to do her clothes. Halston was the hotshot of the day and Liza's a shopper. She came in and they fell in love. She had a great, marvelous sense of the theatrical, and upon seeing his clothes they fell madly in love."

Liza remembered that when they first met, "Halston liked bosoms when bosoms weren't in. Everybody wanted to look like Twiggy, and Halston looked at me and said, 'What are you doing? You've got a great bustline, you have to celebrate it.' And I said, 'What?' Nobody had ever talked to me as if I had any glamour or style or anything. And he really did give it to me, and he continued to give it to me. That was before *Cabaret*. That was before anything."

Halston understood the problems Liza had with the way she looked and helped her work them out. He realized that depending on her temperament and love affairs her figure could go up or down ten pounds in either direction. So he kept several dummies with padding for whatever condition she was in. He knew where she put on the fat, and he designed clothes to show off her better features. During the rehearsals for *The Act* in 1977, Halston reportedly made several sizes of each costume for Liza to accommodate her wildly fluctuating weight. He was also savvy enough to notice that because she was slightly hirsute it was better to cover her arms with long sleeves.

Liza credits Halston for a dramatic transformation in her look and image. Up until she went to him she had a terrible physical self-image and felt as if she had no personal style of her own.

"Well," Halston said, "we'll fix it. Now tell me what you want to look like?"

Liza laughed and said, "A female Fred Astaire." Halston didn't seem the least bit confused by this. "Somehow," Liza said, "he knew exactly what to do, and fit it all into five suitcases.

"At the time my life was complicated with travel and movies and shows," Liza said, "and he told me how to dress and to simplify my life. I had to go overseas and I wanted to look great all the time and Halston said, 'Well, here's what I want you to do. I want you to go over to Vuitton and buy yourself some luggage. "You're going to faint at how expensive it is, but I want you to buy what you can afford and bring it back to me and that's what's going to make your wardrobe. Whatever you can fit in, that's what you'll wear."

Liza went to Vuitton and bought five matching pieces and had them sent to Halston's salon. "Three weeks later," Liza said, "I went to his salon and he had designed something to go to the races in, something to be at home in, something to go to the opening of the casino, something to wear to the polo field, and it all worked, it all fit, and it was extraordinary." Halston had put together not just a wardrobe for Liza, but a stylistic look that she felt comfortable in and could call her own. He even designed a shoe with a five-inch heel that not only gave her height but changed her posture as well. "You have beautiful legs and you gotta show them off," he told her.

Finally, just before she left on her trip, Halston presented Liza with a beautiful leather-bound notebook that contained sketches of all the individual pieces he had made for her, along with a color code and accompanying suggestions on how to coordinate the outfits. The next year, Liza Minnelli was nominated for the International Best Dressed List.

Halston and Liza's friendship, however, went far beyond that of a tailor and his client. Over the years there grew a deep love and real commitment between them. Liza adored Halston. He was father and brother and best girlfriend, and he always had time for her and he was never condemning or mean. Nothing shocked him—they could talk about anything—and he was relentlessly positive and uplifting. Halston had a sensible, straightforward philosophy of "find out what's wrong and let's fix it," according to Liza. "He was like a big brother to me and a lot of women," said Liza. "He taught me to *listen.*" To see Liza and Halston in a room together was to know just how much they loved each other. They were like young lovers, hugging and touching and sometimes Liza would sit cuddled in the same chair as Halston as he whispered bon mots in her ear. Although they would be photographed together on endless nights out on the town, at stellar publicity events and parties, the best moments of their friendship were spent in Halston's kitchen on nights when just the two of them were together, telling each other the story of their lives while Halston cooked pot roast for dinner. They drank wine and giggled and Halston listened and advised Liza on her complicated love affairs, unrequited crushes, and unfulfilling marriages. On these nights Liza marveled at how kind and how smart he was. "You know all those intimate shots of Halston and me with our heads together at parties?" she asked. "Most of the time we were just muttering, 'How the hell do we get outta here?' under our breaths."

Liza had real competition in her affection for Halston in the Italian model and jewelry designer Elsa Peretti. While Halston's relationship with Liza Minelli was paternal and platonic, Halston's friendship with Peretti decidedly was not. In some other fold of Halston's complex nature, his love-hate relationship with Elsa Peretti was the most emotional and sexually tense one that he ever entered into with any woman. If Halston had been heterosexual, Peretti would have been his *grand amour.* Born in

Florence in 1940, Peretti was well educated in European schools before she appeared in New York in 1966 as a model. Funny, smart, and tough, with her short clipped hair and tall, bony figure, she was part Anna Magnani, part Audrey Hepburn. Halston's clothes fit her as if they had been woven onto her back, and she could walk down a runway in his cashmere sweater-dress with one of his capes thrown over her shoulder and bring down the house. But modeling was just a lark for Peretti. In 1969 she started designing jewelry and almost as quickly as Halston found success, she became one of the most highly regarded jewelry designers in the world—perhaps best known for her heart-shaped and equestrian belt buckles, as well as the Peretti "bean" on a cord that could be used as a necklace or a belt. She won a Coty Award in 1971 for jewelry and in 1974 became the in-house designer at Tiffany, where she popularized her "diamonds by the yard." She also started a fashion trend with the Peretti "cuff" of hammered sterling silver to be worn at the wrist.

Not only did Peretti's cool, clean accessories and jewelry interlock perfectly with Halston's clothes, but her hot-blooded and flamboyant nature clicked with Halston's emotional needs, and for a time the two of them couldn't seem to get enough of each other. Peretti was captivated by him, swept off her feet in the beginning and demanding of his time and attention. They were an astonishing pair together, alternately jealous and loving, coveting and protective of each other, but also hot-tempered beyond the normal meaning of the phrase. So delicately was their relationship balanced that anything could set them off, the wrong intonation or a passing criticism, or Halston's inattention. And when the J.E. temper clashed with Peretti's *brio,* spectacular, overblown dramas and fights would ensue, complete with slamming doors, smashing down the phone on each other, and breaking ashtrays for effect—fantastic, overblown dramas that were as passionate as the affection they felt for each other. They liked that kind of interaction because they were both strong people. Peretti could also be impatient and ruthless when confronted with weakness. One friend remembered her encouraging someone who was depressed to jump out the window.

"The only problem was, they never fucked," said Joe Eula. "Everybody said to Halston, 'You should marry Elsa,' said Eula. But Halston just laughed at the thought. Many of their mutual acquaintances believe, or would like to believe, that they actually did have an affair many years ago at the beginning of their friendship, but there is no proof this ever happened. When she was in town occasionally on quick overnight trips from Europe, Peretti stayed on a small bed tucked away in one of the rooms at the East Sixty-eighth Street salon, and when Halston eventually moved out of his East Fifty-fifth Street digs he made a gesture that for a city dweller is the utmost show of affection—he arranged for her to take over the lease of his rent-controlled penthouse apartment.

There also entered into Halston's kingdom a queen mother of mythic proportions: the brilliant modern dancer and choreographer Martha Graham. At the time they met, Graham was already in her seventies. Halston had worshiped her work for years and had often compared it to his own sleek, minimal style of design. Graham was a revolutionary in the arts who broke traditional molds and developed her own distinctive form of modern dance. She was ranked in her accomplishment with Picasso and Stravinsky. However, by the time she met Halston, Graham was an impoverished legend ripe for a rescue. For Halston she was the perfect metropolitan mother figure, elegant and graceful in her old age. Halston became Graham's major patron, ceaselessly supporting her financially, as well as designing and donating the costumes to over a dozen ballets. "She can do it all," Halston once raved of Graham. "She is a genius at dance, at theater, at costumes, at lighting. There is nothing she can't do."

They were introduced by a mutual friend. Graham was going

to present the Capezio Dance Award to Robert Irving, the musical director of the New York City Ballet. "She didn't have anything to wear," said the friend, "and of course, she never had any money of her own. Martha's own dressmaking had been superb, her costumes on stage were absolute innovations. So I thought, who could relate to that? . . . and instantly—Halston. The way Halston cuts and the way he uses fabric—his clothes actually have a dance movement. I rang up Halston and asked if he could possibly lend Martha something."

Graham went to East Sixty-eighth Street and Halston fell in love with her. Graham remembered that first day. "There was a beautiful natural-colored caftan of cashmere and a poncho to wear with it. I loved it so much and I felt so wonderful in it. I asked if I could buy it on time. Halston said no, he wanted to give it to me."

Halston soon became Graham's patron as well as her clothing designer and company costume designer. Sometimes, when things got really bad, Halston not only supported the dance company but paid Graham's rent as well. "I treasure Halston as a friend and as a patron," she said. "He has very much been a patron of mine. Once we were rehearsing in a theater and we had to stop at a crucial time because of union rules. And Halston asked our company director, 'Why is she stopping?' The director said, 'She can't afford to pay the double time.' "

Halston said, "That's ridiculous. I'll pay it."

"When he believes in something," Graham said, "he participates. Of course, he can be ice when he has to be ice."

As for her costumes, "Halston cuts them and watches over them. I've even seen him put the pins in. Every girl is overseen by him. He stayed up half the night making jewelry, and he sewed until his hands bled."

Courtiers, queen mothers, a court magician—all that was needed now to round out the cast of characters was a Black Prince. And Halston already had that in Ed Austin. By now, however, Ed Austin and Halston's sexual liaison had cooled.

Yet, "our relationship never stopped," said Austin. "Only our love affair stopped." Halston still trusted Austin so implicitly that Austin claims he was named co–vice president with Mrs. Marsh on the original incorporation papers of Halston's business, and offered a job in the salon—as his assistant. " 'I'll train you,' is what Halston said to me," said Austin, "and he started me out by picking up pins. Then he let me work in the office, and eventually I started waiting on clients and I became an all-around person. All the staff members knew what was going on, of course. Around the salon he was called the 'king' and I was called the 'crown prince.' Halston had no problem with me working for him because he was all business, but I had a problem with it and I had to adjust. I used to get a little uptight that I wasn't included anymore in certain things."

THROUGH ALL THE passing years of his success, Halston never let his friendship with Charles James lapse. By this point in his life, James was broke and thoroughly dissolute, stoned on drugs most of the time. He was also an exceptionally mean and testy man to deal with, an injustice collector who was apt to lash out at anyone who came near him. Most people with a modicum of sense would have steered clear of the older designer, yet Halston still revered James as a great master, and now that he was in a position to help, Halston decided to resurrect this *monstre sacré*—a project that everyone around them saw as hopelessly doomed. Myrna Davis warned Halston, "You'd better watch out, Charles James has sued everybody." But Halston said he wasn't concerned, that he would be Charles James's patron.

Halston's campaign to bring back James began on December 16, 1969, when he honored James by sponsoring a retrospective of his clothing at the Electric Circus, a super-trendy, psychedelicized nightspot on St. Marks Place in the East Village. Halston said he was producing the show because "Charles James has always been one of my heroes." The clothing in the show was going to be donated to the Smithsonian Institution, and James's beautiful drawings were to be given to the Chicago Historical Society. The poster for the event, which was some sort of private joke between Halston and James, depicted a James drawing of a languidly draped naked figure with a whip lying on it. This kinky combination—the grand *couturiers* Halston and James giving a fashion show in the East Village—turned the evening into one of the great reverse-chic events of that Christmas season, and the tickets, at a steep $40 each, sold out. For those who couldn't afford $40, 100 tickets had been purchased by patrons and distributed free to students at local fashion and art schools who turned out in force to see and meet the legendary James.

It didn't bode well for the rest of the evening when at a preshow cocktail party given at Mrs. William F. Buckley's maisonette on Park Avenue for 100 people, Halston and James arrived separately, not speaking to each other. Whatever had come between them really didn't matter, because James and Halston could get "hissy" with each other over something as insignificant as who got into the limousine first. After the tense cocktail party during which Halston and James stood on either side of the room and made snide remarks, the 100 guests—including Betsy Theodoracopulos, Mrs. John Converse, Giorgio di Sant' Angelo with model Verushka, and designer Dimitri Kristas—piled into two buses and were driven down to the hippie enclaves. Sparks continued to fly between James and Halston as they both threatened to cancel the show. "Halston had done something," said Couri Hay, who had organized the junior committee for the evening and was James's escort for the night. "He had either taken away something or didn't allow the workmen to finish the way James wanted, and there was this madness which was characteristic of Charles's life and his relationship with Halston."

The show did go on, and as beautiful, interpretive sketches of James's clothing by top illustrator Antonio Lopez flashed on the walls, celebrity models like Naomi Sims and Berry Berenson paraded James's stylized costumes. Although the students oohed and ahhed over James's "Ribbon Dress" and "Taxi Dress," on the whole the show was peculiar and a little sad and the entire event anticlimatic.

Yet not long thereafter, Halston announced to the press that he was employing James to work for him in his showroom. "He's an engineer of fashion," Halston raved, "and will help engineer the mechanics of our fashions, such as putting in pockets or working out the wraparound trousers. James will help shape the collection, like Balenciaga helped Givenchy." In fact, considering the risks in bringing James into his showroom, it was difficult to understand why Halston wanted him there so badly, all charity aside. There was one theory that Halston really thought he *needed* James to get his clothes to fit correctly; although Halston's first collections got good reviews, the garments themselves did not fit well when they were delivered to the retailers. Homer Layne, who was Charles James's assistant for ten years, said that "the first collection didn't fit anybody, so everything was returned from the stores." James told Halston his problem was using the tall, angular models instead of "ordinary people or the shape of ordinary people." James later claimed that Halston asked him to help after some of his line "fell apart at Marshall Field." As James later put it, after they had fallen apart, "I was contracted to do consultant work . . . work required to reshape . . . even to restyle his so-called 'designs.' "

In any event, James claimed that Halston promised that every dress James helped work on would bear the label "Shaped by Charles James." As it turned out, James got little more credit than Angelo Donghia did when he designed the first showroom. James was given work space, a so-called "studio" in a small room on the third floor, which a reporter from the *New York Times* described as a cross between "a doctor's office and an artist's workroom with anatomical drawings on the walls, some headless forms of the human body, and a surgical white decor." According to Ed Austin, James was "stoned, stoned, stoned," and after many months, he had turned out only a few styles. "But of course," James said, "once you get the structure right, the things can be reproduced quickly. I believe in mass production."

There was to be no mass production, only mass confusion. Eula remembered, "Of course, the thing wasn't done and we were sitting around at dinner and we said you realize there's no collection. This fool is up there 'creating space' around the figure, but we ain't got no collection. So we went up there and put it together and we indeed did do a show." On June 15, 1970, Halston showed a collection that mingled their work. It was as if everything wonderful about Halston's first collections had been ruined. By general consensus the show was awful, a hodgepodge of styles. *Women's Wear* summed up James's contribution with a brusque "in the soft seventies, who wants engineered clothes?" It was the only negative thing that they had said about a Halston collection in three years. Clovis Ruffin remarked, "I think Halston really thought that Charles James was going to teach him something and show him something, and that he would revive Charles James. At the same time he thought he would get smashing clothes out of the deal. Halston thought James would dip his hand in the 1930s, matte jersey, Madame Grès dress folder, and instead he dipped his hand in the 1952 suede dinner separates folder. It was against the period. Charles James had this perversity of going against the period."

Predictably, James got along no better with Halston than he had with anyone else, and after a clash or two with the J.E. temper, it was over. Said James, "One day Halston walked into the showroom he had given me, which wasn't all that nice, and said, 'You're too old to design. How much do you want to stop being in this business and just live forever?' He offered me two hundred fifty a week for the rest of my life. I declined, I knew he just wanted to steal my work, claim it as his own, of course."

"Halston became Halston after the Charles James show because he realized he was as good as Charles James," said Clovis Ruffin. "He came to the full realization of his talent and he didn't need anybody after that. He did the most brilliant, fabulous clothes after that."

Halston also became the prime villain in Charles James's life, against whom all his vitriol would be directed; if he had been able to afford a lawyer, James would have sued Halston for stealing his designs. Yet even with James's anger turned on him, Halston remained his loyal supporter by continuing to buy James's exquisite erotic drawings of male genitalia. Eventually, James cut him off from that, too. As the years went by and Halston became even more famous, James so focused his hate on him that every time a dress of Halston's appeared on the front page of *Women's Wear*, James made a secret mark on the wallpaper of his room in the Chelsea Hotel. He also kept a list of designs on the wall that he claimed Halston had stolen from him, everything from his figure-eight skirt to a ribbon cape. James would sometimes call Myrna Davis on the phone and complain about Halston to her for hours. He even actually stalked Halston. One summer on Fire Island, Clovis Ruffin and Myrna were sitting on the beach in front of Angelo Donghia's house when Ruffin saw James trudging up the beach with his old beagle dog, Sputnik. Clovis said, "Myrna, watch out, Charles James is looking all over for you. He's trying to find Halston." Myrna made herself scarce.

A few years later Charles James wrote an article for an underground magazine called *Metropolis*, in which among other things, he suggested that Halston had worked as a "night ticket clerk at the old Pennsylvania Station" when he first came to New York. As for Halston's clothes, James said they were "based on the whole 'silent movie swish' and items brought to him by models who had probably acquired them at less than cost price while presenting collections for the Paris *haute cou-*

ture," and that "despite a tearful statement to the effect that slender payments were made for more work than I contracted to do for the kingdom of Halstonia, I have heard, since a sad parting of the ways, many untruths . . ." He finished by proclaimed Halston's designs "fag-hag-drag."

Charles James never made peace with Halston or with the rest of the world. He was found dead of pneumonia and kidney failure in 1978 in his room on the sixth floor of the Chelsea Hotel. He was discovered by his assistant, Homer Layne, lying on the bed in his boxer shorts and dirty undershirt, surrounded by plates of decaying food, dress forms, bolts of fabric, and his fabulous sketches of fashions that never came to be.

"SIMPLY THE PREMIER FASHION DESIGNER OF ALL AMERICA..."

Newsweek **magazine, August 1972**

In January of 1972 a trendy men's boutique called Le Dernier Cri located in the Madison Avenue shop three stories below Halston's salon went out of business. The store had already been transformed into a rather imposing, modern boutique with large open spaces and a small second-floor balcony. The storefront and display windows fronting Madison Avenue and East Sixty-eighth Street had been curiously angled. Impetuously, Halston decided to rent the store himself and open his own boutique to sell his own clothes exclusively. This had only been done successfully once before, by Yves Saint Laurent in Paris.

Halston already had some experience with his own shops. As the demand by the general public for his clothing grew, Halston opened a small, in-store boutique at Bloomingdale's, decorated in a style similar to his showroom. This boutique sold a limited line of ready-to-wear that he was having produced on consignment. Although the clothes were still relatively high priced for the general public, the boutique was an overnight success, and Bloomingdale's biggest problem was restocking orders. Halston was soon negotiating with several other better department stores to open more in-store boutiques, including Halle Brothers in Cleveland, Sakowitz in Houston, Nordstrom-Best in Denver, as well as with five other stores. But despite the fact that sales were good, Halston soon began to feel frustrated with the notion of someone else presenting his clothes. He was convinced that the store buyers were ordering his collection in the wrong way and that sales would be much better if they bought what he felt was a totally coordinated line and not just what struck their fancy. When the opportunity presented itself, Halston decided, he would open his own retail shop and show them what could be done. Now that opportunity had presented itself three stories below his salon.

Halston paid "key money" for the fixtures and moved into the shop within a month. "We really didn't have that much to do because the previous owners had already done it," said Ed Austin, who was by now supervisor of a staff that had grown to fifty-seven people. "Halston put more mirrors in the shop and he had the interior painted an off-white color," Austin said. "He wanted the same exact oyster white as the outside of the building, but the painters said they couldn't do it—it was two different kinds of paints. You should have seen Halston dealing with the painters on that one, that was a trip. 'I don't care what kind of paint,' Halston insisted, 'I want it exactly.' And he got it finally. You *know* he did."

The boutique opened on Monday, February 7, and from the very first day it was jammed with customers. Austin—whom all the rich ladies came to adore—remembered that women would come in from all over the world. "It was not unusual for a woman to drop twenty-five or thirty thousand dollars on each shopping trip," he said. Austin also remembered that one cold winter day so many ladies arrived at the shop wearing mink and sable that when all the coats were thrown on a chaise in the entranceway the pile was ten feet high and worth probably two million dollars.

Although the boutique was in direct competition with the

Halston boutique at Bloomingdale's only a few blocks away, Bloomingdale's continued to do such good business there were no complaints from the department store. This caused Bill Blass to marvel in *Women's Wear,* "I must say Halston has created a lot of firsts in the area of how to sell." With the opening of the boutique, Halston now had three price ranges of clothes under one roof; the boutique level had clothing for as little as $100, the second floor showed clothing at $100 to $400, and in his made-to-order salon upstairs evening dresses could easily cost $10,000.

Women's Wear dubbed the boutique the "latest gathering ground for the Cat Pack" and had Halston purring, "Each time I turn around I find fifty more ladies. It's been terrific. I opened in February, which is a slow month, and my biggest problem is getting stock into the store." Then Halston deftly supplied a list of customers and their purchases. Silk caftans went to Babe Paley, Leigh Taylor-Young, Polly Bergen, Jane Engelhard, Kitty Miller, Liza Minnelli, Marie Hélène de Rothschild, Marisa Berenson, Pat Buckley, Jean Vanderbilt, Sister Parish, Betsey Whitney, Lally Weymouth, Lily Auchincloss, Donna Morella Agnelli, Jan Cowles, and Pamela Harriman. Halston's jersey halter-jumper had been snatched off the racks by Liza Minnelli, Jean Vanderbilt, Amanda Burden, Justine Cushing, Louise Melhado, Marisa Berenson, Lauren Bacall, Minnie Cushing, Betsy Theodoracopulos, Nan Kempner, and Polly Bergen. His new suede coat was purchased by Jackie Onassis, Evangeline Bruce, Liza Minnelli, Betsy Theodoracopulos, Jean Vanderbilt, Pat Buckley, Rocky Cooper (Mrs. Gary Cooper), Mrs. John Converse, Jan Cowles, Pamela Harriman, Ali Kaiser, and D. D. Ryan.

Jackie Kennedy Onassis was probably Halston's most favored customer, and because of her unusual celebrity she was sometimes shown merchandise privately in the third-floor salon. But Mrs. Onassis was also a shopper who liked a bargain as much as anyone, and she would often browse through the racks in the boutique herself. One Saturday she was wandering around the boutique when she noticed a young woman trying on a green cashmere sweater set. As the woman studied the outfit in a mirror, Mrs. Onassis came up behind her and whispered, "You should take them, they go with your eyes."

The startled woman murmured "thank you" and rushed to the cashier and bought the set, no doubt for time eternal to tell her friends, "Jackie Onassis told me to buy this sweater set."

Later, upstairs in Halston's private salon, Jackie told Halston the story and asked him coyly, "Is that all it takes to sell clothes? Just a tiny suggestion?"

CLEARLY, THE SUCCESS of his boutiques heralded a need for Halston to broaden his market. The next logical step for someone in his position would have been to open up his own Seventh Avenue manufacturing concern to produce a mass-market, ready-to-wear line of his clothing in standard sizes that could be bought off the rack—in Halston's case, at selected upscale stores. But this was a step that Halston had long been wary about because, first, it meant taking in partners to run the manufacturing arm of the company, and that meant giving up some element of control. Second, Halston still had great disdain for Seventh Avenue and for the Jews with whom he would inevitably have to be involved in order to expand his business. Eventually, in late May 1972, Halston made his boldest career move yet by teaming up with garment industry kingpin Ben Shaw. Shaw, born Ben Schwartz in Kiev, Russia, seventy-three years earlier, seemed to Halston the epitome of the refugee Jew he so disdained, but Halston also had a healthy respect for Shaw's business acumen. Shaw had bankrolled some of the industry's top names, including Oscar de la Renta, Donald Brooks, and Norman Norell. Shaw allegedly first heard about Halston from Martha Manulis, the important dress retailer, and was brought together with him by designer Chuck Howard.

"I understand Ben Shaw is probably the best person available to work with on something like this," said Halston, and he was right. The new company they formed was called Halston Originals. Shaw also took into the partnership Jerry Uchin, a talented production manager, as well as Guido de Natale, who contracted for various piece goods. This new company, in which Shaw's primary investment was no more than $100,000—according to Donald Friese, who later replaced Uchin as sales manager—would manufacture Halston clothing in a wide price range from $40 to $450. Impressive offices were opened at 555 Seventh Avenue (a building to which Halston dreaded going), and the line was premiered on May 22, 1972. The event was so highly anticipated that the fashion press as well as buyers poured out the front doors of the showroom. Nobody had ever seen such excitement for a new line in the garment business before, and Jerry Uchin was estatic. "I don't know anybody in this business who's had this kind of start," he said happily. "Everybody seemed ready for it." *Women's Wear* certainly was ready for it. They raved, "One of his best collections ever. Halston moved to Seventh Avenue with a spectacular first." Within six months, orders passed the $3 million mark. Even Bergdorf Goodman started ordering his clothing.

The success of Halston's Seventh Avenue business became the talk of the industry. Yet perhaps his biggest triumph of the early seventies was his popularization of the fabric known as Ultrasuede. Halston first saw Ultrasuede at a dinner party in Paris in 1971. Another guest, the up-and-coming Japanese designer Issey Miyake, was wearing a beautiful shirt made of some suedelike fabric so luxurious and light that Halston asked Miyake what it was made of. In his broken English, Miyake told Halston that the fabric was manufactured in Japan. But Halston misunderstood Miyake to say that the fabric was water repellent (instead of washable), which is why Halston first used it to design raincoats. When Halston later discovered the fabric absorbed water instead of repelling it, he was not impressed. "It doesn't rain on the rich," he sniffed.

Ultrasuede was not only washable, it was a durable, light-weight fabric with near-miraculous properties. It was terrific for travel because it was warm in the winter and cool in the summer, it could be thrown in the washing machine and hung out to dry wrinkleless. It was so tough it never seemed to tear or show any wear, yet it was as soft as suede. An unlikely combination of 60 percent polyester and 40 percent polyurethane, Ultrasuede was pressed or packed in layers, similar to the way felt is made. The fabric had actually been around for years but was too stiff and artificial-looking to be successful in its original form and had only recently been perfected in Japan by Toray Industries. It retained its aura of exclusivity in part because of the complicated technology needed to manufacture it. It was also expensive—$19 a yard wholesale for a forty-five-inch-wide roll. The fabric was first shown in America by designer Vera Maxwell, who sold some $50,000 worth of Ultrasuede her first year showing it in small shops.

In the fall collection of 1972, Halston introduced what was to became a fashion sensation: model number 704, a very simple shirtwaist dress with buttons down the front and a little tie at the waist. Suddenly, model number 704 was the biggest fashion invention since the sewing machine. Customers seemed to go berserk. It became what the *New York Times* called a "status security blanket." He sold 78,000 copies of it, which started retailing at $185 and escalated to $360 each as they flew out the doors. Stores would have sold even more if the dresses had been available. Suddenly it didn't seem to matter that women showed up at Le Cirque all wearing the same dress. "The herd instinct is the new chic," rejoiced Eugenia Sheppard. "It's like belonging to a club."

"I'm the ultra-designer," Halston said. "I just can't get enough of it," he crowed. "Each month I'm 10,000 yards behind what I could use." Don Friese said that supply was spread so thin that often they would only be able to fill a small portion of any one store's order, and that many stores began resorting to ordering double and triple what they really needed. Because of Halston, Ultrasuede became so popular that Abe Waters, vice president of Skinner Fabrics, who manufactured it, said, "Sometimes [buyers] almost have me in tears. The way they plead. Unbelievable." Although Halston wasn't the only designer to use the fabric, eventually the names Ultrasuede and Halston became synonymous. He used it for Halston luggage, handbags, shoes, boots, belts, bed covers, picture frames, jewelry boxes, and umbrella covers, to name a few. Eventually he stripped his office of the busy Angelo Donghia fabric, mirrored the walls, and put beigey Ultrasuede over deep, comfortable sofas.

Bernadine Morris wrote in the *New York Times,* "Seventh Avenue often looks like a Halston festival, no matter where you drop in. For women who watch every move Halston makes, it should be noted that Halston's mannequins tend to carry a bunch of violets, especially when they wear one of his pale, mauve Ultrasuede outfits." And on June 7, 1973, only a year after the introduction of his first ready-to-wear collection on Seventh Avenue, Halston showed his fall 1974 collection, which comprised an astoundingly prolific ninety-six pieces. The collection again made the front page of *Women's Wear,* which featured a sketch of the bare halter "dance dress" that had caught Halston's whimsy that season. Longer hemlines were the big story, along with quilted Ultrasuede to add new life. He showed fitted suits in flannel and velvet, step-in shirt chemises, a little black dinner dress in raw silk or jersey and some knockout sequined evening dresses. The *Women's Wear* review could not have been more flattering, calling him the "master of American classics." "It takes a lot of guts to make such a large collection that simple," the review said, "and it takes a lot of talent to keep it from getting boring. Halston has both."

Marlo Thomas, who attended the show, said afterward, "You know, I have to slap my hand away from the phone to keep from ordering more Halston."

On August 21, 1972, Halston experienced his greatest honor yet when he became the cover story of *Newsweek* magazine, entitled "Ease and Elegance Designed by Halston." In coverage unprecedented for a designer, *Newsweek* ran a nine-page article including four pages of color photos. They called him "the premier fashion designer of all America" and quoted *Women's Wear* publisher John Fairchild calling him "*the* snob American designer." Many of his regular customers agreed to model his dresses for the layout, including Raquel Welch, Anjelica Huston, Candice Bergen, Naomi Sims, Liza Minnelli and Lorna Luft. There was also Halston, looking handsome in the photograph, sunglasses perched on top of his head, as he told them, "You're only as good as the people you dress."

Newsweek quoted Halston: "Why, I don't know, but it *is* my time now. I've worked hard for twenty years and I've always had success. I've always dreamed of being a total designer and now it may come true."

FOR A MAN whose career had been celebrated on the cover of *Newsweek,* Halston's personal life was still rather unspectacular and bleak—exactly the way he seemed to want it. He was fast approaching his fortieth birthday and still quite alone. Since his sexual relationship with Ed Austin, Jr., had drifted off, Halston had gone back to his convenient phoning of call boys who would come to the East Fifty-fifth Street apartment, where he would perhaps order them both a steak and a baked potato delivered up, then take them to bed and show them the door. Joe Eula took to calling this practice "dial-a-steak, dial-a-dick," which Halston thought was hysterically funny and began to call it that himself. One night in 1972, the young man who showed up at Halston's apartment from "dial-a-dick" changed his life.

The man's name, improbably, was Victor Hugo—a professional name and a pun, it would turn out, on his "huge-o" endowment. But Victor Hugo was much more than just another big dick. Victor was brilliant, zany, exciting, and dangerous. Because of Victor Hugo, Halston would forever live his life on the edge—on the edge of legality, of propriety, and of sanity. The sex, at first, was spectacular, said Victor, "but Halston and I never had sex after the first three months." He claims, "It was a great love affair, not about sex." And if this is true, and Victor's grip on Halston was purely emotional, then it makes their story even more dynamic and fascinating. "Let me tell you something," said Peruchio Valls, who had known Victor since he was a boy and who later became one of Halston's personal assistants. "The person that Halston loved, more than his own life, was Victor Hugo. And the love of Victor Hugo's life was Halston."

When Victor Hugo arrived at Halston's apartment that fateful night in 1972, he was a handsome twenty-four-year-old student from Caracas, Venezuela. He had coal-black eyes, a milky tan complexion, and curly jet black hair. He was sexy in some burning way, but nondescript-looking except for his legendary endowment, which he had no compunctions about displaying publicly if he thought it was amusing. A boisterous, funny, and explosive young man, Victor was like an X-rated version of all three Marx Brothers rolled into one. Full of energy and enthusiasm, he was in constant motion, chattering in a Caracan accent so intentionally thick and garbled and growled that even his longtime intimates couldn't always make out what he was saying. (Halston used to say, "Even when Victor speaks Spanish the Spanish people don't understand him.") Victor's accent was also calculatedly funny, and in fact, there was something very comical about him, which was a great part of his charm and an element of his personality that he capitalized on. As destructive or outrageous as Victor sometimes tried to be, it was hard to be angry with him for long. At first.

In direct interview, Victor Hugo has told several conflicting stories of his background. He was reportedly born on April 4, 1948, in Caracas, Venezuela, but Victor refuses to be pinned down on any particulars. Halston's younger brother, Donald

Frowick, remembered Victor telling him that as a child in Caracas he was so poor that he lived in a hut with a dirt floor and ate with his hands because there were no utensils. Victor later claimed to the contrary that his father was a Venezuelan "newspaper publisher." Peruchio Valls remembered meeting Victor in Caracas when Victor was an aspiring actor. "He used to work in the theater," said Valls. "He was an actor. He was already twenty, twenty-one, and I was sixteen. He lived in a one-bedroom penthouse in a small building" A few years later, Victor Hugo had appeared in New York where he was a self-professed "artist at large" when he met Halston.

"Overnight we were involved in this thing called Victor Hugo," Joe Eula said, "which I thought was a laugh in the beginning." Obsessed with his art career, Victor was always brimming over with schemes and projects, many of them Dadaesque and surreal. He was a great admirer of Marcel Duchamp, one of the leaders of the Dada movement, who is unjustly perhaps best known for signing a urinal in 1917 and calling it "ready-made art." Victor worshiped him, and Halston delighted in Victor's avant-garde pretensions.

Victor was the first one of Halston's lovers to move in and live with him, although from the start where Victor actually slept at night was not very predictable. Halston also put Victor on the company payroll and gave him a job in the packing room. It didn't take long to discover that Victor wasn't cut out for menial tasks. Clearly, the logical outlet for Victor's artistic bent was to allow him to dress the windows of the boutique, which of course, encroached on Ed Austin's area of pride and joy. "Halston allowed Victor to do a *few* of the windows at first," Austin sniffed. "Halston told me that he would be doing a *few*. I didn't like them, though," was Austin's polite assessment. By now Austin had learned a great deal from working with Halston and managing the boutique, and more than a touch of Halston's grand manner had rubbed off on him. No one called him just "Ed" anymore, but "Mr. Austin," or just a clipped "Austin." Occasionally when one of the favored women clients would call and ask for "Halston," Ed Austin would mistakenly think she had said "Austin" and take the call. When Halston found out about these mistakes, he was enraged. "It would get back to him that I answered the phone in his name," said Austin. "That was one of the little spat things that we used to have. I used to tell him, 'Look, I work for you, you pay my salary, I'm *not* trying to take over.' "

But Victor Hugo *was* trying to take over the windows, and the mixture of Austin and Victor was untenable. By Christmas of 1973 it came to a head. "We had a big fight about the Christmas window," Austin said. "I put in the Christmas window. I had the staff in at seven o'clock in the morning to do it, about a week before Christmas. It took till three o'clock in the afternoon to finish it. It was fabulous, a red window with nothing but red clothing and silver jewelry. We did $50,-000 in one hour. People were coming in and buying and buying. The whole staff was downstairs in the boutique wrapping Christmas packages for customers, and cashmere dresses were flying out the door. It was incredible, absolutely incredible. But Halston came downstairs with Victor Hugo to see the finished window, and he didn't like it. Halston had Victor redecorate it and Victor took all the mannequins and put everything in the window on one side, all the Christmas boxes were destroyed, all the jewelry was bunched to one side. I was in my office while Victor was doing it and somebody came up and told me what was happening. I walked out, saw what was happening, and I went back into my office, put on my fur coat—a beautiful raccoon coat that Halston had given to me—I had a very stiff drink and went home."

When Austin returned to work on Monday, Christmas Eve, one of the girls said to him, "Halston wants to see you."

"I said to the girl, 'You tell Halston I'm in my office.' "

Later that day Halston stormed into Austin's office, the J.E.

temper in full flare. "He was furious," said Austin, "and he told me, 'I want the keys to the boutique. I want my keys, just give me the keys.' Well, it was Christmas Eve, I had packages all over the place, I had a limousine outside waiting to carry me home with all these packages, and I was fired. Christmas Eve, thank you, out the door, no severance, nothing . . ."

Ed Austin never saw Halston again.

In the early part of January the "Eye" column in *Women's Wear* noted that Ed Austin had left his job at the boutique. "We didn't have a good working relationship," Halston was quoted as saying, "but I wish him well. I think he'd be an asset for any fashion business."

He did turn out to be an asset to another fashion business— his own. Eight months later, Ed Austin opened his own boutique, just three blocks north of Halston on Madison Avenue, selling clothes that were curiously similar to Halston's. Joanne Crevelling remembers that Austin's shop was being touted as Halston style without the exorbitant Halston prices. Austin ran the store successfully for several years before it was closed by a water leak. He now lives in New Jersey and continues to work in the fashion business.

"I NEVER TOOK Victor as a serious person," said one executive who worked with Halston for ten years. "I thought that he was just a wild man who had latched on to Halston and found that by acting in a way that was totally antisocial he would make progress in life."

Up until now all of Halston's inamoratos had remained in the shadows. Not Victor. As Halston's infatuation with Victor grew and as Victor's influence in Halston's life solidified, he slowly began to come into the public eye, at first through his job as Halston's window dresser. "I put windows on the map as a pop artist," Victor says, "I looked at it as art. The windows became my paintings, my occupation."

Victor did the windows for the next four years, and it was with the Madison Avenue windows that Victor's artistic sensibilities first began to emerge. Everyone sat up and took note that an unusual personality was emerging. There were some silly ideas, like Halston for President around election time, with signs and balloons, and one with a mannequin who had an apple on her head with another mannequin throwing a knife at it. There was a minimal window with a roll of silk Charmeuse over which a black leather whip had been tossed, which raised a few eyebrows, and a Patty Hearst window in which the mannequins robbed banks wearing Halston's spring line, which raised many eyebrows. Inside the store Victor built a pyramid of twenty-seven toilet seats glued together (an homage perhaps to Duchamp). One window was a hospital scene of either an abortion or miscarriage, in which faceless mannequins stood around a hospital bed where a pregnant, faceless female figure was wrapped in a Halston cashmere blanket. One pedestrian stopped during the night to write across the front window "This is really sick." When CBS local news called about coming down to do a story on Halston's windows, he quickly called Peruchio Valls and told him to change it. Another time, Victor did a window with five mannequins "acting out various forms of violent behavior," in which the mannequins were dressed in black Halston lingerie while they killed each other with guns and knives and whips. Pedestrians complained that the window was degrading to women, and one neighborhood resident sent letters of complaint to six local publications.

Perhaps Victor's most controversial window was the one with droplets of what appeared to be dried semen all over the interior. Passersby the morning of its unveiling could only guess at how it had gotten there, especially in the middle of the night. "To have the come of the lover of Halston on the window!" Victor said proudly.

Victor was shockingly, unpredictably, out of control, and Halston loved it. "He *loved* it," Joe Eula said. "No matter what

Victor did, Halston loved it. He was in love with him." Halston loved flirting with scandal; he even loved the mortification he endured. Victor Hugo was the antithesis of his own public persona: a rigid, formal and proper man who let few of his emotions show. For Halston, Victor was a vicarious jolt, in many ways the same kind of thrill Halston had found in his forays into Central Park so many years before.

There was perhaps only one other person in the world who was more titillated by Victor Hugo's scandals than Halston, and that was Andy Warhol. "Victor wanted to have his name linked to the art world," said Eula, "and the quickest way to do it was to hitch his star to some Goddamn wagon, and it was Andy that Victor hooked on to. He dragged Andy lock, stock, and barrel to Halston's showroom." Warhol had already met Halston in passing in the mid-sixties, plying their respective trades. "It was surprising what a really cute kid he was then," Warhol said of Halston. "We both happened to be at the studio of an art director from some magazine, and I was doing free-lance for them. I thought Halston was so handsome, he looked like a movie star." Although Halston and Warhol shared an interest in rich women—Warhol for portraits, Halston for couture—they never really found very much in common before Victor Hugo.

Even though Warhol was already a great international star in his own right, he was in awe of Halston. He wanted what Halston had, respectability and social cachet. Warhol was actively trying to clean up his sixties' underground drug image, and Halston's scene offered entrée to Warhol's greatest love—internationally rich society women and potential portrait commissions. Over the years Halston commissioned portraits of himself, Victor, his mother, and encouraged Liza Minnelli as well as dozens of society ladies to have their portraits done by Warhol. "It wasn't really a friendship," said an intimate of both of them. "It was more of a business relationship." They never really seemed to talk, or have a heart-to-heart conversation, mainly because Warhol seemed incapable of such kind of inti-macy.

Victor Hugo became the third point of a triangle between Warhol and Halston. While Victor was Halston's lover in name, he played an even more important role in Warhol's life. Warhol was almost totally sexually repressed and shut down, and he lived vicariously for the next decade through Victor's wild sex-ual exploits. "Andy was stranger than Halston," Victor said. "Halston didn't like to watch." In fact, Victor turned into something of a sexual muse for Warhol, who would frequently sponsor Victor's purchase of hustlers or bar tricks and attend and photograph sexual sessions with them. Andy would never participate, but would instead retire to the bathroom where he would privately have what Halston dubbed "his organza."

Around 1974 Halston bought ten little Mao paintings from Warhol for about $2,000 each, and that cemented their friend-ship. Over the years Halston would buy and trade over 150 works by Warhol, and through this private art market they both found a way for them to satisfy Victor. Frequently when there was a transaction between them, Victor allegedly would act as broker and get a commission. In this way, hundreds of thou-sands of dollars may have changed hands over the years.

Halston's association with Warhol first become public on October 19, 1972, at the Coty American Fashion Critics' Awards, where Halston was one of eight designers to be pre-sented with a "Winnie." The plush ulphostered pews of Alice Tully Hall at Lincoln Center were filled that night with an international cross section of the fashion world—buyers, press, store owners, manufactures, and designers. All the other de-signers gave traditional shows on film and with models on a runway, to the great delight of the audience. The show con-tinued seamlessly when, suddenly, everything seemed to come to a standstill. Then began "An Onstage Happening by Andy Warhol," as it was billed in the program (coproduced by Joe Eula). Suddenly oddly blaring music was heard in the wings and, unexpectedly, Warhol actress Donna Jordan, with cropped platinum blond hair, tap-danced wildly down the runway in a Halston outfit—whirling around fiercely until, seemingly spent, she left the stage, soon to be followed by Jane Forth, another staple of the Warhol films. She schlepped her baby, Emerson Forth, to the rim of the stage and left him there in the hot glare of the footlights for several minutes while he happily crawled around hunting for his bottle. The audience began to twist nervously in their seats as another Halston-clad model juggled for a while and model-turned-fashion-editor China Machado played the bongo wearing a Halston caftan. As a buzz of dismay grew like an audible humming through the audience, the people in the theater began to feel insulted at the cheap, embarrassing "happening" from the master of glamour. Before it was over, the smell of frying bacon wafted through the auditorium as social arbiter Nan Kempner cooked breakfast onstage on a real electric oven while dressed in a sequined evening gown. For the finale a huge wood-and-cardboard birthday cake was pushed out on the stage and 200-pound Pat Ast emerged from the cake and belted out "Happy Birthday," although no one in the audience could understand why.

"I refuse to be taken so seriously," Halston fumed when he later heard people were insulted. "It was fun and a camp. God, I hate pretensions! If it shook some people up, goody . . . I loved it. The whole thing freaked me out."

"WILL HALSTON TAKE OVER THE WORLD?"
Esquire magazine

By 1973 Halston was the golden boy of fashion. He was widely considered to be the most influential designer in America and his companies were grossing nearly $30 million in retail sales. In only three and a half years in business he had won three Coty Awards. There were few public figures more glamorous or more admired in business. *Women's Wear* couldn't come up with enough praise for him; he "captured the subtleties of the impressionist period," he was "a master evolutionist," and "one of the greats." Offers flooded in to the East Sixty-eighth Street office from all over the world to design everything from lampshades to christening outfits. Eugenia Sheppard declared 1973 "The Year of Halston," and it appeared that everything he touched turned to gold.

That's why it seemed like yet another brilliant business move when it was announced in early October of 1973 that the huge conglomerate Norton Simon Industries would acquire Halston, Inc., and his design services for approximately $12 million in stock (with his Seventh Avenue partners reportedly receiving a share equal to Halston's). At that time the idea that a fashion designer would sell not only his company but such an intangible commodity as his own artistic talent was startling. *Newsweek* magazine called the deal "Rags to Riches" and *Time,* the "Couturier's Coup," noting that Halston was one of the "best business minds" in the fashion industry. With Norton Simon behind him, *Esquire* magazine asked, "Will Halston take over the world?"

Signed on November 5, 1973, although the complete set of contracts for the deal stood several feet high and took months to sort out, in concept the transaction was relatively simple. In exchange for approximately 280,000 shares of Norton Simon stock worth $7 million, which he was prohibited from selling for several years, and a reported yearly salary beginning at $150,-000 and escalating to $500,000, plus stock options, plus an escalating percentage of profits that would skyrocket into the millions, Halston would get business management, marketing direction, and the vast international merchandising resources of Norton Simon Industries, which employed over 30,000 people. In return, Norton Simon Industries was buying all of Halston's existing companies, his design services exclusively, the Halston trademark, and all underlying rights to it—lock, stock, and barrel—for all time. The contracts also reportedly stipulated that Norton Simon Industries could use the name Halston for products Halston did not create, and that Halston could not use his name on any product without the consent of Norton Simon Industries. Of course, this seemed like a far fetched eventuality: Why would Norton Simon Industries ever put Halston's name on an article that did not come from the hand of the genius?

Privately, Halston was thrilled with the terms of the deal. He was already rich, but now in one fell swoop he would be financially secure for the rest of his life. Overnight, he would be able to live the kind of life most people only dreamed about. Publicly, he kept his usual cool about it. "I was spending too much time with lawyers and accountants," was the way Halston explained the deal to the press. "I needed a better league of businessmen. It's one of the most exciting things that has happened in my life. It will let us take a giant step into the world market. Perhaps even China. People say all kinds of things about the Norton Simon business. They say it was a get-rich-overnight thing, and it really wasn't. I had just gotten to the point where I needed help with my business. I was spending weeks and months with lawyers working on contracts and things like that. Norton Simon is able to help me. I mean, I don't kid myself. The money is important. It's important to live uptown. It gives me the chance to do that little extra thing I might want to do. Of course, I hear a lot of things about myself. I hear that I'm jet set and this and that, and I'm really not. I live a very quiet life."

"He sold his *name*, baby," rasped Joe Eula. "It was *The Devil and Daniel Webster.*"

Norton Simon Industries was not quite the devil. It was a company in the business of buying brand names. Since its inception in the forties by the California industrialist and art collector whose name it still bore, Norton Simon Industries had assimilated dozens of companies, including the Ohio Match Company, Hunt Foods, Inc., the Canada Dry Corporation, as well as Redbook magazine, Wesson Oil, Tanqueray Gin, Avis, and the McCall Pattern Corporation (whose designs by Halston were enormously popular). With assets around the $2 billion mark, Norton Simon Industries had owned many companies before, but it had never owned a *person.*

Yet it was not a faceless conglomerate that was buying Halston. It was a man, David Mahoney, then the fifty-one-year-old chief executive officer of the Norton Simon empire. For David Mahoney the purchase of Halston was an emotional as well as a business decision, for Mahoney felt very *simpático* with the drama and flair of Halston's self-made success story. Mahoney himself was a self-made businessman with a story almost as dramatic as Halston's. A tall, handsome man with brown hair and a battered nose broken playing basketball in a Bronx schoolyard as a kid, he had worked his way through the Wharton School of Business at the University of Pennsylvania and gone into advertising. As a young man he already appreciated that a good social life could enhance his business contacts, and he spent the cocktail hour every day networking the bar at '21,' nursing one drink the whole evening, trying to meet important people. Clever, with a calming but authoritative paternal air about him, Mahoney jumped from a $25-a-week job in the mailroom of an advertising agency to the presidency of the Good Humor Ice Cream Corporation by age thirty-two. After a stop at Colgate Palmolive and Canada Dry, in 1969 Norton Simon himself promoted Mahoney over four other men in the line of succession to take over from him as chief operating officer of the company. Eventually Mahoney became the ninth-highest-paid executive in the U.S., at a salary of $825,000 a year plus incentives.

Mahoney's name was as likely to be found in the social columns as on the financial pages. He and his second wife, a former Miss Rheingold, Hildegard Merill (who became one of Halston's esteemed customers), led a visible and active social life. In some ways, for Mahoney to buy Halston was similar to a CEO of a billion-dollar Japanese company paying $80 million for an Impressionist painting to hang in the boardroom of the company in Tokyo. Indeed, Halston described Mahoney as his "Renaissance patron," a man who would fund the expansion of his company while Halston could give his full attention to his art. The way Mahoney saw it, he bought Halston for his "creativity, his flair, his *class*. Big Business sometimes forgets that what makes them grow are people. There is no substitute for class."

Sniffed Halston, "That's very nice of him. But he got more than that—he got a thriving business."

But Halston was only fooling himself. His name had barely a 17.4-percent awareness level with the general public, according to polls conducted by Norton Simon. Although the name Halston was a glittering addition to Norton Simon Industries' more traditional holdings, the moneys generated by Halston Enterprises represented only "a sliver," as Mahoney put it, of Norton Simon Industries' total income. But there were clearly ways to increase that income—something at which Mahoney and his team of marketing executives were expert. The transformation of Halston into a trademark like Avis or Good Humor was their next step.

Within two months of the purchase, Edward M. Gallagher, a Norton Simon Industries executive whose previous experience ran the gamut from vice president of an NSI-owned ad agency to marketing consultant for a feed company, was named managing director of Halston Enterprises. Interviewed by *Women's Wear* for the occasion, Gallagher came across as strangely reticent and uncomfortable in his role as the new company head. He refused to have his photo taken or even talk about his job. "Halston is the presence here," Gallagher said.

"Sometimes," *Women's Wear* conjectured to Gallagher, "when a public company takes over a small one, the big fish not only swallows the smaller one, it chews it to pieces."

Gallagher denied anything like that would ever happen with Halston. "My obligation," he said, "is to minimize the pain."

He would be gone in a few months, at his own request.

WITH NORTON SIMON INDUSTRIES bankrolling him, David Mahoney bought Halston his first gift—Versailles, so to speak. On November 28, 1973, the same month in which the Norton Simon transaction was completed, Halston was scheduled to take part in an event in France that some believe changed the history of the fashion industry by validating the international importance of the American designer. In any event, it changed Halston forever.

The *New York Times* coyly called it a *"divertissement."* It was, however, no small distraction but a rather grand idea that had been hatched over lunch one day around a swimming pool in the south of France by Halston's publicist, Eleanor Lambert, and Marc Bohan, the French designer. The concept was that, as a gesture of good will, five French designers—Hubert de Givenchy, Christian Dior, Pierre Cardin, Emmanuel Ungaro, and Yves Saint Laurent—would invite five American designers—Halston, Bill Blass, Stephen Burrows, Anne Klein, and Oscar de la Renta, to join them in a mass fashion show. It was a historic union. "To my knowledge," said Halston, "the five French designers have never shown outside of their houses and certainly not in the same salon." And certainly not in concert with Americans. Befitting its momentousness, this Franco-American fashion show was to be held at no less a grand venue than the Marie Antoinette Theater in the palace of Versailles, for the use of which French President Georges Pompidou had to give his special permission.

The event certainly captured the imagination of the press and held international society in thrall. The Baroness de Rothschild was president of the gala committee, and Princess Grace of Monaco was a guest of honor. In America, Marion Javits, Françoise de la Renta, and Mary Lasker were asked to donate their services as sponsors. The 720 seats in the blue-and-gold theater, built in 1769 for Marie Antoinette, were impossible to come by from the first whisper of the event, and were sold out at $235 each. Even the $27 program books were scarce. Along with special contributions, the event would raise approximately $260,000 for the restoration of the building that had once housed the French court. There were to be two fashion shows, one by the French and one by the Americans, of fifty minutes each. Afterwards a supper would be hosted by Baron and Baroness Guy de Rothschild.

"We had a competition," said Joe Eula. "It was the biggest competition in the goddamn century in the world of fashion. It was just *wild.*"

The event at Versailles was also David Mahoney's first opportunity to flex his financial muscle for Halston and, as he would unfailingly over the years, he did it with style. Virtually the entire event took on a Halston–Norton Simon veneer. To begin with, Mahoney donated $25,000 to help defray the cost of the American production. (The remainder of the costs, approximately another $25,000, were to be divided among the five designers with Anne Klein's husband, businessman Chip Rubenstein, as banker of the event.) Then it was announced that all the American models would be wearing makeup by Max Factor, a Norton Simon–owned company. Then Halston's erstwhile court magician, Joe Eula, was hired to design the scenery and sets for the American segment of the show, which naturally did not please all the other designers. While it was agreed among the Americans that the thirty-six models and ten dancers would be shared among them, Halston insisted that there be special celebrity models just for his segment—that the star of the show be his pal, Liza Minnelli, and that the show be directed and choreographed by Liza's godmother and Halston's good customer, Kay Thompson. Also with Mahoney's backing, it was announced that Halston would give a grand and exclusive supper party the night before the show on Tuesday, November 27, at Maxim's at a cost of $25,000. "You can't believe the pressure we've had from people who wanted to be invited," Mahoney told the *New York Times*, "There was nothing we could do. The restaurant only holds two hundred and twenty people." As for his lavish sponsorship, "We've been told the Versailles show will be one of the great things of the world—a happening," said Mahoney, "and as we are new in this business, this is our way of saying we'd like to offer our support. I think this is a wise use of money."

The tension began to mount as several hundred Americans from the top of the Social Register began to pour into Paris shortly after Thanksgiving and check into the Plaza Athénée hotel, the unofficial headquarters of the U.S. contingent. They were followed by an entire army of American models, stylists, seamstresses, assistants, hairdressers, and makeup artists. Finally, as the festivities drew nearer, the international society press descended on Paris for what they billed as "the War of the Coutures." "Paris in a Tizzy," was the *New York Times* full-page headline a few days before the event, "But Then It's Not Just Another Fashion Show."

Indeed, for the Americans it was beginning to turn into a full-scale disaster. First of all, none of the sets designed by Joe Eula could be used. "We had the plans of this marvelous Marie Antoinette Theater," said Eula, "but the plans were in French, so who's going to read these plans? So I got on a plane and went to Paris and took a look at the theater." Satisfied there was an abundance of hooks from which to hang his scenery, Eula went back to New York and designed what he described as "flags on silks and all these sheets." "But when we got there for the show," Eula continued, "it turned out there wasn't one single place to hang a Goddamn fucking sheet and I had done this great big set where I painted a thing of Liza and I did all these flags and these silks. After working like a fool for months when that thing first came down I took one look at it and I said, 'Throw it all away. Burn it.' It looked like Chinese laundry."

Tempers were seething among the American designers when Eula said, "Bring one black backdrop down behind the whole stage." He stood there and studied it for a moment and said, "We're going to do one abstract design of the Eiffel Tower and that's *all* we're going to do." Eula asked for a roll of white photographers' seamless paper, several hundred feet long. Then he got quarts of black paint and dipped a broom—a regular whisk broom—into the paint and drew, freehand, an Eiffel Tower in broad strokes forty feet high. That was it. That was the set. The Americans would have to deal with it.

The set was not the only problem. While the French were using an orchestra that had been rehearsing for weeks, the Americans had never once rehearsed together, and their music was canned on one master tape—and once the tape was started it couldn't be stopped, no matter what kind of mistakes or delays the show might incur. The two-day rehearsal period before the event was a fiasco. The French rehearsals went on all day and into the night, while the Americans sat around in the audience and shivered in the cold theater. "We waited what seemed like several days while the French rehearsed," remembered Tom Fallon. By ten o'clock the night before the show the American models were glassy eyed and grumpy. "We were starving," said Halston's model Chris Royer. Oscar de la Renta and Halston had only just begun rehearsing when suddenly, the French electricians' union announced that the stagehands had worked beyond their overtime, and that they were quitting for the night and shutting everything down.

Chip Rubenstein got on the telephone and tracked down the head curator of Versailles, Gerald Van der Kemp, who coincidentally was hosting a fund-raising event elsewhere in the palace. Van der Kemp immediately arranged for the electricians to stay on, and the rehearsals continued. Van der Kemp also gallantly invited the entire American troupe to join his party whenever the rehearsals ended, and sometime after midnight a band of die-hards led by Liza Minnelli took a bus to the party, with Liza singing "It's Going to Be a Great Day" to everybody on the bus.

The next afternoon, only hours before the event, with the American rehearsals still not completed, Anne Klein was clinging to Kay Thompson for support and asking her for extra time to rehearse her portion of the show over and over and over again. "She was hyper-nervous and she had good reason," said Eleanor Lambert. "She was a sportswear designer, and the other designers all had great big beaded evening dresses." But there were also more compelling reasons for Anne Klein to be nervous; only she and her husband knew at the time that she was dying of cancer. The show at Versailles would be a finale to a triumphant career, so of course it had great meaning to her.

"She kept clinging to Kay Thompson," said Lambert, "and begging her to rehearse one more time, and Kay would give in because she was a wonderful woman."

Sitting in the auditorium smoking endless cigarettes or nervously pacing in the wings, Halston waited for his turn, growing increasingly impatient with all the time and attention being lavished on Anne Klein. Convinced that she was getting favored treatment because her husband was the event's treasurer, Halston flew into a rage and stormed out of the palace, threatening not only to pull out of the show himself but to take his models as well, thereby wrecking it for everybody else. His loyal entourage followed him into the courtyard in front of the palace and stood around helplessly as Halston locked himself in the backseat of his limousine and brooded. The models were torn; they didn't want to disobey Halston, but they also didn't want to ruin the rest of the show. Several tense minutes passed while various people tried to reason with Halston, to no avail; he refused to come out of the car or lower the window. Then Liza Minnelli came out into the courtyard and marched over to the limousine. "Liza banged on the door and stomped her foot," said Eleanor Lambert, but Halston refused to get out of the car. So Liza turned to the models and said, "Listen, kids, we've got a show to do, so don't start this. You're in show business, and the show must go on. Cut all this out and let's go *rehearse.*" Lambert said, "They followed Liza back inside and left Halston all alone out in the car." After a few minutes he relented and returned to rehearsals, but he acted haughty and distant the rest of the afternoon.

That night a caravan of sleek black limousines, silhouetted against the floodlit Palace of Versailles, discharged an elite corps of society into the theater, including Mrs. Winston Guest, Mrs. André Betancourt, Mrs. Pierre Schlumberger, Mr. and Mrs. Prentis Cobb Hale, Dewi Sukarno, Baron Alexis de Rede, Mrs. Harrison Williams, and Princess Grace. There was an expectant hush as the theater lights dimmed, the orchestra began the overture, and the curtain rose on the French show. Within moments the audience was enthralled. The French had outdone themselves. The combined show of the five designers was more elegant and elaborate than anything ever seen in Paris. The sets were glittering, the music voluptuous, and the show unfolded with a perfection honed by skill and months of preparation. As a connecting theme each French designer's show was accompanied by a float, and each float seemed more astonishing than the one before. Saint Laurent used an elongated old-fashioned car filled with models and Cardin used a space ship, which simulated a takeoff. For the finale, fourteen French showgirls from the Crazy Horse Saloon modeled furs by Revillon, designed by Dior, Ungaro, and Saint Laurent. As the show progressed to a climax the furs fell away in strategic places revealing bare bosoms and bottoms and, eventually, a long, pregnant pause of total nudity. Perhaps the most incredible moment of the French presentation came with Dior's segment when a giant, white-pumpkin coach was rolled onto the stage, upon which there was a stem of diamonds and white feathers. At the end of the sequence the stem came alive—and it was Josephine Baker! The pumpkin fell away to reveal a mirrored staircase, which Baker regally descended while a white ermine coat, thrown around her shoulders like a cape, unfurled the entire length of the staircase behind her as she sang "That's Impossible." Then, with a professional jerk, Baker threw the coat out in front of her and brought down the house. "It was elaborate, beautiful, and grand," said Fallon. "Perfect and professional."

While the excited audience sipped champagne in the palace foyer and raved about what they had just seen, backstage the fear among the Americans was epidemic. There was so much tension and unhappiness that some of the models wept and wanted to run off and hide. "Everybody was scared to death," said Lambert, "They were all on edge. Here we were in Paris trying to outdo—not outdo, but equal—the glamour of French couture, and it was awesome. Everyone was terrified the show would be a disaster."

Said Fallon, "At this point the Americans thought they were buried. We were going to lay an egg, and it was going to be an international humiliation."

As the audience returned to their seats in the theater, Liza Minnelli stood in he wings petrified of what was coming, repeating over and over, "I don't know about this, I don't know about this . . ." Curtain up, the unstoppable tape began, and Liza strode onstage and began to lip sync *"Bonjour Paris"* to her own voice. She looked stunning. She was wearing gray cashmere Halston pants, an off-white Halston cashmere turtleneck, a matching hat and several big Elsa Peretti silver bracelets on her wrists. Thrown over her shoulders, Halston style, was a brilliant red cashmere sweater tied around her neck. Although she was lip-syncing, she also began to belt out the song and the clear tones of her voice filled the theater. She was so bold, so full of brash self-confidence that it was impossible for anyone in the audience to know how she was quaking. Behind her the Joe Eula–painted Eiffel Tower somehow looked fine. No, a minute later, as the models dressed in raincoats and carrying umbrellas stormed on the stage behind Liza, the Eula set looked better than fine. In fact, the simplicity of it, the nonchalance of the hand-painted design, made it look terribly chic, a brilliant stroke and a powerful statement about the elaborate fussiness of the French presentation.

That night helped ensure Liza Minnelli's reputation as one of the great entertainers of our age. She gave a brilliant, inspired performance. "When Liza got through with the opening, the audience exploded in rapture," said Tom Fallon. "They started throwing their $27 dollar programs on the stage, they were in such ecstasy. When we saw that, the Americans went wild. From there on in there was so much energy, such exhilaration, we knew that nothing could go wrong." And nothing did. There were no screwups, no disasters. The taped music worked perfectly. As the American models crisscrossed the stage to cheers not one person missed a beat, an entrance, or a cue. The show began with the easy, clean clothes of Anne Klein, who showed beachwear and cool little dresses in her trademark sophisticated prints and lively colors. Then came Stephen Burrows's "absurdities" of multicolored bibs, pop art bodices, and grand, sweeping trains. With "Borsolino" music playing, Bill Blass's clothes filled the room with images of the Great Gatsby, the Hamptons, and Aspen, with luscious chiffons and ruffled blouses, lavish fur, and evening dresses that seemed to be made of sheets of sequins. Next, to the ominous soundtrack from the Luchino Visconti movie about a Nazi munitions family called *The Damned,* there appeared the splashy, theatrical world of Halston, with caped chiffons and swirling satins, and evening dresses of striped palettes "that created their own light effect," according to the *New York Times.* The show closed with Oscar de la Renta's display of gowns of chiffon and crepe which seemed to float and drift down the runway.

The American show that night signaled the coming of age of American designers. "It was generally acknowledged," reported the *New York Times,* "that the night belonged to the Americans," adding that the American show was a "super spectacle and smash hit." There was even a serious offer from a producer to take the show on the road for a world tour, or book it in a hotel in Las Vegas.

"Genius," Ungaro said.

"Excellent," Cardin said.

"I was so proud," said Princess Grace.

"The French were good," said the Duchess de la Rochefoucauld. "But the Americans were sensational. *C'était formidable."*

Backstage after the show, as Halston was mobbed by models and admirers and the international press, his ego seemed to soar as high as his blood pressure. His cheeks turned bright red, his eyes flashed as though they were throwing off sparks, and he

Roy Frowick, age ten; second row, center. *(courtesy of Ron Grimm)*

Ann Holsclaw, Roy, Dana Jo Scism. *(courtesy of Ron Grimm)*

Ann Holsclaw and Roy fool for the camera. *(courtesy of Ron Grimm)*

Madeline Hatcher proudly wears
her thirty-year-old gift from Roy
Frowick. *(courtesy of
Madeline Hatcher)*

André Basil, handsome
and debonair and
completely smitten with
"Fro." *(courtesy of
Sieglinde Sayles)*

Twenty-year-old Roy Frowick
with artwork at the
Ambassador East in Chicago.
(courtesy of Sieglinde Sayles)

Roy with the pedigreed pups of Basil's clients. *(courtesy of Sieglinde Sayles)*

Basil, Roy, and Basil's niece Trude in a nightclub lounge.
(courtesy of Sieglinde Sayles)

"Fro" in his tiny
workroom at Basil's
salon in the
Ambassador. *(courtesy
of Sieglinde Sayles)*

Halston, with Onka and hatboxes, arrives at the
Ambassador Hotel. *(courtesy of Sieglinde Sayles)*

Onka helps Halston choose a pastry. *(courtesy of Sieglinde Sayles)*

Lucia Perrigo, the Ambassador's powerhouse publicist, in Booth Number One in the famed Pump Room. *(courtesy of Lucia Perrigo)*

Halston's brother and sister, Bob and Sue Frowick, see him off on his first trip to Europe. *(courtesy of Sieglinde Sayles)*

Halston all dressed up for Halloween in 1956. *(courtesy of a friend)*

Arthur Williams, Nanita Kalachnikoff, Halston, and friends in a Venice
restaurant in the early sixties. *(courtesy of Arthur Williams)*

Halston in an original design
of a tablecloth and several
napkins in the Fire Island
Pines. *(courtesy of Arthur
Williams)*

Halston with Mr. and Mrs. Michael Lichtenstein.
(courtesy of Michael Lichtenstein)

Victor Hugo relaxing at Halston's house. *(Christopher Makos)*

Victor Hugo in a wig at a
nightclub opening.
(Patrick McMullan)

Simply Halston,
the mid-seventies.
(Christopher Makos)

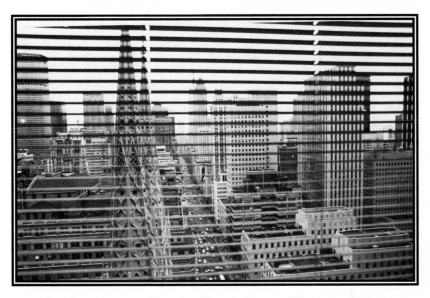

The view downtown from the Olympic Tower. *(Christopher Makos)*

A Halston fashion show at the mirrored Olympic Tower aerie. *(Anton Perich)*

Halston behind his lacquered mandarin red table replete with trademark rare orchid. *(Anton Perich)*

On the way to Studio 54, Halston has a smoke and a laugh. *(Christopher Makos)*

A night at Studio includes a reluctantly photographed Halston surrounded by Pat Ast, Victor Hugo, Dr. Robert Giller, Robert Jon Cohen, and Lorna Luft. *(Anton Perich)*

Halston, Loulou de la Falaise, Yves Saint Laurent, Steve Rubell, and Lauren Bacall. *(Anton Perich)*

Halston, Liza Minnelli, and Steve Rubell at Studio 54. *(Christopher Makos)*

Halston and his fans Martha Graham, Betty Ford, Elizabeth Taylor, and Liza Minnelli. *(AP/Wide World Photos)*

Halston's successor, John David Ridge, at work in the design room. *(Alexander Agor)*

Halstonette Pat Cleveland in a Halston gown and white Saga mink for Ben Kahn. *(courtesy of Ben Kahn Furs)*

Liza, Steve Rubell, and Halston at 101 East 63rd Street. *(Christopher Makos)*

Bob Frowick, Sue Frowick Watkins, Liza Minnelli, and Don Frowick leave Halston's memorial service in San Francisco. *(S. Kermani/Liaison)*

generally held court while he bragged grandly about his contribution to the event. Later, at a party held in the candlelit Hall of Mirrors, with his models still wearing their evening gowns, Halston acted so grandly, he could have been the Sun King himself. At the close of the evening he shared a limousine back to Paris with Bill Blass and Tom Fallon. During this ride to town Halston put on a display in the backseat of the limousine at least as spectuacular as the Versailles show itself. He boasted that the show had been successful mainly because of him and Mahoney and Norton Simon. "He was wild, way over Niagara Falls," said Fallon. Halston began to lapse into the third person and went on about himself that way: "Mr. Halston *knew* it would turn out all right." and "Mr. Halston certainly showed the French a thing or two. Mr. Halston has been coming to Paris for years and years and years. Mr. Halston met Cristóbal Balenciaga years ago. Why, Mr. Halston always told him, I said, 'Cristóbal . . .' "

For Halston, Versailles became his coronation as the king of American fashion. In his mind—and perhaps in the judgment of the world—he *had* become the American Balenciaga. He might not be recognized by the *Chambre Syndicale de la Couture,* but he was surely an ordained *haut couturier,* as big and famous as any of them. *Bigger. More* famous. And now, with Norton Simon and David Mahoney behind him, maybe he just *would* take over the world.

ROYALTY NEEDS A palace, and a few months after Versaille, in March of 1974, as a celebration of his new-found wealth and status, Halston finally moved out of the rent-controlled East Fifty-fifth Street apartment, which he bequeathed to Elsa Peretti, and into one of the most striking and dramatic private homes in Manhattan: 101 East Sixty-third Street, between Park and Lexington avenues. Originally designed by architect Paul Rudolph for a real estate attorney, it was one of the few modern houses built in Manhattan since the Second World War. The multiplaned, multileveled house took a year and a half to design and another year and a half to erect. Halston had admired it for a long time, and when he asked a real estate broker if anything like it was for sale in Manhattan he was delighted to hear that the Rudolph house itself was available. It had a sober exterior of dark glass in elongated rectangular shapes, as well as a metallic-looking two-car garage at street level. Inside the front door, a long, narrow hallway with slate floors and white walls led to a vast, open space—the living room—twenty-seven feet high at its skylighted apex. The rear wall was a spectacular two-story glass greenhouse which was mirrored at the back to reflect a lush forest of bamboo stalks that Halston had planted as thick as a jungle. The natural light, filtered through the skylight, gave the place a cathedral-like atmosphere, and there were hidden speakers everywhere, from which Halston liked to play Mozart. The furniture, also designed by Rudolph especially for the house, was geometric and oversized, gray knit-flannel jersey platforms in shades of putty and gray. There were no little knickknacks or clutter anywhere except for a few Elsa Peretti sterling-silver ashtrays. Hidden away in the hallways were Warhol lithographs, but the main walls were bare except for a Victor Hugo canvas of nothing—a painted white field. Each night at sunset, the houseboy would light over one hundred votive candles in crystal holders, even if Halston was home alone. The high, black onyx fireplace was lit every night, too, no matter what the season—even in the heat of summer when the air-conditioning had to be turned way up to make the heat bearable.

This main living space was surrounded by floating catwalks and open staircases that lead to three other stories, four bedrooms, a rooftop terrace, plus a separate studio for the newly hired houseboy, Mohammed Soumaya. Halston's innermost domain was his two-story-high master bedroom suite, with its own sitting area that overlooked the living room. The bedroom itself was tucked away, completely private and separate. The Ultrasuede-covered bed sat on an elevated platform, altarlike, in front of floor-to-ceiling mirrors. Next to the mattress was a telephone and a sparse and artistic setting of orchid plants and art books. It was a clean, spare, asexual room—impeccably neat, the sheets freshly pressed every day as was his nightshirt and a new toothbrush, which was provided every few days. A walk-in closet held his wardrobe, which was hung impeccably, the garments spaced three inches apart. There were over forty pairs of pants—twenty white and twenty black—eight white suits, two black velvet suits, white tie and tails and tuxedos and thirty pairs of shoes handmade in Italy and France at a cost of over $600 each.

Yet the entire place was cold and had an empty resonance to it, "an eerily deserted stage set, waiting for its players to appear," was the way one visitor described the feeling. Indeed, many players entered and exited the house. 101 became the focal point of Halston's social life. Almost every night there was a chic little dinner party or cocktails for a crowd of twenty. As it was his sanctum sanctorum, an invitation to 101 was highly valued by his friends, and the house assumed almost a mythical aura with his crowd. Over the years the fortresslike beauty of its facade became part of his public emblem. Halston was so dedicated to 101 that once he fought with members of a construction crew who were interfering with the house's serenity. One day he learned that massive excavation was beginning for a subway tunnel directly underneath East Sixty-third Street. This meant not only that there would be drilling and blasting a few hundred feet beneath his town house, but also that all the trees on the block would have to be cut down. An association of home and apartment owners on the street tried to block legally the arborial denudement, but to no avail. Yet Halston had his own, unique plan to stop the cutting down of the trees. Tree chopping, he reasoned, was positively un-American. So he bought fifty large

American flags, which he intended to drape in the trees. Then, he reasoned, the construction crew wouldn't *dare* cut them down. However, the workman arrived one morning at dawn before Halston could drape the trees and began to hack away with jackhammers and chain saws.

When Halston saw them at work from his window, he threw a jacket around his shoulders, ran outside, and began begging the workers to stop, trying to reason with them. Finally, one of them stopped to listen. "But we don't need a subway," Halston told them. "The residents of this block are rich enough to afford cabs."

Halston said, "The construction worker looked at me with murder in his eyes and cursed me for being so rich and said to me, 'None of my kids have shoes.' "

IN ORDER TO take over the world, Norton Simon Industries had to exploit properly the full potential of their assets in Halston Enterprises; thus a new managing director was named to take care of the financial side of Halston's business. Many in the fashion business considered it nothing short of a miracle that until this point Halston had not had what they called in the trade a "back office man." The appointment of a permanent managing director was expected to be a major blessing that would relieve Halston of many tiresome details.

To this end, in March 1974, a calm and sensible man named Michael Lichtenstein was named to the post, a position he would hold through hell and high water for the next decade. Married, in his early forties, Lichtenstein was an honors graduate of Columbia University and Yale Law School, class of '51. A one-time general attorney for Playtex Industries, as well as a lawyer with the Cinerama company, at the time Lichtenstein was tapped for the job with Halston, he was executive vice president of Kleinarts, Inc., a children's wear and notions manufacturer. "Mike Lichtenstein was the perfect balance for Halston," said a Norton Simon executive who worked closely with them. "He was studious, intelligent, low key, and a beautiful counterpoint to the high-fashion world of Halston and the social drama around him. One of Lichtenstein's major tasks was oftentimes picking up the pieces, and a task he did very well."

They first met at Halston's salon on East Sixty-eighth Street and spent several hours chatting. Halston told him the gossip of the day, and as Lichtenstein sat and listened and studied Halston he decided that he really liked Halston the man. "He was very elegant," said Lichtenstein. "Very elegant and charming. He seemed like a person I could work with and I guess he felt the same about me." That was also the same day that Halston closed on the purchase of 101 East Sixty-third Street, and he invited Lichtenstein to walk over to the new house with him. "It was a stunning place," said Lichtenstein, "and I remember telling him, 'Halston, I'm going to like working with you. You know how to spend your money.'"

The positioning of Lichtenstein as Halston's managing director had to be sensitively handled because Lichtenstein worked for Norton Simon Industries and he was not to report to Halston, but to Norton Simon vice president Gary Bewkes. This suited Halston just fine, because to Halston's way of thinking, Lichtenstein had been sent by David Mahoney to work for *him*. And in Halston's mind, he didn't report to *anybody*, except maybe Mahoney himself.

"Our very first endeavor was to create a fragrance," said Lichtenstein. "The main reason David Mahoney bought Halston, Inc., was to create a fragrance." Not coincidentally, a few months before aquiring Halston, Norton Simon had also aquired the cosmetics firm of Max Factor, and neither Halston nor Max Factor had a fragrance. Before he was bought by Norton Simon, a number of cosmetics firms had already talked to Halston about licensing his name to market a fragrance. Revlon, Elizabeth Arden, Palmolive, and Chanel had all approached him. "For a while I was courted by everyone in the business," Halston bragged, "Chanel, Revlon. Charles Revson, Sr., was sure he was in business with me." But none of the companies was willing to give Halston the kind of control he wanted over the product. (Reportedly Halston did sign a deal for a fragrance that had "fallen by the wayside," according to Eula, and Norton Simon bought him out of any responsiblity for $50,000.)

Perfume was the billion-dollar jackpot of the fashion industry because it was a relatively cheap product to manufacture with a huge markup and profit ratio. Unlike a line of apparel, which a designer had to design and manufacture several times a year, it was only necessary to concoct a perfume once. Perfume costs only pennies to manufacture, it is mostly alcohol, and the liquid perfume in the bottle is worth only about 5 percent of the price the consumer pays. It was also, of course, a gamble. Developing and marketing a new fragrance could cost several million dollars hard cash that had to be taken out of the company's cash flow, and industry averages were that six out of seven new scents failed in the marketplace. Many fragrances, even if successful, lasted only two or three years and never earned back the money invested in them.

But Norton Simon had lots of money and believed that the $2-million investment to launch a Halston perfume was more than worth the gamble. "Of course, it wasn't my two million," Halston said. "It was just my name, which is worth a hell of a lot more than two million." Thus, Halston's first assignment was to "design" a perfume for Max Factor—and enhance the Factor image as well. Unfortunately for Halston, Max Factor would do nothing to enhance *his* image. It wasn't exactly a premium cosmetics house. With annual sales of $200 million, Factor was sold mostly overseas or in the U.S. at chain-drug-store counters. The scent Halston was being asked to design would elevate the company to sales in better department stores, where the markup was 40 percent compared to approximately 30 percent in drugstores or supermarkets. "Factor . . .

is a powerhouse in drugstores and drugstore chains, probably number one in that market," said Orhan Sadik-Khan, then a senior vice president at Norton Simon Industries, "but it's never had the fashion image of, say, a Revlon or an Estée Lauder. It is Halston's ability to raise the fashion image of Max Factor that is important."

The design and launch of the fragrance became emblematic of everything that was to follow. A separate contract was negotiated between Halston Enterprises, Inc., and Max Factor for the fragrance that ran sixty-four pages and gave Halston final control over every minute detail, including what the packaging would look like and how the copy in the magazine advertisements would read. Halston's position in the matter was that although the perfume was going to be manufactured and distributed by Factor, he was a separate entity and there was no one at Factor to whom he was responsible. In fact, it was the Factor people who were bound to consult with him—every step of the way. He was, after all, *le grand couturier* and it was his taste and opinion they were paying for in the first place. "This meant," groaned Lichtenstein, "getting all the approvals from Halston every day, day by day." Halston didn't care for it much, either. "Sweetheart," he told a journalist, "it was absolutely horrendous. For months and months and months I worked. It was an *incredible* experience."

Six fragrance firms bid for the chance to help Halston create his new scent; Halston chose the large, prestigious firm of International Flavors & Fragrances, with headquarters in New Jersey. Every week representatives from IF&F brought precious oils to Halston's office for him to smell. "It had to be original," said Halston, "and not a derivative of X which is a derivative of Y, which is a derivative of Z." According to Halston, he spent two months sniffing various oils before he could even begin to discriminate among smells. "I must have smelled hundreds and hundreds of perfumes," he said. "They were either too green or too hot or too dull or too boring. Nothing seemed right. It was endless." Finally, after six months, the chemists at IF&F made a startling—and timely—discovery of a new essential oil. "It was a fantastic break for us," Halston enthused. "It was perfect. It was right. And it makes the perfume smell like nobody else's."

The next step was to design the bottle in which the perfume would be sold. Conventional wisdom in the fragrance industry was that although the actual smell of the perfume was important, it meant less in terms of the perfume's overall commercial success than the image projected by the packaging and advertising. Max Factor had on staff a team of packaging designers who decided that the bottle should be a faceted rectangular shape— what is known in the business as a "classic Chanel rectangle," the much copied look of the ever-popular perfume Chanel No. 5. But not Halston. "I said no, no, no." Halston "didn't believe" in the use of square bottles, he informed the Max Factor designers. "I want a bottle that will be a collector's item." Halston wanted to use instead a bulbous teardrop shape designed by his pal Elsa Peretti, for whom he arranged a reported $25,000 fee. At the time, Peretti was hitting her stride at Tiffany, where her design of a small pendant in the shape of a bottle, like a silver glass vial, had became a huge best-seller. The shape Peretti designed for Halston's perfume was similar and quite unusual. It was an off-centered, round form with a slight indent that was also somehow askew. The shape begged to be touched and fondled and fingered, and it became one of many classic and beautiful shapes of Peretti's distinguished career. But the Factor people didn't like it, they didn't think the public would like it, and they heatedly lobbied against it, dubbing the shape "the blob" and claiming that the off-centered hole on top would make it "impossible" to fill with the existing assembly-line equipment. "I hear that twenty times a day," Halston said. "There is always a way, but you have to know it yourself. You can be creative, but if you yourself don't know how to handle the technical side, you are at the mercy of your workers. It was like any big business exercise, you must prove it wrong. I didn't believe in square bottles or spheres," he insisted.

"Halston became passionate about the Peretti shape," said Paul Wilmot, vice president of promotion and marketing for Max Factor. "He decided to spend his own money finding a way to get it filled, and he spent almost $50,000 to develop a technique to fill it. Although it took virtually redesigning the filling nozzles, the blob it was."

"It was horrendous," Halston said. "But I'm a fighter. And after nights of work, we finally worked it out."

Halston's next dictum was that there be no name or imprimatur on the bottle whatsoever. He was "so sure" of his reputation, said one observer, "that he didn't think the bottle needed it." This was, of course, anathema to the marketing-conscious people at Factor. How would they ever show the bottle in a print ad or TV commercial without a name on it? "They were ready to kill me," said Halston. "They said I was stark, raving mad. And how dare I sabotage the project? A new fragrance? New essential oil? And no *name?*" But Halston remained adamant. "Women don't like to see a designer's name on their dressing table every morning," he insisted. "They don't want to see Mr. X, Y or Z hanging around on their bureau." On this issue a compromise was reached. "My name appears on a small band on the neck," Halston allowed. "You must take the name off when you open the bottle."

Each step of the way followed the same excruciating pattern, and it astonished the Factor people that Halston gave every detail of the fragrance equal weight. In the name of "perfectionism" Halston didn't seem to care to differentiate when it came to levels of priority. He obsessed about even obscure details: the quality of the cardboard that would go into the package, the thickness of the cellophane, the way the bottle nested in the box. "He had his standard," said Linda Wachner, who was president of Max Factor. "He didn't want models to appear in the print ads, just the product. He wanted bottle shots, he didn't want people in them. He wanted it to look *separate.*" He chose the photographer—his friend Hiro—for the product shots and okayed the advertising copy. When one copywriter from Max Factor's advertising agency showed up at Halston's office with a mockup of an ad that had the catch phrase "Simply Halston," he took one look at it and roared, *"Why, there's nothing simple about me!"*

Halston even chose the time of the year to release the perfume, insisting on a spring launch when the Factor executives wanted to wait until fall. When it came to the New York launch party, Halston pondered several locations and then decided that no place would be chicer to hold it than his own home. He fussed over food, flowers, and liquor. When he was told that gift packages of the perfume would have to be given away at the party, Halston refused, saying that to hand out perfume in his own home was too crass and commercial a gesture. He insisted that the perfume be sent to each guest the day before. He personally chose the little shopping bag that the perfume would be put in and even picked out the expensive grosgrain ribbons used to tie the handles closed and determined where the gift card would be tucked in. The Max Factor people became so dependent on his decisions that one day one of them asked, "How should we deliver these to people?"

Halston looked down his nose and sneered, "With midgets."

"He had a very good sense of humor," said Lichtenstein.

One night in late February 1975, Halston filled his new town house with hundreds of guests including fragrance buyers, press, department store executives, and a cadre of friends and fans to help launch the scent. It was a successful party at which the rave reviews for the perfume were only surpassed by the reviews for his new house. Yet the fuss in New York hardly compared with the West Coast launch, which took place two weeks later in San Francisco. Billed as an "Evening with Halston," a dinner-dance to benefit the San Francisco Museum of Modern Art was held at the I. Magnin department store. I. Magnin's president, John Schumacher, said of the party, "It's the first time we've attempted anything on this scale since Dior was over here in forty-six." "This scale" meant that the store removed every single sales counter in the pink-marble first floor to make room for several hundred tables and the construction of a hardwood dance floor, then draped the ceilings in pink chiffon. There was a five-course dinner and Dom Perignon 1962 was served exclusively. "There were only eleven magnums left in California," said Schumacher proudly, "so we flew it in from Las Vegas and Phoenix." The party cost upwards of $50,000, and a $25,000 check was donated to the museum.

After all the parties, the perfume officially went on sale at Bloomingdale's on February 24, bolstered by purchase-with-purchase promotion according to which the customer got a piece of Elsa Peretti costume jewelry every time she bought one of the $60-an-ounce vials, or the 2¼-ounce spray cologne at $10. Max Factor started rather cautiously by only shipping $1 million worth of retail to twenty-nine better department stores. Everyone sat back and waited and watched tentatively.

What happened next was like a fairy tale. In the first two weeks, Bloomingdale's sold $40,000 worth of Halston perfume—a volume, said a store executive, "beyond our largest estimates." Salespeople reported that women were snatching the toilet water at the counters without even smelling it. One salesperson asked, "What other ten-dollar Halston can you buy?" Within ninety days $1.5 million worth of Halston perfume was sold, and within two years, Halston perfume would be generating over $85 million in worldwide sales, making it the second-largest-selling scent in history. Irwin Alfin, president of Halston Fragrances (at Factor) said, "It's the most successful launch in the history of fragrance." As for Max Factor, Halston's perfume catapulted the company into competition for the third-best position in department and specialty store sales, right behind Estée Lauder and Revlon. For more than a decade, the Halston scent would always be in the year's top ten sellers, the smell synonymous with class.

So incredible was the public reaction to the fragrance that an outside research firm was hired to analyze its popularity. They discovered that 64 percent of the women who tried the perfume purchased it. Why? The scent was wonderful. It was distinctive, clean, and elegant. It was different and, well, simply Halston. The packaging was beautiful, too, and everyone loved it. The Peretti bottle became famous in itself, and one of the most highly acclaimed shapes ever to come out of the fragrance industry. For years the Halston fragrance and its success story would be legend in the industry, hailed as a brilliant coup—and Halston's reputation as a genius, at anything he put his mind to, seemed to have been confirmed beyond any question of a doubt.

With the success of the women's scent, a line of Halston cosmetics was immediately put into the works, as well as not one, but *two*, men's fragrances to be marketed at different price points with different scents. Named for their bottle numbers at International Fragrances, 1-12 and Z-14, the scents each smelled different. Launched a year after the women's scent, and backed with a half-million-dollar advertising budget, the two fragrances won three awards from the Fragrance Foundation that year, for advertising, packaging, and the most successful limited launch of the year. Sales were predicted to continue at $1 million a year each, which in the men's field made it a blockbuster. There were plans for full lines of 1-12 and Z-14, including after-shaves and soaps and talcum powders.

It was only when the men's fragrances had become such a tremendous hit that Halston looked back and shuddered at the thought that the perfume might have failed: "The responsibility was all on my shoulders," Halston said. But, "It's my fragrance and I made it. It was the most difficult design I've ever done."

PLANET HALSTON

The blockbuster financial success of the perfume sent everyone at Norton Simon Industries into ecstasy. It sure made David Mahoney smell sweet, because the $12 million he paid for Halston had already been recouped many times over. For Halston's part, the huge grosses seemed to justify all his overbearing control, and he grew more smug with more superior airs than ever. The world was his oyster! And if the perfume was such a smash, what else could they tap into? "Up at Norton Simon," wrote Jerry Bowles in *Esquire* magazine, "the plan is to turn Halston into the biggest marketable name since Mickey Mouse."

There were several different possibilities available to Halston and Norton Simon for "growing" his company, and it was decided that the safest and easiest way to expand Halston Enterprises was not by further enlarging Halston's own company, but by licensing his name and designs and letting other companies have the investment, manufacturing, and distribution woes. What's more, with a little bit of luck, licensing could prove very lucrative. There was usually a handsome cash guarantee up front, and a typical license could pay 7 percent of the net sales, with sliding royalty payoffs the bigger the volume. In return, licensees expected design direction, advice, and, most of all, samples from which to mass-produce the line.

"At the time," said Lichtenstein, "aside from one or two American designers, like John Weitz, there was little licensing. Halston was really one of the first to go into it heavily, and it was my job to develop strategies and make it work. What we had as an asset was Halston's time, so we tried to spend it wisely. We wanted to choose fields for licensing where the esthetics of the product would make a difference, where the product would have sufficient volume so that it would generate income, and thirdly, where Halston felt he could make a contribution." Halston turned down literally hundreds of requests for licenses, including, for example, separate offers from all four major automobile manufacturers to design luxury car interiors, because it was time-consuming and didn't offer high-volume returns. "So," said Lichtenstein, "statistical services broke retail merchandise down into a hundred and twenty-one categories sold in stores, and found that some eighty-four of them had relevance to Halston. We then put those into A-B-C priorities and went after the A business first and then the B's and so on. Sometimes there was luck involved. For example, *Time* magazine did an item on a Halston bathing suit and we immediately went into swimsuit licensing, even though it wasn't an A category."

"I don't think I've broken any records in licensing fees," Halston said, "although there's a temptation with a name as famous as Halston's." What followed over the next several years was simply an onslaught. By this point there were already existing deals for licenses with McCall's patterns and Hartmann luggage made out of Ultrasuede. Then came a scarf license for Daniel La Foret and a license for tennis towels for Fieldcrest, as well as Fieldcrest sheets which were imprinted with a white-on-white letter "H" all over them. There was a line of elegant loungewear for Dorian Loungewear. Then a license they called Halston III was signed for better blouses with Manhattan Industries. Soon a deal followed for hosiery for Kayser Roth, as well as another contract for fifteen styles of gloves in cashmere and Ultrasuede. There was a line of luxurious furs for A.C. Bang and later another hugely sucessful line for Ben Kahn, where a Russian lynx coat could cost upwards of $100,000. There was an extensive menswear license granted to the giant Rapid American Corporation and given a gala preview at the New York State Theater at Lincoln Center. That line was later relicensed to J. Schoeneman.

In 1974 Halston also designed the uniforms for the American athletes in the Pan Am Games, and the next year he designed the uniforms for all the American teams in the 1976 Winter Olympics, the parkas of which were being sold for $50 at Montgomery Ward. He designed new sleek and modern uniforms for Braniff flight attendants, and a five-part, washable polyester uniform for the Girl Scouts of America troop leaders that was practical yet feminine. ("Everybody has got to love the Girl Scouts. After all, it's the biggest ladies' organization in the Free World.") In 1976 Halston signed up to create a dress and sport shirt line for Cluett Peabody & Co. (which was later switched to Garey Shirtmakers, Inc.) and a line of belts and wallets for Paris Accessories. In 1977 he signed a license for sleepwear and a robe line for Weldon. There was also beachwear for Jonathan Logan, a line of bras and panties for Vassarette, and for Commodore, a collection of hats, his *spécialité*. He designed one of the most successful wig lines in the business for Designer Collections, and in 1977 he formed his own company to produce and design handbags and leather goods with H.B. Accessories.

There were also eyeglass frames for Bausch and Lomb and rugs for Karastan and foundation garments for Formfit Rogers. Sportcraft was a Halston dress line established exclusively for sale and manufacture in Canada, and Garolini, Inc., got his designs for shoes (some high heels, in which Victor Hugo appeared in public). He also opened his own free-standing boutique at the new Water Tower Place complex in Chicago, where he was feted like the Prodigal Son returned. In between all this he managed to turn out two or three made-to-order collections a year for private customers, as well as all the seasonal collections for for his own Seventh Avenue company, Halston Originals. He still found time to design an entire wardrobe around Elizabeth Taylor's jewels as well as the glittering gold costumes the wedding party wore for rock star Sly Stone's wedding at Madison Square Garden.

In an article in *Signature* magazine, writer Sylvia Auerbach noted, "You can wake up on a Halston sheet, toss off a Halston blanket and put your feet down on a Halston rug (licensees—Fieldcrest Mills, Karastan). You could put on a Halston shirt (Cluett Peabody) and a Halston tie (Tucker Ties), and pack a Halston suitcase (Hartmann Luggage) for a trip on which you'll be served by a Braniff stewardess in a Halston uniform. Your wife might serve you breakfast wearing a Halston bra under her Halston robe (Vassarette, Dorian Loungewear) before going shopping in her Halston raincoat (Misty Harbor). And you could bring her Halston perfume in the famous tear-shaped bottle."

"As I recall," said Lichtenstein, "we had thirty-one licenses and many more product lines than that because some licenses had more than one product, most of which was seasonal and had to be designed two to four times a year."

Naturally, getting all these different lines out was a nightmare. There were hundreds of tiny deadlines to be met each week. The glove house wanted to know how much fabric to order by Wednesday, the belt house needed him to pick out the buckles and tell them how wide to make the alligator belts; the robe house couldn't find faux mother-of-pearl buttons; the made-to-order collection was scheduled in ten days; and the windows at the Madison Avenue boutique needed to be changed. People streamed in and out of his office, twenty or thirty a day. Although he told the press he made his appointments "like a doctor," he complained in the office, "I feel like a hairdresser."

This already untenable situation was made much worse because next to "You're only as good as the people you dress," Halston's favorite dictum was "There are no little designers." Little designers are what he called the design team that many designers employed to help them with the enormous turnover needed to meet seasonal collections. "Because Halston found it very difficult to delegate authority," said Lichtenstein, "he could never develop a staff of independent designers to do the line and then come in and edit."

Although Halston had many talented assistants through the years—including Bill Dugan, Vincent Caraballo, Peruchio Valls, Stephen Sprouse, who went on to his own success on Seventh Avenue, and actor Dennis Christopher, who put in a short stint at Halston's side before going on to fame in film and on Broadway—while they worked for Halston they remained only that, assistants. "The result was the work became an impossible burden for Halston—or anybody," said Lichtenstein. Yet the burden certainly began to pay off. By the mid to late seventies, Halston's combined companies were grossing close to $100 million dollars a year, and with salary and royalties, Halston personally was earning a reported $2 to $3 million a year. The vigorous licensing program brought in not only lucrative fees, but also increasing visibility and influence. His power in the design field was unparalleled. And unmistakably, everything that came out of his office was wonderful—classically inspired, yet somehow fresh, whether it was the sleek look of his new Halston sunglasses, or his asymmetrical necklines, or the sexy, cut-high-on-the-hip "Savage" bathing suit that caused such a controversy when it made the cover of *Time* magazine. From 1973 to 1980, Halston turned out a prodigious number of innovative designs and collections, and season after season, from both the *New York Times* and *Women's Wear Daily,* he invariably received the most favorable reviews and raves. He

revived argyle, he reintroduced the cape to modern fashion. He
flattered customers with loose caftans and asymmetrical necklines. He reinvented the sweater set. After his fourth Coty
Award he was elected to the Coty Hall of Fame. It seemed that
no customer was immune to his appeal. "I have no ideal
woman," he said emphatically. "I have a public which is north,
south, east, and west." Fashion had finally found the universal
American designer.

His influence was so great that on Christmas Eve of 1977, the
New York Times asked Halston to redesign Santa Claus's famous red outfit, with drawings by Joe Eula. The *Times* printed
Halston's verbatim response to the question, "What should
Santa Claus wear that isn't so dreadfully boring?" which he
spoke into a tape recorder. First, Halston wanted to do a little
grooming on Santa himself. "After all, when you think of it," he
said, "Why couldn't Santa Claus be *really* good-looking . . . I
think realistically Santa could be a little bit younger—he could
look a little more groovy—there's no reason he has to be so fat."
He also thought Santa's beard could be trimmed more fashionably and that his hat could simply be changed to a ski cap in
which he'd look *"awfully* cute." Halston also prescribed various
Santa outfits for different locations throughout the world. In
Miami he envisioned Santa in a red wetsuit with water skis—"It
would be *fabulous,"* he said. In Egypt Santa would have a red
caftan with white fur trim and a big hood lined in white, which
would "look *fabulous."* The Chinese Santa "would be *fabulous"*
with "a little Mao suit in red" and a "nice little red Chinese hat
and a white little beard—*far-out."* And the Japanese Santa
would be *"fabulous* in a red kimono lined in white," and the
African Santa would wear one of those *"marvelous* robes they
wear, and a *marvelous* hat," and in India Santa would wear
"marvelous spats and a red vest, why it would be "fabulous."
For South America, "gaucho pants." Finally, Halston asked,
"Why does Santa have to come from outside? Why can't he
come from the *bedroom?"*

★ ★ ★

THROUGHOUT THE SECOND half of the 1970s Halston defined the word *superstar*. Never before in history had a clothing designer become quite so famous, or amassed as much power and influence socially and in the fashion world. At Andy Warhol's up-market *Interview* magazine, editor Bob Colacello claimed Halston's clout was so great that when he started advertising in *Interview* in the mid-seventies, all the other designers followed and their advertising revenues doubled. Indeed, by his friend Andy Warhol's standards of fame—gossip columns, *People* magazine, supermarket tabloids—Halston had become one of the most famous people in the world, his name synonymous with elegance and taste around the globe.

On a personal level, it would be hard to say that Halston's success went to his head, because he had long been full of himself. In private, of course, with his old friends, he could still be a down-home boy from the Midwest with a good sense of humor, optimistic and looking toward tomorrow. But as time went by, a change did become apparent in him, even to his close friends. What had at first been an affectation of speech or gesture had now taken on the grand manner of a true monarch. He became almost a caricature of a sissy homosexual fashion designer, haughty and superficial, blowing kisses into the phone and calling his famous ladies "Sweetiecakes" or "Pussycat" or "Gorgeous."

Halston also seemed a bit more petulant and on edge, easy to lose his temper and spit out invectives like "moron!" or "idiot!" at those who displeased him. No doubt Halston's fuse had been shortened because around this time he began to snort cocaine on a regular basis. He was first introduced to cocaine during his summers on Fire Island, but now, instead of an occasional weekend treat, cocaine became a constant in his daily pharmacopoeia of drugs, along with two packs of True cigarettes, a few joints, and many scotch-and-sodas to try to take the edge off the hectic life he was leading. Taking the edge off, putting it back on, became the typical seesaw balancing act of the addicted, but Halston didn't seem the least bit worried by it. He could handle it. He could handle anything. He was Halston. Anyway, it was no big deal. By the mid-seventies, in certain circles, dabbling in cocaine had attained newfound respectability. It was a seemingly harmless, physically nonaddictive "social drug" (it made you speed-talk) with a well-deserved reputation as an aphrodisiac. It was becoming the demimonde's version of a martini before dinner, and there was no telling in whose pocket or Bendel's purse a little amber vial might turn up.

Halston was afraid that his startlingly green eyes would betray that he was stoned on drugs—as they often did—so he began to wear sunglasses all the time, even indoors at night. Chris Royer, one of his favorite models, came to the salon one day wearing a pair of cheap mirrored sunglasses she had bought as a lark from a street vendor, and Halston liked them so much he had several expensive pairs made for himself. With his black turtleneck sweaters and black Ultrasuede jackets, and the slash of dark, mirrored glasses hiding his eyes, he took on a *Star Wars'* Darth Vadar look, ominous and intimidating. Now he was rarely seen without a limousine or an entourage, and with a flair worthy of a rock star, he added a new and brilliant affectation to his act: the Halstonettes. This was the name the writer Andre Leon Talley gave to the models who seemed to follow Halston everywhere he went, as a pun on the Rockettes, Radio City Music Hall's synchronized dance team. The models in the Halstonettes considered it a great honor to be included as part of Halston's corps. It started when Halston began bringing four or five models with him, always dressed in coordinated Halston outfits, to important store openings, or publicity appearances. It was a smashing look, to have beautiful people hovering around him wearing his clothes. "Since I do have my girls around a lot and they have to wear *something,* I certainly don't want them wearing another designer's clothes," he said, "and I love to be around beautiful people at night. Who doesn't?"

Soon the so-called Halstonettes began to accompany Halston more frequently, to nighttime social gatherings as well as business events. They all arrived at the same moment in limousines, and Halston would emerge from the lead car dressed in black, rigidly tall and immaculate, the mirrored sunglasses sheathing his eyes. Close behind appeared a panoply of equally immaculate and rigid-looking men and women, one more chillingly beautiful than the next, all in coordinated outfits, right down to the mirrored sunglasses that mimicked those of their master. They glided behind Halston in a cluster, and when he stopped, the girls surrounded him like a squad of protective sequined bodyguards. This loosely defined group of Halstonettes included Shirley Ferro, Nancy North, Chris Royer, Carla Aroki, Martin Snaric, Tony Spinetti, Pat Cleveland, and Connie Cook.

As the greatest star in fashion, it was only appropriate that he now snare the greatest star of them all for his client, and new friend, Elizabeth Taylor. Halston and Taylor had first met in 1975 when one of the producers of the Academy Awards ceremonies asked Halston if he would design a dress for Taylor to wear to the awards ceremony. Halston said he'd be delighted, but that, of course, "Miss Taylor will have to come to New York for the fittings." Word came back that, no, Halston had to come to Los Angeles, and he said he was sorry, but he was too busy. The next day the phone rang in his office and it was Elizabeth Taylor. She said, "Is this really Halston?" and he said "Is this really Elizabeth Taylor?"

They hit it off from the start. Taylor asked him on the phone what kind of a dress he had in mind for her if they did manage to get together.

"I think a strapless dress," Halston said, "which is flattering to any woman with good shoulders."

Taylor liked this line a lot and began to use her powers of

persuasion to get Halston to come to Beverly Hills and fit her. Finally, Halston sighed and said, "Only for you, I'll come to California."

Taylor chews up weak people who act goofy and impressed around her, and she found none of that with Halston. Although he always felt Taylor was "royalty" compared with the rest of his clients, he treated her the same way he treated all his "Sweetiecakes" and "Pussycats." "We have such rapport," he said, noting that at the time they were both forty-four years old. "We're made for each other. I'm in love with her."

By then Taylor was romancing and about to marry Republican Senator John Warner, on the rebound after Richard Burton had married model Suzy Hunter. Although she was dabbling in films—she made *A Little Night Music* in 1977—Taylor was mostly interested in being the fat and blowsy and seemingly happy Virginia housewife of John Warner. She was also drinking heavily and eating as much as she pleased, and in one well-publicized incident she had almost choked to death on a chicken bone as she was gorging herself. When Halston first laid eyes on her, Taylor was unmistakably *saftig,* and her clothes were ill fitting. "That's because she's been in European clothes that are overpowering," Halston said defensively. "I found her to have a terrific figure," he said, "well endowed and with *bazooms.* She has a small waist and hips and beautiful legs."

Halston not only designed the gown she wore to the Academy Awards, but he also escorted her to the awards ceremony where they were seen together on live TV by hundreds of millions of people around the world, Taylor popping out of Halston's low-cut, strapless dress, with Halston himself beaming his perfect smile at her side. After the ceremonies were over they went off to a round of gala parties till the wee hours of the morning, where Taylor discovered that Halston could keep up with her in the alcohol department. Soon afterwards Taylor commissioned Halston to make some seventy gowns for her, many of which were designed specifically for the colors of the gems in her jewelry collection. Although, according to one intimate of Halston's, the relationship between them was mainly based on business, they did become occasional carousing partners, both with a taste for nightlife and cocktails.

They made a handsome pair, as well, the night in 1977 when Halston was Taylor's escort for the tenth anniversary of the founding of the American Film Institute, held at the Kennedy Center in Washington, D.C., to which Taylor wore one of her seventy Halstons. After the gala affair was over, Halston, Taylor, and their friend, public relations executive Barry Landau, went to a little French restaurant on M Street to have dinner. Later, after several bottles of wine and many cocktails, they all went to the house on F Street that Taylor shared with her husband, John Warner, to have a few brandies in the library. Taylor slipped out of her Halston dress and curled up on the sofa in her nightgown and bathrobe in front of a roaring fire. Halston was feeling patriotic that night and began waxing grandly on the subjects of Washington, D.C., and how great America was, and then suddenly he had an irresistible urge to see Washington, all lit up at night. Although the weather was freezing and it was nearly two in the morning, Halston was determined they would go out *now*, and he talked Taylor into throwing a mink coat over her nightgown. Along with Landau, they got into Halston's waiting limousine and went off to see the Lincoln Memorial.

While the limousines waited, Taylor and Halston and Landau ascended the steps to the huge monument of the seated president and stood in silent respect for a moment. Then, unexpectedly, Elizabeth Taylor began to recite the Gettysburg Address aloud.

Suddenly, from out of the shadows, appeared a Washington, D.C., Federal Buildings' guard, who began to rush up the steps toward them shouting, "Hey, you! The memorial is closed! You're on government property. You have to get out of here, now!"

Taylor didn't even flinch. She turned toward the policeman, blinked her violet eyes, and in her most dulcet tones straight out of *National Velvet,* said, "I'm terribly sorry, Officer. I was reciting the Gettysburg Address. Am I doing something wrong?"

The guard began to explain about federal laws and trespassing on government property when a flicker of recognition crossed his face and he stammered to a halt, stunned that he was face-to-face with Elizabeth Taylor. Finally he managed to say, "Gee, I'm sorry. Would you do me a favor and continue?"

Taylor nodded and turned back to the statue and recited the entire Gettysburg Address out loud. By the time she was through, all of them were in tears. They thanked the guard and drove off.

Next, Taylor directed the limousine driver to take them to an all-night flower stand on Wisconsin Avenue where she and Halston bought a huge bouquet of flowers. Then they drove to the entrance of the National Cemetery where America's honored war dead are buried. Taylor and Halston got out of the limousine and laid the flowers by the locked gate along with a note they had written in the car to the boys who were buried there.

Finally, with the sun nearly coming up, they directed the driver to find the nearest White Castle hamburger stand and go in and get them doughnuts and hamburgers and coffee. When Taylor unwrapped her order in the back of the car, something was missing, and she and Halston decided to go into the deserted White Tower and get it themselves. The girl behind the counter was incredulous at the sight of Halston in a tuxedo and Elizabeth Taylor in nightgown and mink coat in a White Castle at five in the morning. "Pardon me," the girl asked, "are you really Elizabeth Taylor?"

Taylor said, "Yes, I'm fucking Elizabeth Taylor. Now where's my ketchup?"

★ ★ ★

ELIZABETH TAYLOR ALSO became an occasional visitor to 101 East Sixty-eighth Street, which had become a virtual clubhouse for all the women in Halston's life. It was at a dinner party at 101 that Elsa Peretti and Elizabeth Taylor first met. From the start Peretti was jealous toward anyone Halston paid attention to when she was around, and the fact that it was Elizabeth Taylor didn't make any difference. Peretti was prickly and difficult all night when she saw the way he and Taylor fawned on each other. Taylor was wearing her famous Krupp diamond ring that night, and when the conversation unavoidably turned to the ring, as it frequently did, Taylor took it off her finger and let everybody around the table try it on. When the ring came to Peretti she slipped it on and allowed as how, "It looks so much better on my hand than on yours." The moment of silence that followed was so thick it could, as they say, have been cut by a knife.

As time went by, Halston's friendship with Elsa Peretti became even more delicately balanced. Peretti had long been a star in her own right, yet Halston only acknowledged how successful she had become by saying "I gave you your start." Peretti, for her part, always found something to criticize or complain about with Halston, but most of the complaints were some variation on the "You don't love me as much as I love you" routine. There was also a backlogged agenda of hurts and slights and petty arguments between them. One recurring bone of contention had to do with Peretti's $25,000 fee for designing Halston's perfume bottle; she didn't feel it was enough, since the shape had become synonymous with the perfume and she had never seen another penny. To soothe this rub, Halston gave Peretti a $35,000 sable coat for Christmas, although she was miffed even more when she discovered that Halston had talked Norton Simon Industries into buying the coat for her wholesale, at $25,000. To make matters even more delicate between them, Peretti and Victor Hugo had become good friends—so close that she even gave Victor a key to her apartment. Peretti later regretted this when she discovered that Victor and his friends had worn her best dresses out dancing at a discotheque. Victor, who told Warhol he liked to create turmoil for the fun of it, began to play Elsa and Halston off each other. According to Eula, Peretti was always bailing Victor out with money and then going to Halston and saying, "You created this monster, you should take care of it." It got worse and worse.

Another reason for Peretti's growing animosity toward Halston was the competition she was receiving from his growing harem at 101. There were so many "Halston girls," as Warhol called them, that Warhol dubbed 101 "Halston's Home for Wayward Women." Another glittering addition to Halston's coterie was Bianca Perez Morena de Macias, better known as Bianca Jagger, the thirtyish estranged wife of Mick Jagger. Bianca had married the Rolling Stone in 1971, four months pregnant with their daughter, Jade. Beautiful, sassy, and a flashy but fashionable dresser, Bianca had become a celebrity in her own right. When Jagger left her in 1978 for Texas model Jerry Hall, Bianca had fled their West Side home to the arms of Ryan O'Neal for a time. Back in New York, homeless, she practically took up residence at 101. Bianca was a vivacious and glamorous addition to Halston's inner circle, and it was even reported in the *New York Post* that Halston was playing matchmaker for Bianca. "Halston Set as Matchmaker for a Mickless Bianca" proclaimed the headline. "Those who care think Halston has only one mission in life at the moment," said the columnist. "He is determined to find Bianca a rich husband. After all, Halston has tailor-made Bianca's clothes for ages now, so why not her life?" It's doubtful that Bianca Jagger needed anyone to find her a date, especially since at the time it seemed she so adored Halston himself. "Homosexuals make the best friends," Bianca said, "because they care about you as a woman and they are not jealous. They love you but don't try to screw up your head." Andy Warhol thought their relationship was so close, "it was like a romance," and one night when someone in the crowd suggested that perhaps Halston should marry Bianca, Halston put his hands on his hips and said, *"I'm* the hostess here."

Bianca's only real competition for top cat in Halston's pack was Liza Minnelli. Over the years, as Halston and Liza's predilections kept pace, he became not only a Dutch uncle to her but also an enabler and coconspirator. Robert Jon Cohen, who was Halston's twenty-year-old unpaid assistant at the time, remembered Halston bringing a Gucci binocular case with several ounces of cocaine to Liza Minnelli's apartment. "I've heard all the rumors," Liza said. "I know they say I'm shooting up, pills—the whole works. How dare they? They're gonna try to grind me up. Well, I won't step into their grinder."

Minnelli was already in her own grinder. By the end of the 1970s she was going through one of her most frantic and self-destructive periods. She had recently finished work on the film *New York, New York,* film director Martin Scorsese's first musical. Although Minnelli was still legally married to Jack Haley, Jr., at the time, she and Scorsese began to have an affair during the filming of *New York, New York,* which became an ill-kept secret in the press and entertainment industries. To complicate matters thoroughly, Scorsese was also married to screenwriter Julia Cameron, who eventually named Minnelli as a co-respondent in her divorce from Scorsese. In early 1977, to further exacerbate this complicated and sticky situation, Minnelli and Scorsese decided to collaborate again, this time on a Broadway musical called *The Act,* which Scorsese—who had never worked in the theater before—would direct. All the various embroilments made the rehearsal period of *The Act* a field day for gossip columnists and publicists, and the show was sold out months in advance. In an almost Byzantine twist, Minnelli's husband-to-be, Mark Gero, was stage manager of the show, literally waiting in the wings for her. All of Minnelli's entanglements, however, did not discourage her from having a brief liaison with dancer Mikhail Baryshnikov. Halston, who was father confessor and referee in Liza's wars of love, listened to every episode of her adventures, dried her tears, and dispensed his best advice.

Liza asked Halston to design the costumes for *The Act*, for which he charged a $100,000 fee. He asked her to come to the showroom during rehearsals and run through the whole show for him, telling him exactly what it was she had to do in each costume. Liza remembered how the idea for all the sequined gowns started. "By this point in the show you're hot and wet," Halston told her, "so we'll put you in sequins so the sweat won't show. If you're going to be shiny, you might as well shine all over. And if your hair is wet," he added, "it's going to look stupid if you're standing there in a jersey that shows wet spots."

No ONE GOT a bigger kick out of watching the nightly celebrity sideshow at 101 East Sixty-third Street than Andy Warhol, who was probably Halston's most frequent guest. By now Victor Hugo seemed to spend as much time with Warhol as he did with Halston. Victor told Andy everything that went on between him and Halston, and Warhol fed on each word of it, often tape-recording his phone conversations with Victor. Victor was up to his usual shenanigans; making silkscreens of the Mona Lisa wearing Halston dresses, arriving at the opening of Warhol's Hammer and Sickles show in a cut-up shirt, or wearing a plastic garbage bag to a retrospective at the Metroplitan Museum of Art. Once, Victor even managed to insult Warhol by defacing a portrait of himself that Halston had commissioned. But for the most part, Warhol couldn't resist encouraging Victor's outrages. He would say to Victor, "Do something crazy, take off your clothes and I'll give you a painting," just to spice up the evening. One summer night, when Halston was away for the weekend at Joe Eula's Connecticut country house, Victor held an orgy in Halston's house and invited Warhol over to photograph some of it. Halston came home to find "greasy handprints on the walls and come on the Ultrasuede," according to Warhol. Even worse, his cocaine was missing from the safe. "Halston didn't even know Victor knew the combination," said Warhol. Eventually, for his own peace of mind, Halston moved Victor out of 101 altogether and into a co-op loft on Nineteenth Street and Fifth Avenue. This loft then became the site of much of Warhol's voyeuristic picture taking.

Halston's inner circle at 101 now included its own doctor, a curly-haired young physician named Robert Giller, "the acupuncturist who is needling his way into society," as *Women's Wear Daily* put it. Boyishly handsome, with curly hair and a bemused smile, the doctor was about thirty-five and had a successful practice. Giller's medical degree is from the University of Illinois Medical School. He reportedly also served in the army and spent a year in Hong Kong studying acupuncture. Reportedly, Giller had been practicing in New York since 1973, specializing in holistic medicine. He and Halston met at the gymnasium of the stars, the spartan workout parlor of Radu Teodorescu on East Fifty-seventh Street.

Over the years Giller had attracted a large celebrity clientele. "A lot of times celebrities are friends of one another," Giller explained. "You get one and they tell their friends." Giller had luxurious Park Avenue offices from which he dispensed his famed vitamin shot whose revitalizing effects were becoming well known in certain circles. Halston swore by these injections and became Dr. Giller's patient. Other patients of Giller reportedly included George Hamilton, Liza Minnelli, Judy Collins, Carrie Fisher, Mikhail Baryshnikov, and occasionally some of the Halstonettes. "I didn't like Giller," said Chris Royer. "I got very bad vibes on this guy. I don't know what the vitamin shots were for. He said they built up your resistance." Model Connie Cook also went to Giller on several occasions but decided to discontinue the vitamin injections.

Andy Warhol, in his diaries, describes one passing, slightly surrealistic moment at 101. Dr. Giller arrived at Halston's house and, according to Warhol, Giller "started to find Halston's energy center, and while he did that, Halston was having white powder, so finally when Dr. Giller announced that he'd found Halston's energy center Halston had had enough white powder so that he did have energy." Moments later Victor Hugo rang the doorbell in his underwear, and no one seemed to notice.

THE NIGHT OF March 12, 1977, the public got a startling yet funny glimpse of what it was like to be part of Halston's inner circle. That winter, WNEW TV, a local New York television station, premiered a new live show called *Friends of . . .* This was the exciting but risky concept of TV producer Alyce Finell. The idea was that each week a central personality of some renown or expertise would hold a live, on-the-air dinner party with six or seven friends attending. It was hoped that the friends would also be accomplished and witty and the dinner conversation would be riveting. Broadcast from WNEW's studios in Manhattan, the element of the show's being live lent added excitement, and if things went well the viewers would be able to feel that for an hour and a half every Saturday night they were eavesdropping on the private lives of famous people.

After just a few weeks on the air, *Friends of . . .* picked up something of a cult following among the Manhattan congnoscenti. There had already been a "Friends of . . . Dick Cavett," whose dinner table included Charlotte Curtis, Jerzy Kosinski, Garson Kanin, Bibi Andersson, and Peter Glenville. Composer Cy Coleman hosted a table with guests Bob Fosse, Russell Baker, Madeline Kahn and Paddy Chayefsky as his guests. The show really seemed to pick up viewership the week that magazine publisher Clay Felker hosted an entertainingly witty and clever dinner party that David Frost, writer Gail Sheehy, designer Milt Glaser, and Norman Mailer attended. This last show received the best rating so far as well as some good press, and with word of mouth building, *tout le monde* was expected to be watching the next show—"Friends of . . . Halston."

Alyce Finell had learned that the only way to make an improvisational show like *Friends of . . .* a success was to plan ahead carefully for each show. Finell spent many hours interviewing each host to find out who his or her friends were and help develop an interesting cross-section of dinner guests. From the start, however, there were problems with Halston. He didn't want to give a pre-interview—he'd been hosting dinner parties his whole life—and when Finell finally did get to talk to him his only concern was that he be allowed to decorate the dinner table. Finell had almost as much trouble with the dinner guests: Bianca Jagger, Dr. Robert Giller, Joe Eula, Baby Jane Holzer, and Victor Hugo. Halston had asked Andy Warhol to be on the show, but he had refused because Warhol claimed he had had a similar idea himself about hosting a dinner party on television each week and that the concept had been stolen from him.

The most difficult guest to deal with for Finell was Bianca Jagger. "She gave me a pretty hard time on the phone," said Finell, "because she didn't want to be presented in an improper environment and without dignity, or whatever she felt she deserved. I assured her that this was not anything to be concerned about." Eula, Holzer, and Dr. Giller were easy enough to talk with, but Finell came away completely mystified by her interview with Victor Hugo, who uttered hardly a single understandable word.

The night of March 12, Halston's dinner table at the studio had been set to every last detail of his directions, with his own linen and china. There was a simple gray linen tablecloth, flatware from Tiffany, and Baccarat crystal. The centerpiece was a single gorgeous spray of white orchids. About an hour before the broadcast, the dinner guests began to arrive alone or with a support group to wait in the studio's Green Room. There were many more attendants than expected, and the Green Room began to fill up quickly and take on a party atmosphere. The buzz and excitement grew when Bianca Jagger stripped to change her dress. "Bianca Jagger, who was so concerned about the propriety and her public demeanor," said Alyce Finell, "was very busy prancing about bare breasted." In the meantime, Finell tried get the guests' attention. "I wanted to suggest some areas of conversation they could move into if things began to fall apart, which could happen very rapidly, but nobody wanted to listen." Finell got the distinct impression that Halston and his friends seemed to be in on some sort of inside joke. Doggedly, Finell showed them some prearranged hand signals in case things got slow. They all assured her things wouldn't.

At 10 P.M. the show went on the air. The first fifteen minutes was incredibly stiff and boring; Halston and his guests looked pale in the bright TV lights and painfully self-conscious as they sat there like cardboard figures. The slowness of the conversation was in itself discomforting. "They weren't saying *anything*," said Finell. "They were speaking, but it was nothing of any consequence." Finell tried the prearranged hand signals, but the group ignored them. Even Andy Warhol, watching at home, was struck by how boring it all was. "It was a real-life dinner with a seven-second delay," he dictated to his diary. "The only real-life thing missing at the table was coke, and no runs to the bathroom."

There was one almost painful moment when Victor announced that he was no longer doing Halston's windows, and that he was now "an artist for hire." At that moment the camera cut to a close-up of Halston; his face looked hard and angry. During commercial breaks Finell rushed out of the control booth and onto the set with her suggestions for conversation, but she was again summarily dismissed. Then about half an hour into the show the guests started to do something that Finell had begged them not to: the conversation started getting louder and the guests all started talking at the same time, creating havoc for the sound man. "Soon nobody could be heard clearly with three or four people talking at the same time," said Finell. Halfway through the show the group's behavior began to change dramatically. "This group was suddenly in their own stratosphere," said Finell. "They were speaking gibberish."

Victor Hugo claims that the combination of the hot lights and the champagne hit the dinner guests all at once and made them giddy. Whatever it was, the tone of the party suddenly shifted gears and Victor did the most unusual thing: he took off his moustache. It turned out that he had shaved his real moustache earlier in the day—reportedly because Dr. Giller had one—and had come to the studio wearing a professionally applied fake.

In the control room, the baffled director asked, "Who's that?" Finell couldn't understand it; a new guest seemed to have appeared at the table. "Where did he come from?" the director asked. Then, when the camera was on someone else, Victor stuck the moustache back on. In one shot Victor had a moustache, then fifteen seconds later he didn't. No one could figure out what was going on.

During the next commercial break Finell begged the group to behave, but when they returned chaos reigned once again at the table. Victor and Joe Eula started arguing about whether or not Andy Warhol had had the idea for this kind of show first and Eula snapped at him, "Let Andy speak for himself, why he's not here." And then Victor loudly announced that the whole show was ripped off from an idea by Warhol.

"The champagne, the lights—whatever else it was," said Finell, "I don't know which one started it, but there were champagne bottles on the table and Victor began to shake the bottles and spray champagne at everyone across the table. It was childish, but there was some terrible black decadent secret to it. Then it started to get very boisterous, and Victor Hugo pulled an ugly, scrawny rubber chicken out of his tuxedo jacket and started masturbating with it on live TV."

The control room went berserk as the director screamed to the cameramen not to photograph Victor and the floor manager frantically motioned for Victor to get rid of the chicken. They quickly went to another commercial break. Victor Hugo claims that the chicken was a prearranged signal with Halston's houseboy of the moment, who was in the hospital because "a wire in a dildo had broken through and punctured him and I took out the chicken to say hello to him watching TV in the hospital."

"Finally the ninety minutes of eternity was over and I was numb," said Finell. The show was canceled a few weeks later, but the day after "Friends of . . . Halston" aired Alyce Finell called writer Pete Hamill and asked him what he thought. Hamill told her that the Halston show had made an important sociological contribution: it showed beautiful people to be not quite what they perceived themselves to be. "When they started throwing champagne at each other," Hamill said, "I thought, 'Aha, this is where the Nazis come in.' "

STUDIO DAYS,
STUDIO NIGHTS

Halston didn't want to go to Studio 54 that fateful night of May 2, 1977, when Joe Eula dragged him there for the first time. Halston was not a big fan of discotheques or nightclubs. "Too tall to dance," he would say, and anyway, although he liked having Chinese food at Pearl's he wasn't the type to hang out in smoky clubs or dine at celebrity restaurants like Elaine's. Even at this point in his life, Halston still followed much the same schedule of getting up early in the morning and arriving in the office around eight. He would work hard most of the day, dine with friends at 101 before dismissing them around eleven, and then have a sex date for an hour before going to bed by midnight. "You couldn't get the guy out of the goddamned den," Joe Eula said. "I was the one who went everywhere. They couldn't open a new place without finding me on the doorstep. And one night I dragged Halston to a new place. I said it was perfect for him. It was so big he could get lost in the crowds."

There were, indeed, crowds. It was a balmy Sunday evening the night Halston's limousine first turned down West Fifty-fourth Street between Broadway and Eighth Avenue, and the scene that greeted him seemed nothing less than apocalyptic. The street, heretofore best known to Halston as the male porn-theater district, was a snarl of limousines and taxis and private cars inching their way toward a silver-and-black art-deco marquee with the STUDIO 54 logo on it to disgorge their passengers. There were several hundred people spilling out under the marquee in a scene right out of *Day of the Locust,* pushing, shouting, squashed against barricades. Across the street, keeping a wary eye on the crowd, were four New York City policemen inside their patrol cars, the rotating beacons splashing the crowd in waves of red light. A pack of paparazzi, cameras held high above the heads of the crowd, raced to and fro, strobe lights freezing the scene in bolts of lightning as they hungrily descended upon the rich and famous emerging from their limousines. Halston was astounded; what could be happening inside to cause *this*?

Halston and Eula navigated their way through the mob up to the marquee where they were greeted by an almost surreal scene. In the middle of a brightly lit no-man's-land delineated by three lengths of velvet ropes on movie-theater-style stanchions stood a little man with sad eyes and a crooked smile, flanked by a team of hulking bodyguards. This unprepossessing-looking figure dressed in a Lacoste shirt and blue jeans was Steve Rubell, thirty-four, the discotheque's co-owner, and the anxious crowd was chanting his name in a desperate cacophony: "Steve! Steve! *Steve!* STEVE! *STEVE!*" When Rubell spotted Halston, he ordered the guards forward to part the velvet ropes and wade into the crowd to usher Halston and Eula to safety. Rubell was effusive and giddy at the sight of Halston. "Oh, I'm so excited to meet you. I'm your biggest fan," he told him over and over again in a pervasively loud, nasal voice that sounded like a record being played at too slow a speed. Then he whisked Halston and Eula away from the screaming crowds through the blacked-out glass doors of his nightclub.

Once inside the club, like Alice down the rabbit hole, nothing seemed real. It was a cross between an amusement park and a nightclub, Mardi Gras on laughing gas. Even the sheer physical size of the place was overwhelming. It was a cavernous, former opera house and one-time TV studio, which easily held 3,000 people. And what people! An ever-changing cast of beautiful and exotic types who looked as though they had been sent by Federico Fellini's casting department. There were businessmen in pin-striped suits and women in gowns, and diplomats, and foreign royalty, and men in leather, and drag queens with beards and debutantes with West Pointers in uniform. There were couples of every sexuality and denomination in passionate embrace all over the huge, darkened balcony that hung over the pandemonic dance floor. The young, muscular bartenders, stripped to the waist, danced and twirled as they served drinks to music so loud it seemed to carbonate the air. As Rubell showed Halston around the lounges and hidden passages, the subterranean VIP room, the coed bathrooms where private parties were being held in the stalls, Halston hadn't been that amused in *years.*

An idea came to Halston. The next night was Bianca Jagger's birthday, and Halston was giving her a dinner party. Wouldn't it be amusing to bring some people to Studio 54 after the party?

"I'm sorry," Rubell said, "but the place is closed on Monday nights."

Halston arched an eyebrow and said, "Well, then open it!"

Rubell hesitated only a beat before he said, "Of course!"

The next night, after a buffet dinner catered by Glorious Foods at 101, Halston and thirty guests including Jacqueline Bisset, Fernando Sanchez, Mick Jagger, Mikhail Baryshnikov, Margaux Hemingway, Alana Hamilton, and Diana Vreeland piled into a convoy of limousines shortly after midnight and went to Studio 54 where they were greeted by Steve Rubell and several dozen frenzied paparazzi whom Rubell had managed to tip off. Inside, the club was already well populated by a couple of hundred fun-loving revelers Rubell had thoughtfully invited for background effect. In honor of Bianca, a naked black man painted in brilliant colors led a white horse across the huge dance floor. On the horse sat a naked black woman, also painted in brilliant colors. Not to be upstaged, Bianca told the woman to dismount, got up on the horse herself, and rode bareback around the Studio 54 dance floor as red and white balloons fell from the ceiling and the disc jockey played "Happy Birthday."

After that night, Studio 54 became as much of a narcotic in Halston's life as any other. The club would be in existence for only twenty months under Rubell's regime, but for that time Halston became one of its central figures. "Halston fell in love with it right away," said Eula, "all those people and personalities. It was right up his alley. From then on that became our second home. We'd leave the office and go straight to Studio 54." Night after night Halston was there, sometimes with the Halstonettes in tow, frequently with Liza or Bianca or Andy or Victor Hugo. Sometimes Halston would go to "Studio," as they began to call it, several weeks in a row without a break, and never get bored with it. He would sit in a banquette or he would stand by the bar, or sometimes watch for hours from the disc jockey's booth, half hidden in the shadows of the colored lights, a frozen half smile on his face as the dancers whirled below him. There was always something amusing. Henry Kissinger in conversation with a fairy princess on roller skates. Elton John doing poppers on the dance floor. Robin Williams mooning from the balcony. Capote and Tennessee Williams having a tiff. Jacqueline Bisset being twirled in the air by her date. Rubell, a little drunk and stoned, lying in Yves Saint Laurent's lap. The estranged wife of the Canadian prime minister, Margaret Trudeau, clinging to Ryan O'Neal. Elsa Peretti laughing at Victor Hugo, who was naked except for a garden hose and blindfold. The Hells Angels and Leonard Bernstein and Vitas Gerulaitis and Raquel Welch. Diana Vreeland. Streisand. Christina Onassis. The sideshow was so great and never-ending that often Halston would stay at Studio 54 until closing time at four in the morning, when he would stumble out the doors into the deserted street. A lone limousine would be waiting for him there, to drive him off into the dawn.

When asked by the press about the ineluctable lure Studio 54 held for him, Halston said, "It's a democracy. You see a David Bowie there, Liza, unemployed actors. It generates energy. Everyone just blends together in a curious sort of way. I can always hide in the deejay booth. No one bothers me there. I think that people must be entertained. It isn't necessary that you be serious all the time. At Studio 54 you can find a range of personalities from Queen Juliana to Princess Grace. They go to be entertained just as they might go to the theater or ballet for entertainment."

SOME BALLET. STUDIO 54 was the embodiment of the most decadent social period of any city in modern history. By 1978, Dionysus had hired a press agent and New York was headlong into an era of staggering permissiveness. As the result of two liberal mayoralties in what was already one of the most liberal cities in the world, any carnal pleasure, dream or nightmare, found acceptance in New York. The city was host to increasingly open street prostitution, and because of newly passed Federal Communications Commission regulations, local cable television stations were permitted to lease access to producers who could cablecast virtually anything, even hard-core sex as long as the penetration was blotted out by an electronic black dot. The gay movement had reached the zenith of its cultural power and gay ideology held great sway with the New York media and fast-lane crowd. With Gay Liberation came great sexual indulgence. By the end of the seventies there were perhaps several hundred gay bars and discotheques in the New York area, and a score of bathhouses as well. There were heterosexual pickup bars and bathhouses, too, like Plato's Retreat with its mattressed orgy room, and sadomasochistic sex clubs, both gay and straight, like the Anvil and the Hell Fire Club, which were flourishing in the meat-packing district with no community interference. So acceptable did these seem, that one night Andy Warhol took Bianca Jagger to see the Anvil with his dog, Archie. Gay Liberation helped set a wild tone at Studio 54, with its exaltation of beauty and youth, and promiscuity was so venerated that being called "trash" was considered a compliment. There was so much copulation in the balcony at Studio 54 that the *real* reason it was eventually covered with rubber was so that it could be washed down with disinfectant more easily in the morning. The gorgeous bartenders, each of them personally interviewed by Steve Rubell, slept with the celebrity customers, men and women, and then compared notes. "The customers think they're passing us around," one bartender said, "but it's *us* who's passing *them.*"

Social drug taking was also de rigueur. There was a whole slew of designer drugs on the black market, with alphabetical names, that made you feel woozy or rubbery or elated; MDA, Special K, the good old LSD. And at just about the time when Studio 54 opened, a prescription "hypnotic" sleeping pill called Quaalude came on the market. A thick, white tablet, the "Lude," as it was called, was said to be the perfect disco drug. Just the right mixture of lude and cocaine and alcohol gave the user the perfect, slippery, glimmering sensation for a night out at Studio 54.

Steve Rubell was the king of the lude. He handed them out to customers and employees like candy or free drinks, tickets. In public, his speech was frequently slurred, and he looked very stoned and sleepy eyed. A phenomenon in his own time, Rubell had become the arbiter of New York nightlife—the sociological link between the Stork Club's Sherman Billingsley and Walt Disney. Paradoxically, at the core he was also something Halston hated the most: a loud, Jewish nerd, the son of a Brooklyn mailman who grew up in a three-room apartment and happily admitted he would probably turn himself away from the doors of his own club. Formerly, he had also been a nationally ranked amateur tennis player and a successful ex-stockbroker who had owned a chain of steak houses called the Steak Loft. Several years earlier, he had teamed up with an old college chum, attorney Ian Schrager, and begun opening discotheques, first in Boston and later in Queens, New York. In 1977, with $400,000 from private investors, Rubell and Schrager made the leap to Manhattan with Studio 54.

Rubell's capricious door policy immediately made headlines. It all had to do with who was allowed to pass through the portals of his disco. Although whimsy played a great part in whom he let in, there was also a secret basic set of rules. No "bridge and tunnel" people from the five boros, no "Quiana from the Americana," by which he meant the wealthy South American tourists who stayed at the nearby hotel. The *verboten* "bagel nosh" crowd meant Jewish-looking people. Those who were smiled upon were the exotic, the pretty, the young, and the rich—although none of those attributes could necessarily guarantee admission. Among the many turned away at the velvet ropes was family of the shah of Iran, who offered to buy Rubell a house anywhere in the world if he could guarantee their nightly admittance without a fuss; several sons of mafiosi; the president of Cyprus; and John F. Kennedy, Jr. One determined woman drove to Manhattan from New Jersey with three different outfits in her car and kept changing in the backseat, hoping one would strike Steve Rubell's fancy. When Rubell told one man that it was his polyester suit that was keeping him outside, the man offered to let Rubell burn a hole in the lapel if he would only let him and his date inside. Some people had the temerity to offer Rubell a bribe, but that was the last way to get inside. It was said that when the club first became a success—reportedly grossing $600,000 a month, most of it in cash—Rubell took home shopping bags full of twenties and hundreds, dumped them on his bed, and cavorted nude in the pile like a kitten with catnip before he jerked off over the cash. "Money," he told Halston the next day, "is the best sex."

Halston and Rubell were, on the surface, a most peculiar pair for New Best Friends, yet for the next few years they were inseparable. Frick and Frack, they shared houses on Fire Island and boys in Manhattan, they vacationed together in Mustique (*Women's Wear* called the pair a "much in need of a rest duo"), and they flanked Liza Minnelli in her seat at the 1978 Tony Awards. (When she won for Best Performance in a Musical, Rubell literally flew a foot out of his chair, he got so carried away.) In truth, Halston and Rubell were not so much friends as business associates who profited from each other's services; Halston was the centerpiece of the most glamorous clique in the city, and Rubell was the innkeeper that that clique helped to make famous. Like Warhol, Rubell was enamored of celebrity. "With Halston, it's class all the way," Rubell said, grinning. "The man's middle name is *taste.*" But his attraction to Halston went beyond his admiration of taste. Even Rubell's partner, Ian Schrager, said "Halston had magic."

"The publicity was coming our way hot and heavy," said Joe Eula, "and everybody got on the bandwagon with us."

The nights at Studio 54 began to meld into one snowy blitz of cocaine and scotch and Quaaludes. Every night there held some new, small titillation: a fat Elizabeth Taylor in a silly flowered hat with Halston in the disc-jockey's booth playing with the lights all night; Mick Jagger falling asleep on Baryshnikov's shoulder; Truman Capote giving a party for his own face-lift. There was the party for *People* magazine, and the Halloween party, and the Academy Awards party, and the opening-night party for Liza when *The Act* opened on Broadway, and parties for Liza's birthday, Liz Taylor's birthday, Andy Warhol's birthday, and Steve Rubell's birthday. On April 26, 1978, the club celebrated its own birthday: a scene of tumultuous chaos inside and out as five thousand people tried to get in the doors. Inside, Liza Minnelli, surrounded by

Andy Warhol and Bianca Jagger, sang Happy Birthday to Steve Rubell, and later, in a special tribute to Halston, crooned to him, "I'm always true to you, Halston darling, in my fashion!" For the birthday party Halston threw for Steve Rubell the club was turned into a child's fantasy world which included a circus with live ponies, toy soldiers, and huge stuffed giraffes. The banquettes were reupholstered in quilted blue-satin, and circus clowns handed out toy balloons. At one point sixty members of the Galaxie Twirlers marching band stormed across the dance floor playing "Happy Birthday to Steve Rubell." There was also Elizabeth Taylor's birthday party at which Bianca Jagger wrapped her legs around one of the lighting fixtures that descended onto the dance floor and clung to it as it was hoisted high above the dance floor. And a party for Liza's solo performance at Carnegie Hall, and a New Year's Eve party when everybody was still at Halston's house and they heard it announced live on the radio that they were arriving at Studio 54 and entering the doors—"It's Halston! And Andy! And Bianca Jagger, folks!"

The tales of drugs and sex that began to emanate from Studio 54 were sometimes lurid. "The stuff that happened was much worse," said Rubell. "You couldn't believe it." One night, after the club closed, Rubell held a contest between some of the more attractive male employees and customers to see who could ejaculate the farthest, the winner receiving a vacation trip with Rubell. The openness with which Rubell and Halston flaunted their unsavory activities spelled flirting with danger. Rubell's feelings of omnipotence eventually did him in one night when he bragged on a local New York TV station that what the IRS didn't know wouldn't hurt them. Again, in the summer of 1978, Rubell was so convinced of his power to control the press that he and Halston decided to hold a drag party at 101 East Sixty-third Street where men would come dressed as women and women as men. Halston said he was giving the party to show his "appreciation" to the staff of Studio

54, and a select crowd of beauties including bartenders, security guards, and busboys were invited along with some of Halston's and Andy Warhol's friends. As word of the party spread through the disco crowd and Rubell started fielding phone calls from reporters asking if the upcoming drag party was for real, Rubell issued an edict to the press: he wanted a complete blackout on the party—no press coverage whatsoever, particularly no photographers around Halston's town house so that the guests would not be self-conscious about arriving on the street in front of 101 in their drag.

That hot Monday night in July Halston greeted guests in an off-the-shoulder matte jersey blouse, skinny-legged evening pants, and black spike heels, which brought his height to six foot six and on which he seemed to have no trouble balancing. Victor Hugo came as Régine, "the other disco queen," he said. Rubell wore a $15,000 red sequined gown, slit to the thigh, that had originally been designed for Liza Minnelli to wear in *The Act*. Rubell was said to be miffed that the same gown in blue had been given by Halston as a birthday gift to one of the Studio 54 bartenders. Warhol came in a Dolly Parton getup complete with blond bouffant wig and giant boobs. The doormen from Studio 54, some of them heterosexual, moonlighting cops, were all in ill-fitting dresses but didn't seem the least bit self-conscious. Out on the rooftop terrace a twenty-year-old busboy entertained with continuous, nonstop push-ups. The highlight of the party may have been when a candle ignited Steve Rubell's feather boa and gave the rest of the guests an excuse to throw their drinks on him. The party went on far into the morning of the next day. As the sun came up one guest was so confused he admitted, "Before tonight, I thought I was only bisexual."

One of the party guests that night—whom neither Halston nor Rubell wanted to invite—was Bob Weiner, a notorious spoilsport and mean-mouthed columnist for a downtown newspaper. But Weiner was desperate to be invited to the party, and he swore that he would never print or speak a word of what took place if he was allowed to come. Three days later, much to Halston and Rubell's chagrin, Weiner described the party at length in his column under a pseudonym. The column included many references to the taking of Quaaludes and the use of one of Halston's guest bedrooms as an orgy room. Weiner was quickly dispatched from the hallowed halls of Studio 54 for all time, but he had done his damage. Rumors about the party and orgy became so widespread and persistent that *Women's Wear* felt pressured to send a reporter to see Halston for his comments about it. "I love gossip and hearsay, but I hear I've done so many raunchy things it's unbelievable," he said, sidestepping the issue of the party. But when pinned down about whether he actually wore an off-the-shoulder dress, Halston said, "No one knows what I wore except people who were there." And then, unable to resist, he whispered, "A black cashmere body stocking."

The Studio 54 period might have reached some sort of dizzying height in late May of 1979 when Halston became the recipient of the third Martha Graham Award. It was, essentially, a meaningless award, particularly since Halston was Graham's biggest financial supporter. Still, it was a festive, happy night, and an incredible tribe of supporters turned out for him. "All the great ladies of the world were with me," Halston gushed, and indeed, Studio 54 was so crowded with stars surrounding him on the banquette that Betty Ford sat on Liza Minnelli's lap, much to the delight of the paparazzi swarming all over Halston, Elizabeth Taylor, Andy Warhol, Martha Graham, Ruth Carter Stapleton, and Bianca Jagger, as guests like Truman Capote, Mayor Edward I. Koch, Barbara Walters, Kitty Carlisle Hart, Gloria Vanderbilt, Patricia McBride, Eleanor Revson, Sandra Payson, Elizabeth and Felix Rohatyn, and the designer Valentina came to pay homage. At about one in the morning, Liza Minnelli took to the microphone to present the award to Halston, but instead of coming on strong with the big brassy personality everyone expected, she could barely be heard and what she said made little sense. When she finally introduced Halston, Liz Taylor turned to him and brayed, "Get your ass up there and talk loud." Halston talked "loud," all right, but he sounded as unintelligible as Liza, and the audience was more amused than shocked at their altered states.

Nothing could dilute Halston's passion for Studio 54, even when in the summer of 1979 he was visited at home by the FBI who questioned him at length about Steve Rubell and his business dealings. It seems that bragging on TV about skimming funds had done him in, and it was also widely rumored that Rubell had turned away the wrong IRS man at the velvet ropes one night. The Feds came after Rubell and Schrager with all they had, and even with Roy Cohn representing them, they were sent to a blue-collar prison for tax evasion. Ever the loyal friend, just before Rubell's sentencing for tax evasion, Halston threw a going-away party for him, at which Diana Ross sang to them from the disc jockey's booth.

In May of 1979, it was announced by the Coty Awards committee that Halston would receive a special citation for his Hall of Fame membership that year, but he rejected the award, following Calvin Klein's lead. Klein was to have received a Coty that year, too. The problem was that Coty had recently launched its own cosmetics line with nine products called the Coty Awards Collection, and the package was stamped with the image of the "Winnie" award. Both Klein and Halston felt that Coty was "trading on the awards commercially." But Halston had a wonderful idea for the fashion industry in lieu of the Coty Awards. "I hope this doesn't sound pretentious on my part," he said, and then went on to frame the concept for brand-new fashion awards, held by a democratically elected committee of peers and presented at a spectacular televised ceremony, just like the Academy Awards or the Tonys. Halston even hinted that he might sponsor a fund-raising night at Studio 54 to raise seed money of $250,000. But no one took him up on it. No one was taking Halston very seriously just now.

By the end of the seventies, there was some imperceptible moment, some small threshold of time, when Halston crossed the line of ubiquitousness—when he was too much in the news, at too many parties. There came a point when Halston's popularity turned a corner and his whole persona started to wear thin, when the smugness and self-congratulatory behavior, the grandness, the pretensions, the snotty superiority of his crowd became tired. "They were playing at fame," Eleanor Lambert said. "I'm famous, you're famous, isn't it glorious we're all so famous." There was even a Fradon cartoon in *The New Yorker* magazine on May 29, 1978, picturing a wife remarking to her husband over the morning newspaper, "I dreamt I was sitting in on a National Security Council meeting, and guess what, Liza Minnelli and Halston were there too!"

John Fairchild remembered that around this time Halston complained to him about his fame. "He used to say he was fearful to go out on the street because everybody would recognize him. I remember one day we had lunch at the Four Seasons and he said that he had to take a limousine back to the office because people would ask him for his autograph on the street. And that disturbed him. He thought."

Halston couldn't understand why they were picking on *him*. "You see and hear the craziest things about everyone—but I'm just a person like everyone else. Well, not like everyone else. There's much more publicity, more picture taking. That's sort of the hardship part sometimes. Everyone knows who I am; but I don't know who *they* are."

IN JANUARY OF 1978, at the height of Halston's Studio 54 period, he left his cozy salon on East Sixty-eighth Street and moved into a floor of a skyscraper high above Manhattan—a move that many of Halston's inner circle regard as a symbolic turning point. "It was when we moved to the Olympic Tower," said Chris Royer, "that it all began to spin out of control. I hated the Olympic Tower. I remember coming in there and dreading it. It was like the Wizard of Oz. It was so cold." In fact, the environment of the Olympic Tower was so sleek and minimal that when they moved in, Joe Eula renamed Halston simply "H."

The move was precipitated by the Norton Simon safety engineers, who had completed an extensive inspection of the East Sixty-eighth Street building, which they had purchased for Halston. The engineers were concerned that the building was not safe for a business that had grown as large as Halston's. There were over thirty-five employees, only one elevator, and extremely poor fire-escape routes. Halston was more than delighted to move to newer and larger quarters, and he and Mike Lichtenstein began to scout various parcels of real estate. "It was difficult to find a space that was suitable to Halston's sense of what he thought the ambience of his salon should be," said Lichtenstein, "and then a broker took us to the twenty-second floor of the Olympic Tower."

The Olympic Tower is one of New York's most photographed buildings, standing as it does shoulder to steeple with St. Patrick's Cathedral on Fifth Avenue and Fifty-first Street. A dark glass monolith fifty-two stories high, it spectacularly reflects the cathedral in its imposing facade. Funded in part by the estate of Aristotle Onassis—thus the name the Olympic Tower—the top twenty-two floors of the cooperative building were reserved exclusively for residential use, with a separate entrance and lobby in which a one-story waterfall poured into a pond.

The floor that Halston leased was even more dramatic than the rest because it was the top commercial floor of the building and, in order to accommodate the requisite utilities, the ceiling had been specially built one and a half times as high as on any other floor. The mammoth 8,000 square feet of space was in a huge U-shape, with sealed floor-to-ceiling walls of windows that looked south, north, and west. "Once Halston saw that floor he wouldn't think about any other place," said Lichtenstein. The price was $16 a square foot, about $3 more than most other space, and the rent came to what was at that time a whopping $128,000 a year. "To some people it was outlandish," Mahoney said, "but I thought it was a great stroke for public relations."

With the assistance of Gruzen & Partners, architects, the showroom took nine months to build, and Halston designed the interiors and furniture himself. The main north-to-south space was separated into four sections by mirrored walls fourteen feet high weighing several tons each, yet each so perfectly balanced that they moved with the touch of a fingertip. It took one month just to put the mirrors in, and getting them up twenty-two stories in industrial-sized elevator shafts without shattering them was a tactical nightmare. The massive doors also had to be hung absolutely on-the-true to avoid a funhouse effect. When they were finally installed, a team of maintenance men had to be hired to keep them free of fingerprints. *Women's Wear* said that there were enough mirrors "to keep any self-respecting narcissist happy." There were also facilities for a maid and a cook, a complete kitchen with Baccarat crystal and Tiffany china and flatware, and a vast and beautifully appointed design room second largest in the world only to Yves Saint Laurent. "The sewing area was vast," said Lichtenstein, "and just before we moved in we took all the sewers up to the Olympic Tower for a Christmas party. I remember the sewers weeping—really weeping with joy at how beautiful the space was."

That's because the sensational wraparound, panoramic view of Manhattan and Fifth Avenue stretching all the way to Washington Square Park and up to Harlem was truly stirring. And when the sun set in the west, the building was bathed in a burnished orange light reflected ad infinitum in the mirrored walls. With the ornate carved spires of St. Patrick's Cathedral hovering just outside the window, sunset seemed like a truly religious experience. At night, with the city ink blue on blue, glittering like a carpet of diamonds, visitors to the salon spoke of feeling suspended, as if they were in a spaceship hovering over a silent city. It was Andy Warhol who suggested they carpet the floors in a dark color so as to "anchor" the showroom in space, it seemed to float so much, and Halston designed the carpets in a deep persimmon color, woven with tiny *H*'s linked at their serifs.

Halston didn't really have a separate office. His area was at the south end of the enormous room, and his desk was a large, sparse, blood-red lacquered Parsons table with two sterling silver Elsa Peretti candlesticks on it, a sterling silver Peretti ashtray, and several sprays of white orchid plants. Halston sat serenely behind the table in his dark glasses, while just behind his head, like a special effect in a movie, the crosses at the top of of St. Patrick's Cathedral loomed against the clouds. This was such an awe-inspiring sight that once when a young advertising executive was ushered past the mirrored two-ton doors into Halston's immense throne room for the first time, the woman was struck mute. "She fell apart," remembered Lichtenstein. "She stammered and left." Later, Lichtenstein asked her what had happened, and she said that the sight of Halston was so frightening she couldn't speak.

Halston decided that there was to be no sign on the front doors. He didn't think it was necessary. "People aren't going to wander in off the street," he reasoned.

When Mahoney saw the salon finished for the first time he told Lichtenstein, "Mike, you've got the most expensive loft in New York."

The official opening party was held in mid-February 1978, with the international fashion press in attendance, as well as Warhol, Bianca, Victor, Elizabeth Taylor, and Steve Rubell. The showroom received spectacular reviews, as did Halston's newest collection, perhaps one of his best in years. Toward the end of the show Liza Minnelli came striding down the long runway in a slinky black Halston dress singing "New York, New York" and the room went wild. In the middle of the runway in her seat of honor next to Warhol, Minnelli handed Liz Taylor, "who was clapping madly for her sister—movie star turned model," as the *Times* described it, a red rose and it brought down the house.

"This new home elevates my position in the fashion business, literally and figuratively," Halston told the assembled press after the show. "But it does more than that. I think it elevates all American fashion. A lot of people put me down for waving the flag, but gee I love our country."

It was when Halston first moved to the Olympic Tower that the changes in his behavior and schedule seemed to become more apparent. Up until the advent of Studio 54, Halston faithfully adhered to the same schedule he had kept since he first started working. He was in the office around eight and stayed until six or seven. "Now he would get in around ten or eleven," said Lichtenstein, "and finally not until noon."

Said Bill Dugan, "At this point the workroom had been there half a day waiting for work."

"He would work longer into the night," said Lichtenstein, "but this was a strain on the staff who had to stay later with him. This especially caused problems with the sewing staff because Halston wouldn't get started with the fittings until six-thirty in the evening."

" 'H' would stay out until two or three in the morning and come in hung over on cocaine," said Peruchio Valls. "And he wouldn't take orders from anyone. He was Halston, the emperor of the fashion world, and nobody gave him orders."

Whereas before Halston was just acting grandly and being demanding, now he was becoming an unpredictable terror. "His behavior got worse over the years," said Paul Wilmot, who was executive vice president of marketing for Halston's fragrance. "If you talk to people who are aware of the problems of people who are deep into drug addiction, Halston's behavior was *textbook*. He had no sense of priorities. It was as bad to him to have a window in a store that wasn't right as it was to have a whole line fail."

Employees walked around on eggs as the J.E. temper flared, magnified by the effects of cocaine. "Idiot!" he would scream. "You untalented fool!" "Get out of here!" "Get out of my sight!" And everyone would go scurrying for cover. Halston also became suspicious at this time that his office phone might be bugged, or that there might even be microphones hidden in vases. Who, specifically, he thought might be doing this to him was unclear, but there was some business foe he suspected, so he hired a specialist in industrial espionage and had the entire office swept for bugs. When the report turned out to be negative and there were no bugs, somehow his belief was confirmed that they had been there in the first place. "See," he said, "they found about about the sweep and they took them out."

By late 1978 speculation that Halston was using cocaine was so widespread that David Mahoney had been told about it. "Obviously," said Mahoney, "if you hung out at 54 at the time, it had to be so, and it was also at a time in the seventies where he wasn't alone in it . . ." But, added Mahoney, "I never saw it. I can't see where it was true that he was on drugs. Maybe I didn't want to believe it."

In any event, when Mahoney had a private conversation with Halston about the drug rumors, Halston didn't even seem upset. He denied taking drugs, he told Mahoney not to worry, and Mahoney, wanting to believe him—and being helpless to do anything about it anyway—let the subject drop. But the rumors persisted. Eventually a reporter from *Women's Wear* even asked him about it, and he felt obliged to respond on the record. "I put on dark glasses and everyone thinks I'm the number-one cokehead of the city," he said. "Everyone gossips about everyone else. You can't take drugs and work, to keep up my pace. Everything it gives you it takes up." Halston said he got his energy from vitamins.

Joe Eula remembered differently. "We used drugs and a lot of it. Of course you had to deny it," he said, "Anybody who said 'yes' blatantly had to be a goddamned fool." Did it hurt Halston's business? "Of course it hurt his business. On the other hand, I think it did his business a lot of good because it was the time of the drug parade."

"He began to think like a rock star," said John Fairchild, "and when anybody starts believing their own publicity, they're in deep trouble."

"He began to believe his own press," said Peruchio Valls.

"He began to believe his own press," said Chris Royer.

"He began to believe his own fucking press," said Joe Eula. "It was sitting on that fucking Catholic cross that brought him down. He was too removed from the real world. There wasn't even any air up there in the Olympic Tower. The windows were sealed, and I had a dream of chiseling a hole in one of the windows and sucking the fresh air in out of New Jersey."

It was only six weeks after Halston's move to the Olympic Tower that he had a penultimate falling out with Elsa Peretti. Relations between Peretti and Halston continued to be strained, with Victor carrying tales between them and fanning the flames of their jealousies. Joe Eula remembered that one snowy winter's night in 1978, "The three of us were having dinner and Elsa was having problems. Elsa was truly in love with Halston and Elsa was starting to feel her oats, because she had become a big star in her own right. Halston was criticizing her stuff and saying she wasn't working and they were both having problems with Victor. So we were invited to dinner one night to see if we could calm ourselves all down because he and Elsa were really openly dueling. It was a very simple dinner of caviar, baked potato, and cocaine. It was always the same— caviar with watercress, champagne, and coke." With that menu it didn't take long for dinner to dissolve into a screaming fight. "After the first dozen Tiffany glasses had been broken with Elsa yelling, 'You don't love me and I love you and you have no sensitivity and you're all for yourself. I hate you, you can't think of anyone but yourself, all you think of is the material things in the world,' " said Eula. "Elsa yelled, 'I'll show you what I think of all your material things!' " Before Halston or Eula could move, Peretti dashed across the room and snatched the sable coat that Halston had given her for Christmas from one of the Futons and threw it into the roaring fireplace.

"It must have been a very dry old fucking sable because before I could get to it it was nothing but flames," said Eula.

As the fur went up in a blaze Halston staggered to the landing, "absolutely catatonic, shocked," said Eula, who started laughing hysterically. "I thought it was the funniest thing," he said.

Peretti now demanded that Eula take her home immediately, and in her confusion she began to look around for her coat, which was on fire. "I threw my own coat on her," said Eula, "and I took her scarf and wrapped it around me and we went out in the snow. We went to her place and drank two bottles of champagne and continued to get drunk and stoned until the next day we laughed at the whole thing."

Three months later, on April 14, 1978, Halston and Peretti ran into each other again in the basement at Studio 54. As recounted in detail in Bob Colacello's book on Warhol, *Holy Terror,* Peretti reportedly misunderstood when Rubell called her "Honeypie" and took offense and began snarling and cursing at him. When Halston tried to calm her down, Peretti screamed at him, "I am not going to be thrown out of a basement by a faggot queen like you! You're nothing but no-culture cheap faggot dressmaker."

Bob Colacello reported that Halston replied, "And you're nothing but a low-class cheap jewelry designer for Tiffany."

Peretti then began to chant "Faggot, faggot, faggot" at Halston as she poured a bottle of vodka over his $600 shoes, smashed the empty bottle on the floor, and then smashed herself on top of the shards as she wept, "I've done it! I'm finished with them! I'm finally free!" She fell asleep exhausted in a corner until Colacello woke her later and took her home at 5

A.M. It was, for all practical purposes, the end of their friendship.

Not long after that ugly incident, Joe Eula and "H" parted
company for good as well. According to Eula, as Halston got
more on his "high horse," the tension in the office between
them grew onerous and the two of them were constantly bicker-
ing. "It was like an Italian couple," said Chris Royer. "There
were always fights between Joe and Halston." One great matter
of contention between them was that Halston had of late
become very disapproving of Eula's other business endeavors.
Eula had recently involved himself on a consulting basis for a
new modeling agency called Xtazy. Reportedly, Eula received a
$50,000 fee for his work, in cash, all in twenty-dollar bills,
delivered to him in a shopping bag. Now Xtazy was suing Eula
for $6.1 million for breach of promise, and because Eula's
name was synonymous with his work for Halston, Halston felt
tainted by association. Even more alarmingly, Eula had lately
become acquainted with a man named Alan Finkelstein, who
was then the owner of Insport, a Madison Avenue sports clothing shop. Finkelstein reportedly had unlimited amounts of cash
at his disposal, and he had come up with $1 million in cash to
back a $1.9 million Broadway "disco" musical called *Got Tu Go
Disco*, which was to star the real doorman of Studio 54, Mark
Benecke. Eula was named the director, set designer, and costume designer of the show, which made Halston very unhappy.

Still, things held together until April 24, 1978. That night,
after a forty-sixth birthday party for Halston at Eula's house
which was attended by William Paley of CBS, Barbara Allen,
Andy Warhol, Steve Rubell, and Alan Finkelstein, among others, Finkelstein was arrested in an East Side apartment by federal agents. Within fifteen minutes, fifteen other people across
the country were arrested by the Organized Crime Strike Force
who accused Finkelstein and others of being part of a multimillion-dollar marijuana ring that may have earned upwards of
$200 million. Halston went through the roof.

Eula refuses to discuss the actual moment when he and Halston parted, but during a tumultuous confrontation, the J.E. temper—augmented by generous amounts of cocaine—was unleashed on Eula. Halston and Eula said such nasty things to each other that Halston felt he could never forgive him. Not the least of the barbs was "You're starting to believe your own fucking press." Eula was summarily banished, and in the long run, it was Halston's great loss. Eula was perhaps the last clear and unintimidated voice in Halston's entourage. The absence of his verve, his creative spirit, and his iconoclasm would leave the Olympic Tower barren. Eula always regretted that Halston never relented. One night a year or so after their big fight, Eula saw Halston across the crowded dance floor of Studio 54, but Halston wouldn't even look in his direction. Eula asked Ron Ferri to intercede between them and go over and ask Halston to let bygones be bygones and bury the hatchet. But Halston told Ron Ferri no, he was not interested in knowing Joe Eula again.

TROUBLE IN PARADISE

I t wasn't only drugs that affected Halston's personality. The huge amount of stress exerted on him by his business responsibilities got to him long before the use of cocaine did. "Rather than to say to us, 'The amount of work has gotten out of hand,' " said Lichtenstein, "Halston would often react in a way that was sometimes not appropriate." This inappropriate behavior manifested itself in screaming tantrums, vicious insults to employees, and occasional random firings. Often just the slightest thing would set him off, or else he could suddenly turn icy cold or cruelly cutting. Don Friese remembered that the first time Halston yelled at him on the phone, Friese yelled right back. But many people were too intimidated to challenge Halston. "He was a bully," said Friese, "a talented, brilliant, bully, and if he thought he could push you around, he would."

There were several representatives from his licensees that he refused to deal with because they had slighted him in some way. Occasionally these were real offenses, but frequently he just didn't like the way somebody dressed or spoke. Once, when Halston had a meeting with a woman from an advertising agency whose haircut he disdained, he refused to address her directly and spoke to her only through Mike Lichtenstein. She never turned up again. On another occasion, the Hartmann luggage people ran a print ad for his Halston Ultrasuede luggage using models dressed in another designer's clothes. Halston was justifiably upset; his punishment was to forever ban the Hartmann organization and all their representatives from his offices. Thenceforth, he decreed, they could only deal with Halston Enterprises through Mike Lichtenstein.

Sometimes Halston's capriciousness would cause real mayhem in the companies he dealt with. Such was the experience of Richard Cole, the former president of the women's division of Manhattan Industries group, a $100-million-a-year shirt and blouse company. Cole's experience with Halston—which started long before the Studio 54 era—could serve as a paradigm of the problems licensees would endure with the designer. Cole had licensed two potentially very profitable lines: Halston V, a "better" blouse line, and Halston VI, a two-piece dress line. A suite of offices and furniture was rented at 1411 Broadway and an extensive staff of showroom, marketing, advertising, sales, and road people was hired to man the company.

The first time Cole met Halston, "there was genuine enthusiasm on Halston's part," said Cole. They discussed the scope of the line, and Cole presented Halston with a "line plan" of how many fabrics they would use, how many short-sleeved blouses they needed, how many sleeveless, and what their time schedules would be since they were manufacturing in Japan and working eight months ahead of the shipping date. Lo and behold, Halston not only delivered the samples for the first collection on time, they were "perfect," according to Cole. The line, which arrived at the stores on schedule, was a "smash," said Cole. "We sold out to the piece."

But the second line never materialized. "Halston was on to his next game," said Cole. "He had signed a shoe license or something—whatever the next license was, that's what he was focusing on. We were left out there fluttering." After a month of Halston's dodging him by phone, Cole demanded a face-to-face meeting, but over the next few weeks, half a dozen appointments were broken or postponed. When Cole finally got to see Halston—who was still on East Sixty-eighth Street at this point—it was after five-thirty and Cole claimed the salon reeked of marijuana smoke. "It was a snake pit up there on Madison Avenue," said Cole. On this second visit to the salon, Cole was greeted by a much cooler Halston. "I no longer had his enthusiasm. Now I was looking at a pair of sunglasses that reflected my own face back to me." Halston told Cole that when he was good and ready he would eventually make up his mind as to what designs he would supply for Manhattan Industries in the future. As for the line that was due imminently, he suggested that Cole "adapt" a collection from Halston blouses he already had. But it was already too late. "First season a smash," said Cole. "Second season I was out of business."

Yet Cole still held out hope for the next, and potentially biggest, season—fall. This time Cole was ready. He hired a woman designer who had been a successful blouse designer at another company and asked her to prepare a line for Halston's approval or tinkering. One afternoon the designer presented the line to Halston at his salon. She hadn't been out of his office ten seconds when Cole received an irate phone call from him. "Don't you ever send me another 'diesel dyke' designer," Halston told him. Cole had never heard the derogatory phrase for a masculine lesbian before, and when he found out what it meant he was even more mystified because the woman who had met with Halston was heterosexual and married with two children.

Finally, a fall blouse line was put together for Halston's approval, and all that was left was for him to choose the colors and fabrics. Cole and his staff had put great effort and marketing research into this aspect of the collection because blouses are an accessory item that have to coordinate with whatever the season's trendy colors might be. Cole brought a palette of colors for Halston to choose from in that season's popular "dusky" shades. Halston sniffed and said, "I don't believe in dusky colors. I only believe in primary colors. I don't care if that's what they're showing for fall, I don't believe in those colors. I won't do a line in those colors."

Said Cole, "This egomaniac is sitting up there with those glasses that you can't see through, that you want to throw a rock through, and all you can think of is I want to kill this human being—and I guess I really tried to kill him. I threw a chair at him. Unfortunately I missed him. But he was scared to death. After I threw the chair at him there was really nothing left to do but to leave."

Later that day Cole got a phone call from Lawrence Leeds, the CEO of Manhattan Industries, who said that Halston had called him to say that he felt very sorry for Cole who was obviously overworked and tired, and suggested that Cole hire a "merchandiser" or a special "president" for the division. Thus Crawford Mills was hired.

Mills was an ex-Navy man from Sioux Falls, South Dakota, and he and Halston hit it off well from the start. Mills was a strapping guy with a red face who seemed to be able to coax work out of Halston. "We were always two guys from the Midwest who just got along," said Mills. "Within five minutes we were no longer talking about me, we were talking about the line and getting it out and the problems and so forth." Mills and Halston decided that the only way to catch up was for Halston to design two seasons at one time, doubling an already enormous workload. Eula worked on prints. "Things finally began to smooth out," said Mills. "We turned two divisions around, we were shipping on time, and we were making a better-quality product. Once Halston got working he would work very fast," said Crawford. "If he wanted to, he could design two seasons at once to catch up." Yet whatever charm Crawford Mills had with Halston eventually wore off. Halston would get bored and ornery and, eventually, the licensees would give up and let their contracts lapse. "In those days," said Mills, "he would lose four or five licenses a year. The companies would give it a try for a couple of years and then move on." Finally, Halston V and Halston VI languished due to Halston's own disinterest, and they were eventually folded.

Now an even more unlikely solution to the problem of Halston was proposed. "In 1979," said Mike Lichtenstein, "a decision was made that since [the licensing wasn't working out] we would increase the ready-to-wear business by going into designer sportswear, which is what Calvin Klein and Anne Klein were doing."

This was, of course, a complete turnaround from their original strategy of *not* opening their own cost-intensive business, but the licensing was falling apart, and Norton Simon could afford the gamble. So, with very little choice left, most of the licenses were allowed to lapse or were bought out at great expense and a new division was opened called Halston Sportswear—which would do exactly the same thing as the licensing, except in-house. Crawford Mills was hired as president of the new division, and as was their wont, Norton Simon poured a huge amount of money into opening it. Tours were made of thirty-five different manufacturing plants in Hong Kong where part of the line would be produced, including silks, leathers, and knitwear. One million dollars was poured into fabrics and piece goods, and offices were opened at 530 Seventh Ave. "We had to protect his image," said Mills. "We couldn't start off with something that wasn't right for Halston."

It quickly turned out that Halston didn't much like designing sportswear—or, for that matter, any other kind of line in which constant change in style and look is necessary. In fact, the great irony of Halston's designing sportswear was that his trademark was the certain sense of redundancy in style—not a good attribute for a high-turnover, seasonal line. "We recognized the problem of delegation might be severe here," said Lichtenstein. "You have to design a lot more pieces for a collection of sportswear, and you need a staff. The fact that there were 'no little designers' finally came to a head when they entered into sportswear."

Halston agreed to have a small design team to help back him up and edit. Several young designers tried the job. One lasted only a few days before he began to feel ill and then quit; he eventually died of cancer. Another became famous in the Halston lore when Halston threw the hapless young designer's samples on the floor and jumped up and down on them. The designer disappeared during lunch. "I can't come back," he told Lichtenstein. "I just can't do it."

"I think the strain was too much for Halston," said Lichtenstein. "This wasn't like a life-insurance company. This was dramatic, and every day there was a new drama there."

"The first full year in business was 1980, and we did five million in sales," said Mills, but the start-up expense was so great that they didn't make any money. "The second year we wanted to improve by fifty percent, but we only went to six million, and Halston made the decision just to wind it down."

"Halston made the decision to close the sportswear division by walking out," said Lichtenstein. One day in late November of 1980, just before Thanksgiving, Halston had a tantrum about something that had happened in the office—no one can remember what it was specifically. He picked up the sterling silver Elsa Peretti Tiffany candlesticks that sat on his red lacquered table, put them under his arm, and marched out the door—vowing never to return.

"He expected somebody to come get him," said Don Friese, "or somebody to call him. But nobody did."

Halston grew especially peeved that he did not hear from David Mahoney, whom he expected at least to call and ask what was wrong. When it became clear that Mahoney wasn't going to call him, Halston started to call Mahoney. "Mahoney was at his house in Bridgehampton," said Paul Wilmot, "and Halston called him Wednesday, Thursday, Friday, and Saturday. Finally, on Sunday, Mahoney took his call."

"Halston was more than petulant," Mahoney said of the phone call. "He was a prima donna at the time. Everybody was saying they'd hold my coat while I knocked this guy down. If anybody else walked out, I'd tell them to stay there. But this guy wasn't a businessman. We were dealing with a creative genius who we had built up into this. So I told him, 'You can't go off petulantly like that, Halston. It's not good for the company and it's not good for you.'"

According to Mahoney, Halston said, "You're right," and he was back at work the next day. Nevertheless, Halston Sportswear was folded after only a year in business, Crawford Mills left the company, and thousands and thousands of unshipped garments had to be sold off at a loss.

STILL THE SPENDING was profligate, and in the summer of 1980 the grandest—and most exhausting—expedition of Halston's career was staged when Halston became the first American designer to visit the People's Republic of China. Not only had the communist Chinese never seen a three-ring circus like the Halston entourage, neither had the fashion world. Under Halston's Barnumesque direction, the trip ballooned into a round-the-world, three-week, three-continent tour of rock star proportions that cost Norton Simon Industries an estimated $600,000.

It began as a relatively simple idea one day when some representatives of the Chinese silk industry came to Halston's showroom in New York to see his famous silk dresses. When Halston complimented the Chinese by saying, "The Chinese produce the greatest silks in the world," a rare invitation was extended to him from China's silk industry to visit various silk-producing centers in China. It was what Halston described as "a friendly hands-across-the-ocean exchange." Around that time Halston had also been toying with the idea of going to Japan on a promotion tour for his Japanese licensees, Kosugi Sangyo Co. Ltd., and suddenly the idea for *le grand tour* was born. Halston decided to add a stop in Los Angeles for a blast through Beverly Hills, then on to Japan for a fashion show and some business promotion, next to China where they would visit the silk factories and see the Great Wall, and then to Paris where they would cap it all with a five-day social whirlwind. "I want to have it like a little movie," Halston explained. "It makes it *amusing,* and removes the whole curse of it being just a 'business thing.' If we directed our whole planet the way we would a play or a movie, it would make life more interesting for everyone."

Halston populated his movie with a cast of thirty-two. The players included Liza Minnelli and Mark Gero; Victor Hugo; Bianca Jagger, whom Halston identified as the "official stager and choreographer"; the photographer Hiro; nine assistants and seamstresses, including Peruchio Valls; the Halstonettes, which included twelve models; "the kids," which included assistant Bill Dugan, D. D. Ryan, his secretary Faye Robson; executives Michael Lichtenstein and Michael Pellegrino; 130 pieces of matching brown Ultrasuede luggage; and an NBC news crew which filmed their every move for a documentary about Halston that was never aired. It took nine limousines just to get Halston's troupe to the airport, and a separate truck for the luggage. When asked why he needed to travel with such an extensive entourage, he told a reporter, "A visual statement would be more effective than my going and talking, saying I like different shades of red."

Every little detail was planned months ahead—a nonstop schedule of fashion shows, promotional lunches, and public appearances that was choreographed with the "madcap precision of a Busby Berkeley musical," said *Women's Wear.* This included coordinating over five hundred outfits for the Halstonettes, which took up five bulletin boards at the Olympic Tower. Halston kept all the details in a black loose-leaf book which he bragged would by the end of the trip be "this thick." "Work clothes, dinner clothes, party clothes," said Halston tapping his book. One day everyone would wear red-and-black cashmere and shiny mirrored sunglasses, the next, the entire entourage would be in different shades of ivory. For each event, say a day trip to the Great Wall of China, or dinner at Maxim's, the entourage would have matching outfits.

The group left Kennedy Airport for Los Angeles at 9 A.M. on the morning of September 4, minus Bianca Jagger who turned up several days later in Tokyo. In L.A., Halston staged a charity fashion show at Bullock's Department Store in honor of the Costume Council of the Los Angeles Art Museum. The following morning they took off on the long flight to Tokyo, where they arrived on September 7. Halston discovered that the Japanese were a more difficult audience to impress than he had expected. Japanese designers were already a growing fashion influence in 1980 and they had already seen all the grand couturiers from Paris. Even Halston's spectacular fashion show, held at the Imperial Hotel ballroom, which was outfitted with a giant mirrored runway reminiscent of the Olympic Tower, with all the Halstonettes in their sequined gowns, "failed to create media dazzle," reported *Women's Wear*. Later, at a press conference, a Japanese journalist asked Halston, "Don't some of your clothes look a lot like Oscar de la Renta's?" Even that question didn't seem as embarrassing as what happened later: At a charity auction for the Red Cross, an autographed copy of *Deep Throat* porn star Linda Lovelace's autobiography was quickly sold, but nobody bid at all on a $3,000 Halston dress. Halston finally had to buy it himself for $1,000 to save face. "Frankly we were had," Halston said. Aside from Pat Cleveland's throwing a magazine at Victor Hugo at lunch one day, the Japanese leg of the trip was uneventful. In fact, the most fun they had in Japan was dinner at one of the better geisha houses at which Victor Hugo made Bianca Jagger up as a geisha girl.

There was also a rumor among the traveling cortege that one of the more unpredictable members of the group was going to try to attempt to smuggle cocaine into China anally. "I knew that it was very likely that somebody along the line was carrying something that they shouldn't, and I told this to Halston," said Lichtenstein. "This was Red China, and they would go to jail and we'd have to wave good-bye. I had been at the Beijing airport a few months before and knew how tough customs were."

The day before the group left Japan for China, Lichtenstein called a meeting of the entire touring party and laid down the law. He said, "Look, I'm not asking you, but I'm telling you, if any of you plan to bring any illegal substance into China, there's a body search of each person as they go in. They take you into a little room and search you, and if they catch you with anything it's going to be good-bye, Charley." Some of the Halstonettes resented Lichtenstein's advice, however, and a wicked suggestion spread among the group that they should hide their drugs in Lichtenstein's luggage.

Luggage was another concern of Lichtenstein's. "There was absolutely no service at the Beijing airport," said Lichtenstein, "and I told my Chinese counterparts that we would need some assistance with our luggage, that we had a great deal of it, and they said, 'Yes, yes, we understand.' But when we arrived at the Beijing airport with one hundred and thirty pieces of luggage, out came one assistant with one supermarket cart."

The group also discovered that there were no limousines and no private cars in Red China—only government buses to take them to and from destinations. The group did not stay in a hotel, either, but in "State Guest Houses," which the Halstonettes called "prisons" because no one was allowed in or out without passes. When the models did leave their rooms the doors had to be left open and guards stood in the hallway to make sure no one went in or out. "This is China!" Halston admonished his balky troupe. "And this isn't a hotel. This is a guest house. This is a guest house."

On day twelve of the journey there was a sort of fashion summit in Peking at a banquet given by Chinatex, China's state-owned fabric industry. The tables were furnished with Mao Tai, a potent and legendary Chinese wine, and Halston took to toasting every course in the dinner, knocking back at least a dozen shots of the 110-proof wine. "Even we don't usually drink this much," said the host, Wang Wing Jung, to Halston.

In Shanghai the group arrived in green Mao Red Army tunics with green hats and red Halston sweaters. In this industrial city they gave a fashion show for 1,400 Chinese in the textile business—all dressed in virtually the same state-approved costume. ("One could suffer a severe identity crisis," D. D. Ryan said of the trip.) On stage there were many outfits made from Chinese silk, and although there were some reserved murmurs from the crowd, for the most part the clothing shocked the audience, particularly because of the necklines. "This is not necessary," said one of the Chinese, "That is not nice, not subtle." But when two of the girls came out in see-through black-net outfits the "silence was almost painful." One of the Chinese whispered, "Never for China." When it was announced that one of Halston's dresses could easily cost the Chinese equivalent of $10,000, the crowd was even more appalled. "Why, that could feed an entire village," an outraged man said.

Although Victor Hugo and photographer Hiro sat in the audience and applauded wildly, the Chinese hardly made a sound. In fact, when it was over the Halstonettes wildly cheered Halston backstage, while the entire audience sat in silence until a voice over a loudspeaker told them they could leave. Directly afterward, however, at a question-and-answer press conference, a fascinating thing occurred. Chris Royer wore one of the silk jackets from the show into the audience, and the crowd virtually stripped the jacket from her body to see how it was made. Halston quickly sent someone for more and more clothing and each time a model walked out into the audience whatever she was wearing was virtually torn from her shoulders, the Chinese were so fascinated by Halston's construction. This pleased Halston a great deal and warmed him to the moment. He sat and watched and smoked cigarettes for a half hour as the

Chinese picked apart his garments, telling them through an interpreter, "We are all laborers here. We are all workers."

The Halstonettes didn't look exactly like a busload of laborers when they went to see the Great Wall of China the next day wearing coordinated taffeta "Great Wall" windbreakers. They were transported there in a bus provided by the tourist board that had a loudspeaker on the top. One of the crew got on the microphone, and they all sang "Diamonds Are a Girl's Best Friend" at the Great Wall; anyone who heard it must have been mystified. Bianca scribbled graffiti on the wall with her lipstick. NBC TV was there, as were reporters from the Associated Press and United Press International. When they pressed Halston to comment on his feelings at the moment he said with a smile, "I think it's a great wall."

The Chinese leg of the journey ended with an American-style banquet that Halston threw for his hosts, "with American music and apple pie and roast pig because we just couldn't get turkey," obtained by the American embassy. All the Halstonettes dressed in red, white, and blue ("Not flaggy—chic," was Halston's description) and wore "I Love New York" buttons. Halston's final speech startled his guests when he announced that his hosts were "just like Americans. Wang Wing Jung was the first one to order a scotch-and-soda and the first one to the buffet." The Chinese were embarrassed.

Now that Halston had conquered China, Paris lay ahead. Although he had been to Paris dozens of times over the years since his triumph in Versailles, he had not been there in such a high-profile and visible professional capacity. There were lunches and dinner parties and promotional events galore for him to conquer. "I'm not afraid of Paris," Halston said. "Paris is afraid of me."

Hardly. Over the years Halston's attitude toward his Parisian colleagues had become rather snippy. When asked about Yves Saint Laurent's talent, Halston once said, "Yves designs nice raincoats." For his part, Saint Laurent said Halston "isn't a designer." Over the years there had been various other put-downs of European fashion, and the French were also a little jealous of the international success of his scent. In fact, one of the perfume's weakest markets for its size was France, and the plan was to make the most of the visit with a series of closely scheduled promotional lunches and parties.

The platoon arrived on September 21, and at Halston's first big blast, a black-tie dinner at Maxim's for 200 people thrown for him by disco queen Régine, many of the guests didn't turn up. With the French nobility and jet-set fashion crowd pointedly absent, Halston and his crew nonetheless partied until 4:30 A.M. when they went on to Régine's until the sun came up. The next night, a huge "Black Party" was held at Régine's in Halston's honor for nearly 500 people. "In Paris they like you to have a theme," Halston said, and wore a black dinner jacket, a black tie, black shirt, and black carnation to the party where he sat fanning himself with a black fan. Alas, the other big-name guests did not show: Hubert de Givenchy declined his invitation, and Yves Saint Laurent was "too busy working" to attend. Karl Lagerfeld sent flowers with his regrets, and by the time the Black Ball was over, Halston had been slapped roundly in the face by the French. The embarrassment was not soothed any when it was reported that a firm called Energy International, allegedly jointly owned by Régine and the Baron Alexis de Rede, had been paid $100,000 to organize and publicize the Paris trip for Halston and his entourage.

Yet the greatest embarrassment came the final night of the trip. The Baron de Rede had planned an elite dinner party to be held for fifty people at the Hôtel Lambert, a magnificent seventeenth-century mansion on the Ile Saint-Louis where the Baron and Baroness Guy de Rothschild lived. Dinner guests included Oscar de la Renta, Christina Onassis, and the Duke and Duchess of Bedford. It seemed that this party might come off successfully until that afternoon, when Victor Hugo said he had met some friends in Paris and asked the Baron de Rede to add table settings for four more guests. An hour later Mike Lichtenstein was having lunch at Maxim's when he was called to the phone and told that the Baron de Rede would not have Victor Hugo to the dinner that night. As for why Victor was suddenly disinvited, "I have no idea," said Lichtenstein. "For someone not to want Victor Hugo at something didn't really require an explanation." Lichtenstein was stuck with having to be the person to tell Halston, and he did so in a private moment with him on the way back to the Plaza Athénée. "I'm sure dinner tonight will be a wonderful event," Lichtenstein said, "and by the way, it will be rather crowded and they won't be able to accommodate Victor Hugo."

Halston stormed off without saying a word. Lichtenstein went to a museum or two before returning to the hotel, where he found everyone in a state of chaos. The models were in their rooms weeping, everyone was on Valium, and Halston was absolutely refusing to go to the party, no matter what happened. There were hundreds of unanswered phone calls waiting for Lichtenstein from hysterical participants as well as the press who wanted to know what was going on. "There was a point where God himself couldn't make Halston do something," said Lichtenstein. "Whether it was his feelings about Victor or not, I really don't know. I tried to contact him, I called him in his suite and he was there with his secretary and she said, 'He will not speak to you. He will not speak to anyone.' "

The dinner party was thrown into turmoil. Not only didn't Halston show up, but neither did Marie Hélène de Rothschild, Paloma Picasso, André Oliver, São Schlumberger, and many others. Instead, Halston took his entire "corps de ballet" out to a surprise birthday dinner for Chris Royer at Club Sept. Later they went to the huge, gay Palace discotheque where they danced until dawn. At the Palace, Chris Royer hiked her beaded sheath up so she could dance better and tied it around her waist with an Elsa Peretti silver chain and "the boys of the Palace just went crazy," said Halston, who incorporated the look into one of his next collections.

Publicly, the excuse given for Halston's not showing up at the party was that he had food poisoning, and indeed, some members of the entourage remember that toward the end of the trip Halston actually didn't feel very well physically and was just as happy to cancel the dinner. Chris Royer remembered specifically that Halston had a cyst on his back. Whatever it was, the strenuous trip had contributed to the poor health of several members of the entourage who arrived back in New York with bad cases of the flu and colds, including Halston.

Halston's health never seemed to improve after the trip to Paris. By March of 1981 his condition worsened when he developed a large, infected cyst on his right leg where he had been repeatedly injected—or perhaps had injected himself. Halston told Warhol that he and Martha Graham both "shot up B_{12}" and that "a syringe he'd been sent was contaminated with lead." Halston also told Warhol that he went to the doctor, who said he should go to the hospital, but Halston went home instead. Halston stayed at home for several days, during which time the infection spread and his other leg began hurting.

"It was Mohammed who realized there was something wrong," said Chris Royer. "Mohammed called up a real doctor and he described his symptoms and his fever and they rushed Halston to the emergency ward and the cyst was ready to explode and he could have gotten blood poisoning."

"The next thing I knew he was in the hospital," said Lichtenstein. "Apparently he had developed a cyst from an injection and he didn't treat it properly. Mohammed probably saved his life by calling a doctor. He was seriously ill, and I realized later what a close call it was."

Halston was in in New York Hospital for approximately ten days. Although he said he did not want visitors, he was seen nevertheless by Martin Snaric and a very concerned David Mahoney. "It came from needles," said Mahoney, "but he convinced me that it had nothing to do with drugs. It was vitamin shots. I said, 'Were they drug shots?' and he said, 'No, they were vitamin and balance shots.' " Mahoney even asked to speak with Halston's doctors. "They were highly critical of whatever it was he was doing and the medical treatment he was receiving," said Mahoney. But whether or not he continued to use injectables was anybody's guess.

"STRATEGY SHIFT:
FROM CLASS TO MASS"
Daily News Record **headline**

Halston Enterprises moved into the eighties alarmingly off kilter. Fashion, they say, has cycles and tiers, and by this time the whole concept of *haute couture* seemed stuffy and old-fashioned. Many of the women who had been Halston's best customers in the sixties and early seventies were now turning elderly, and his made-to-order business was dying away. The new crop of younger well-dressed women were now shopping at the salons of younger, more contemporary designers, like Calvin Klein and Giorgio Armani; even Bianca Jagger had joined Calvin Klein's group of friends and was seeing less of Halston. Ali MacGraw, who had once called Halston "great," now said Calvin was "the best," and now Calvin Klein's face graced the covers of national magazines. A cruel blow fell when Halston offered to give a gala dinner party for the reopening of Studio 54 in September 1981, and Rubell told Halston he preferred Calvin to throw the party for him. *Women's Wear* even reported that Halston had "problems at the box office," and indeed, the Seventh Avenue ready-to-wear business grosses reportedly dropped below $5 million for the first time. Halston Enterprises was a glittering elephant, "front loaded" with expensive showrooms, limousines, superfluous employees and servants, orchids, and publicity events—so much image-making machinery that it ate up what little profits there were. Although the company's estimated volume was over $90 million a year, $75 million of it was from the worldwide sale of basically one product line—Halston's fragrances. In fact, the popularity of the fragrances were helping keep Max Factor afloat, accounting for one-third of Factor's pretax profits.

Even in the fragrance division there were problems, however. A new, $100-an-ounce prestige fragrance dubbed "Halston Night" was introduced into the market at great expense and subsequently died on the vine. The cosmetics line was only a short-lived success, and around that time a dangerous and corrosive problem called "diversion" began to threaten Halston's original best-selling scent. Diversion occurs when huge amounts of perfume are shipped out of the country at greatly discounted rates and then either legally or otherwise are shipped back into the United States where they appear at drug and discount chains at prices far below those charged at better department stores. The problem seemed especially prevalent with Halston because Max Factor did such a large overseas business and great quantities of his fragrance normally left the country. Better department stores got very upset if one of their expensive brands turned up at a cheaper price in a drug-store chain, and one store, Balliet's, phased the line out completely because of diversion. There was a growing danger that the fragrance would soon lose its cachet and cross over to mass market.

Yet it wasn't only Halston's perfume that was losing its luster. There came a moment in time when the endless licensing had cheapened his name. "When something becomes so popular and so universal," said one Norton Simon executive, "by its own definition it loses its specialness. The fashion world is a fickle one. There were those who felt Halston had lost his edge as a designer."

One of them was John Fairchild. After nearly twenty years of superlative reviews from *Women's Wear Daily,* Halston was getting scathingly bad write-ups. Now Halston's clothing ran under the headline "The Worst of the Best." According to Fairchild, "Halston started to get repetitious. He started to get grander and grander in his concept of fashion. This business is like Russian Roulette. One season you sell, one season you don't. But Halston had season after season after season where he had no impact and it didn't sell. People didn't want it anymore." Perhaps the most dreadful headline of all appeared on the front page of *Women's Wear* after Halston's fall collection showed in April of 1981: "At Halston's It's Déjà Vu" The review pointedly complained that at a Halston show, "there are always the interchangeable front-row, front-page faces, often peering over big black, dark glasses and the perennially cool *cabine* of the models, all of whom are reflected and reflected and reflected in the endless hall of mirrors that is Halston's showroom. No surprise then that on Wednesday morning—with the Cassandra-like Martha Graham, Amazonian Carol Channing and free-again Steve Rubell holding front-row court—everyone had that rather comforting feeling of 'We have all been here before.' The problem was the clothes seemed to have been there before as well."

"The problem was too many orchids and too few threads," said Joe Eula. "Too many people who didn't know how to say no. Too many people that were yes people."

Robert "Kam" Kammerschen was not a "yes" person. He was an elegant, well-spoken executive who had recently been put in the newly created position of executive vice president of five Norton Simon Industries holdings; Hunt-Wesson Foods, United Can Manufacturing, Max Factor Cosmetics, the McCall Pattern Company, and Halston Enterprises. Originally from Chicago, Kammerschen had been president jointly of Chanel and Christian Dior in the United States, vice president of marketing for cosmetics at Revlon, and most recently, president of Max Factor for several months. Although there were always vice presidents at Norton Simon in charge of Halston's business to whom Lichtenstein reported, so far Halston had reported to no one. But now, Halston was told that from here on in if he needed anything—translated, "if he wanted to countermand one of Lichtenstein's demands"—he was to go to Kammerschen. Naturally Halston hated this idea. "In his mind he sold his business to David Mahoney, not a company named Norton Simon," said Kammerschen, "and Halston was a strong-minded individual and a very complex human being." Kammerschen discovered that the situation at the Olympic Tower was out of control and "we had to step in and make him understand that the company was in dangerous straits."

Coincidentally, this seemed like an excellent time to use some leverage on Halston; his ten-year employment contract with Norton Simon Industries was up for renewal in 1983. His salary had reached its limit, a paltry $500,000 a year, and although that was subsidized by royalties and perks, Halston was hoping to get a large raise. To this effect Kammerschen made a complete business presentation to Halston at the Olympic Tower, a "state of the union presentation," according to Paul Wilmot. "At least, the state of the Halston nation."

"The headline for the whole exercise," said Kammerschen, "was that this ship was out of control and we were on a voyage to oblivion. That wasn't going to serve him well, and certainly it wasn't going to serve Norton Simon well. We had to start operating by the rules and have some focus." Kammerschen also presented a series of tables and figures which showed that "for all practical purposes, the apparel part of the business was going nowhere. I showed Halston the numbers to prove my point was right." Kammerschen also presented a set of figures that hypothesized if Norton Simon Industries had put the same amount of money into Certificates of Deposit instead of funding the enormous showroom, it would have thrown off more income and have been worth more than what they ended up with. While all these alarming facts and figures were basically true, this so-called "State of the Union" presentation was part of a setup, a softening-up of Halston for the next step, because Kammerschen, Mahoney, and Lichtenstein had a solution: give in and go mass market.

Recently, Mike Lichtenstein had been approached by a representative of the huge department store chain of JCPenney (as they like to be spelled), about making a deal with Halston. Penney was an $11 billion company with over 600 stores, most of them in suburban shopping malls. They grossed 15 percent of their business through mail-order catalogs. After undertaking a survey of 7,000 customers, Penney executives discovered that they were losing the lucrative, fashion-oriented buyer, so beginning in the late seventies, they started a $1 billion "modernization" program to upgrade their image. They had also recently commissioned a customer-awareness study which revealed that for the JCPenney customer the name Halston was the leading one in terms of recognition and believability (right up there with Gloria Vanderbilt). Penney's proposition was, in effect, that Halston become Penney's exclusive in-house name designer.

At that moment there was a retail frenzy for name designers. As the designer became available to the mass market through licensing, the average consumer had grown accustomed to buying status merchandise. By 1983 designers were responsible for 60 percent of all the labels on the market, with sports or entertainment names another 25 percent and name brands only 15 percent. Sears Roebuck had had enormous success by tying in a clothing line with model Cheryl Tiegs, and JCPenney wanted Halston.

Mahoney and Kammerschen had no idea how Halston was going to react to the notion that America's greatest *haut couturier* design clothing exclusively for JCPenney, but they sure didn't intend to push the issue. However, they were determined that if Halston did agree to the deal, he would absolutely, positively, have to agree to hire and maintain a design staff of "little designers" to help him with all the work so that the same thing wouldn't happen that had happened with the licensing and sportswear division. "Kam and I decided to sit down and present this to Halston," said Mahoney. "We wanted to make it clear that going mass market had a lot of risks. If Halston said 'No,' no it would be."

Mahoney and Kammerschen had dinner with Halston one night at 101 to discuss the specifics. "We had a very open discussion with Halston about strategy," said Kammerschen. "Halston listened, and then suddenly in the middle of dinner, he started to embrace the concept. In fact, it became something of a love fest with him saying things like 'JCPenney is part of the American fabric, and I'm part of the American fabric.' Midway through dinner Halston seemed to adopt as his own the idea that Penney was the best thing to do." He also, added Kammerschen, "saw the handwriting on the wall."

Mostly, Halston liked the figures. "The essence was that Penney guaranteed a huge amount of money over a five-year period of time," said Kammerschen, "and regardless of the success of the line, Halston Enterprises and Norton Simon Industries would see a lot of money." The licensing agreement represented a staggering projection of $1 billion in retail sales over six years, with a guarantee of an estimated $16 million to Halston Enterprises over the term of the contract. "And that was the *down* side of it," said Kammerschen. "The *up* side, the bigger side was, Halston would share in the money personally, because I negotiated a piece of the action with Halston." Halston's personal salary would be boosted to a guaranteed $1,250,000 a year, with increasing step payments and royalties if the Penney deal was a hit. "He was incentivized," said Kammerschen, "that if this thing clicked, and he was obviously the key to making it click, the compensation was geared to make him happy too."

The scope of the project seemed daunting. It started with a

complete women's sportswear and dress line that would be in the stores for the fall of 1983—just over a year away. Menswear would be added in 1984, followed by home furnishings and children's wear in 1985. The clothing would be sold exclusively in specially constructed Halston boutiques in 550 Penney stores, as well as in their catalogs. But Halston was not afraid of the bigness of it all. In a way, to him, this was an even better dream than just being an *haut couturier*. Now Halston would dress the world.

WHEN THE JCPENNEY deal was announced in September of 1982, it was met with disbelief up and down Seventh Avenue. The thought of Halston designing for the moderately priced retailer was like Maria Callas doing a striptease at a stag party, and the gossip in the trade was that this move spelled Halston's certain doom. As the shock waves reverberated throughout the fashion industry, Halston tried to put a good face on the deal. "You know me," he said. "I'm as American as apple pie. When I was a kid, I always shopped in JCPenney. Remember, I come from Des Moines, Iowa."

How would he keep up with the tremendous volume? He would do it, he said, and he would do it all by himself. "I'm a very prolific designer. I didn't sell myself out like some of the others did. As long as you keep your style and your standards, it can only enhance your name by reaching a broader audience." And would it hurt his higher-priced appeal? "I believe there is room for everyone in the world of retailing," Halston said, "and that Halston Originals and Halston III for JCPenney are in no way competitive and embrace totally different levels of trade."

For one, Bergdorf Goodman didn't see it that way. After helping him start his career and carrying his clothes for over a decade, they dropped his line and his fragrance completely with the announcement of the Penney deal. Ira Neimark, the president and CEO of Bergdorf said, "We decided that designers as well as retailers must decide who their customers are. They made their decision and we made ours." According to Kammerschen, the loss of Bergdorf was "more of a blow to Halston's pride than it was a monetary issue, because Bergdorf's wasn't selling that much." (Bergdorf reportedly sold $500,000 a year in apparel and $100,000 in fragrance, not an infinitesimal amount.)

Nevertheless, Bergdorf's decision to drop Halston was a terrible public slap in the face. "A $2,000 beaded dress is quite different from a $90 wash-and-wear dress," he pouted. "It's so noncompetitive. Penney's does not even have a store in New York City," Halston said. "I wish Ira Neimark well, but I don't understand why he thinks he's in competition with Penney's."

Suddenly, several other retailers were grousing in public about canceling him. Said Lasker Meyer, CEO of Foley's department store, "I think there are very few people in life who can have it both ways. I would think there was a terrible danger to Halston, from his viewpoint, of being perceived as a 'product of Penney's.'" Even Bernadine Morris at the *New York Times* conceded that some of the designer's fans might "supplement their wardrobes from a few pieces from Penney racks."

Others disagreed. Lynn Manulis, president of Martha, Inc., said, "If you're clever you can do many things. We can't live in an ivory tower anymore. The world has changed." Yet eventually sales of Halston clothing lagged so badly at Martha's New York store that they dropped his line.

"There are two ways to look at the Penney's deal," said one executive. "It's either the capping of a brilliant career or an attempt to secure some income before the talents completely wane. The second seems to me closer to the truth."

Privately, Halston was torn between the real pride he felt about clothing millions of Americans and the fact that it looked as if he had sold out. One night soon after the deal was announced, Halston was having dinner with Andy Warhol and was feeling especially insecure. He was going on and on about all the billions JCPenney had, trying to impress Andy. "I don't know what it means," Warhol wrote in his diary, "except he let things slip about 'selling out,' and I guess he *has* actually sold out and will be having his name on cheap stuff." On another occasion, flying out to Montauk with Warhol in a private plane, Halston looked down at all the houses below them and said, "Oh, darling, wouldn't it be grand if your paintings cost a dollar and you could just cover houses all over the world with them, and a big one for over the fireplace would cost $50—but think of all the homes in America that you could just fill up."

Now, more than at any other single moment in his career, Halston had put himself on the line. Every newspaper and magazine, every retailer and department store in the country was waiting to see what would happened to Halston III for JCPenney. As the June 1983 launch date approached, the Olympic Tower became a pressure cooker. Neither the vicissitudes of the myriad licensing agreements nor the in-house sportswear line had prepared Halston and Lichtenstein for the problems they now faced with Penney. "The Penney deal had unforeseen scope to it," said Lichtenstein, "and it put Halston under a great deal of tension."

A "great deal of tension" was a typical Lichtenstein understatement. The imperial Halston dealing with JCPenney turned into a major nightmare. At the start of the venture Halston applied himself with the usual enthusiasm he had for projects at their inception, but he was soon to learn that JCPenney was vast and bureaucratic and decentralized. Halston was forced to interface professionally with literally hundreds of people: senior merchandising managers, catalog people, division chiefs, buyers, marketers, advertising executives, suppliers, and store managers. "There was one person to speak to about buttons and another about buttonholes," said someone who worked on the project. For Halston it was "like dealing with the Chinese government."

"They started coming in at the same time," said Mahoney. "Christ almighty, fifteen Penney people, each wanting a different part of Halston. Of course, the Penney people said, rightfully, 'We have the rights to Halston.' So there was a guy from shoes, a guy from raincoats, a guy in ties, a lady in sportswear . . . It was *worse* than licensing."

As far as Halston's promise to set up a design studio with "little designers" was concerned, there was no one on earth who could live up to Halston's standards. A merchandiser, junior designers, and organization people were all fired or quit. The necessity of constantly trying to teach new employees their jobs wreaked havoc. "We should have hired another eight to a dozen people," said Bill Dugan, "but we didn't, and it just about killed us." With the continued onslaught of demands on Halston, the line fell weeks and then months behind schedule. This drove the Penney people wild. "They were disciplined, professional managers," said Kammerschen. "Things had to be done on time because they have to mass-produce. It's not like what Halston was used to, waiting until the eleventh hour at his fashion show, stitching up some garment backstage."

With more pressure on Lichtenstein from the outside than ever before, the tension between him and Halston became explosive for the first time in ten years. Now, if the Penney project failed, not only would Halston be blamed, but so would Lichtenstein—and he could easily lose his job. "The only time that I was really upset," said Lichtenstein, "was about JCPenney. I really thought that we had to have a strategy." Within a few weeks of the start of work on the Penney line things were already beginning to go badly and Halston started to get very temperamental. Lichtenstein suggested calling in the help of an old colleague of his, Martin Rubenstein, who was vice president of Werner Management. "Rubenstein conducted several fruitful meetings with Halston about organization," said Lichtenstein. "Then they wanted to bring in consultants about analyzing stress and stress management."

After several conferences and two consultants lurking around the Olympic Tower for a few weeks, the Werner report was presented to the company. Reportedly, it characterized the situation at the Olympic Tower as some sort of controlled mayhem, run like an informal, privately owned business with no consideration for expenditures or profits. Halston abided by no rules, no timetable, no budget. Worse, the stress consultants reportedly suspected that Halston was using drugs—although they had no concrete proof, they admitted—but that was the impression they got from their research around the office and spending several hours with Halston.

Again, Mahoney confronted Halston about his alleged drug use. Halston insisted it wasn't true, and Mahoney felt he was obligated to take Halston at his word again. Mahoney's deference to Halston at this juncture may seem a bit disingenuous, considering the number of times this kind of accusation had come up, but Mahoney understood relatively little about addiction then. In retrospect, Mahoney says, he is now a lot wiser about drugs, and realizes that Halston's blanket denial was part of his problem. Since then, said Mahoney, "I came to accept that somebody who has an addiction might not steal your money, but they're going to lie to you. Addicts don't think that enabling the habit is really lying."

Kam Kammerschen was not so trusting: "I confronted Halston a couple of times," said Kammerschen. One one occasion Halston and Kammerschen were up at the Olympic Tower at the end of the day, having a drink and sharing a quiet moment together when Kammerschen brought it up again. "Halston kind of winked at me and said, essentially, 'It's none of your business.'

"I said, 'No, it *is* our business if it affects the operation.' "

Halston scoffed about there being any effect on the operation. Fixing himself another cocktail and puffing away at a True cigarette, he went on at great length about "creative inspiration." "He said that he was under enormous stress," Kammerschen remembered, "and that he was on a treadmill to constantly produce fresh, new creative ideas, and certain things served to stimulate his creativity, that it was a catalyst for him, and that he could control it. I realized then it was the 'Golden Superman Syndrome,' of somebody dangerously out of control who refuses to believe they can't possibly self-destruct." Kammerschen said to Halston, "Recently you haven't been managing your business too well. Your behavior is becoming more erratic."

Halston pulled himself up straighter in his chair. His cheeks filled with color, his glare turned frosty, imperious, impenetrable, those green eyes like ice. Kammerschen shortly left the office with a heavy heart. He was convinced Halston was a true and rare genius, but completely lost. "To see the self-destruction of an individual before your very eyes is a very humbling and disconcerting experience," Kammerschen said. "Short of firing him, there was nothing we could do."

WITH THE ENORMOUS pressure of national attention focused on him, Halston hunkered down and got to work. In the summer of 1983, Halston III for JCPenney was unveiled to the world in a manner befitting the scale on which Halston did such things. A $10-million advertising campaign was launched—Penney's largest marketing effort in its history, which included intensive TV, radio, and magazine campaigns. Even *Vogue,* which heretofore had resisted advertising from mass-market retailers like Penney, was making an exception because of Halston's importance in the business and was running his ads. On June 7, individual parties were held simultaneously in twenty-one cities across America for a total of 6,000 guests. In New York, the party was held at the American Museum of Natural History's Hall of Ocean Life where 1,000 guests milled about and drank champagne underneath a huge blue whale suspended from the ceiling. Halston's allies, Andy Warhol, Steve Rubell, and Liza

Minnelli, attended the party as well and watched with the rest of the packed museum as Halston's new clothing was paraded down a runway built under the blue whale.

As the Halstonettes came sailing down the runway in the new Penney clothes it became immediately clear that the collection was vast, detailed, and prodigious. Each garment was quite handsome, clean and simple, each blessed with the master's touch. The next day *Women's Wear* gave the collection a rousingly approving review, albeit noting that for the first time Halston was selling jeans and sweatshirts. "Halston sent out a lively parade of bright, sensible clothes that should have women with an eye for price-conscious class glutting the floors of JCPenney stores across America. Halston III is top form classic Halston transformed with disarming ease and shockingly low price. It is, quite simply, the best thing Halston's done in a long time."

"This is for the American people," Halston said before the show began. "Over half of America goes into that store at some point. When I think of these clothes, I think of my family. I have a sister in Little Rock, Arkansas, and a sister-in-law in Gainesville, Florida, and they're dying for these clothes to come out."

When the line hit the stores it sold so well that everyone could hardly believe what was happening. "We are really elated with the reception of the Halston merchandise in our stores," said John McConville, a vice president of Penney. Within one month all the JCPenney stores had achieved a 33 percent sellthrough. There was indeed a huge Penney audience out there for Halston. A black wool dress with a red suede belt sold 3,000 pieces at $105 each, and a polyester crepe print with hundreds of tiny *H*'s on it also moved about 3,000 pieces at $90 each. In Youngstown, Ohio, they sold out Halston's buffalo-check wool-and-polyester skirt at $58, and in Chattanooga, Tennessee, his $34 print polyester blouse with the tiny *H*'s across the bodice walked out the doors. Even the most expensive article in the Halston III line, a wool crepe suit at $200, sold 500 pieces.

In his tower overlooking Manhattan, Halston was once again

reassured and smug. Despite the predictions of doom and the tactical nightmare of getting the line out, Halston had triumphed after all. In a game where the bottom line was sales, he had won. The Penney line had not been his Armageddon. It was yet another glory. But instead of building steam and enthusiasm with the warm reception of the line, Halston seemed to regress to his old ways. "The first collection was a boom success," said Lichtenstein, "but the tension was getting so bad that Halston and I were practically not speaking to each other."

The second collection now began to turn into a bigger nightmare than the first. Halston battled with the Penney people every step of the way. He felt the Penney people were disrespectful to him and that they "needed to be punished." He said, "If they want the treat, they'll have to take the treatment." The waiting room at the Olympic Tower filled with Penney representatives unable to get in to see him.

"It was Louis Quinze, imperious behavior," said Paul Wilmot. "Even his politeness was temporary and superficial. The people in the office walked around on eggshells all the time because they never knew how they stood personally with him. It got worse over the years."

Now it was Mike Lichtenstein's turn to fall victim to Halston's temperament. "A gap of sorts started to form between Halston and Mike Lichtenstein," said Kammerschen, "because Mike had a lot more pressure on him to make the Penney deal work. That was his job. Up until now it was still small-scale, in-house things, but the Penney deal was so well publicized, they were out front-and-center."

"The only time I ever became angry," said Lichtenstein, "was with the Penney deal. He wanted to design a whole world of products, and I saw the peril in this and I said you cannot run this without delegation. And I went out and hired a group of two or three merchandisers and so on. We also hired a couple of assistants and rented space for them." But one day not long after they had been hired, Halston fired the entire merchandising department that Lichtenstein had set up for him over some claimed mistake or ineptitude.

"The great problem with Penney," said Kammerschen, "was that the job of doing this line in a very short time involved enormous demands on Halston. All those things in concert with some other things going on in Halston's life—and I wasn't aware of what those things were—increased the frequency and amplitude of the mercurial nature of the man."

It was around that same time that Patricia Alexander, a businesswoman in her thirties who was the chief financial officer of Halston Enterprises, struck up a friendship with Halston. Alexander, who joined the company in 1980, had originally been a Norton Simon executive under Gary Bewkes, and up until now she had kept a relatively low profile with Halston. But as time went by Halston seemed to "take Alexander up" according to one employee. He invited her and her two children for weekends in Montauk, he suggested new hairstyles and made her clothing. The two of them seemed to develop some sort of empathy, and this made certain other executives in the office nervous for reasons they could not quite name. Alexander became a new addition to the innermost Halston circle, and "as Halston was getting more aggravated with Mike Lichtenstein," said Kammerschen, "Pat Alexander formed a kind of alliance with Halston. It became obvious we needed some person who could operate outside of Mike, and that became Pat Alexander."

One day in June 1983, Lichtenstein was at lunch with some executives from Penney when he received a phone call from Halston. "He called up screaming and announced that I was never to come back," said Lichtenstein, who returned to the office after lunch anyway. "He sent Bill Dugan in to apologize," said Lichtenstein. Naturally, Lichtenstein forgave Halston, but the die had already been cast. Despite intervention by both Kammerschen and Mahoney, Halston decided that he could no longer work with Lichtenstein—that he could no longer even bear to see him around—and Lichtenstein was banished from the Olympic Tower. He was moved to the Forty-second Street offices of the fragrance division, and Halston reportedly had Lichtenstein's old office turned into a closet, as if to erase his very existence. For a time, indeed, Halston would not hear the name "Lichtenstein" uttered in his presence, and everyone had to refer to his loyal business associate of a decade as "It."

ON JUNE 6, 1983, the day before Halston's big Penney launch, David Mahoney set into action a plan that would shake Halston's world to its very foundations. Along with several other investors, David Mahoney made an offering to take Norton Simon Industries private at $29 a share in cash and preferred stock for all of the company's outstanding 25 million shares. This deal, totaling $725 million, would make it at that time the largest company ever taken off the stock exchange and put into private hands. Not coincidentally, since June of 1980, David Mahoney and his associates had quietly purchased back 24 million common shares of Norton Simon Industries' stock worth around $60 million—cutting the outstanding shares in half. Mahoney paid prices ranging from $13 to $22 for Norton Simon stock, but always less than book value. This buying spree, totaling $460 million, had provoked wild speculation on Wall Street that Mahoney and partners were going to try to take the company private. *Fortune* magazine even ran an article entitled "Incredible Shrinking Norton Simon," but Mahoney refused to comment on what they were doing. "To the question 'Are you going private?' " Mahoney said, "We always consistently answered there is no plan and I stand by that."

Yet now he *was* going private. Moreover, there appeared to be a conflict of interest, since as the shareholders' representative Mahoney's responsibility was to get the best possible deal for them in a leveraged buyout—yet as the buyer himself, he wanted to acquire the company for as little as possible. Reportedly several shareholders' suits were lodged against him. Yet according to securities law, Mahoney had no legal obligation to tell the stock sellers what his plans were. None of this made Mahoney a popular guy in certain circles. The stock was trading at around $26 anyway, and the $29-a-share bid was so low it was greeted with private disbelief. There were "wails of indignation" on Wall Street according to *Time* magazine. *The Wall Street Journal* noted that "Mr. Mahoney has been the object of amazed reaction among Wall Street investment bankers over the terms of his own $29-a-share leveraged buyout proposal," in which Mahoney retained up to 60 percent interest in NSI when it went private. As soon as Mahoney announced his bid, Norton Simon stock began to trade feverishly, and a week later closed at $32.13, up $5.75 a share.

If Mahoney's low-ball figure for the stock was an attempt to smoke out other potential buyers, he found one almost immediately. On June 14, the firm of Kohlberg Kravis Roberts upped the bid for Norton Simon to $33 a share, in a deal worth $100 million more than Mahoney's. KKR, as they were called on Wall Street, was a relative newcomer to the takeover field in which the potential buyer borrows money against the assets of the company he wants to acquire in order to buy it. Afterward, the company is disassembled and the pieces sold off to pay the debt. In 1983 this practice was still rare enough for *The Wall Street Journal* to explain a leveraged buyout each time it was mentioned. If Mahoney decided to take Kohlberg Kravis's offer, he could turn a profit of nearly $14 million on his stock alone. But for Mahoney $33 a share wasn't high enough, and he kept his eye out for other investors. He reportedly had heard on the street that Donald P. Kelly, the chairman of Esmark, a huge consumer goods conglomerate much bigger than Norton Simon Industries, was contemplating making a bid, and Mahoney called Kelly in Chicago to see if it was true. With Mahoney's invitation it was.

On June 27, the day before Bergdorf Goodman canceled

their relationship with Halston, Esmark entered the fray by upping the ante to a bid totaling $903 million. By July 1, Kelly had sweetened the deal at a price of approximately $35.50 a share, totaling $925 million, and Mahoney sold Norton Simon Industries to him. By this sale, Mahoney stood to profit by $13.3 million on his options to buy 770,000 shares of Norton Simon Industries stock at $15. He also owned about 48,000 shares outright, which would be worth another $1.6 million. Mahoney immediately announced his plans to leave the company following a transition period, and he placed a personal phone call to Halston to say good-bye.

Mahoney says that Halston was not angry about the sale of Norton Simon Industries, and that Halston understood the exigencies of business. "Besides," said Mahoney, "I don't think he sold any of his Norton Simon stock in the ten years, and Halston was making a lot of money at $35 a share. Don't forget that." Mahoney and Halston remained on good terms, but he and Halston rarely saw each other after the sale. "Halston thought he and David Mahoney would work together for all eternity," said Eleanor Lambert. "Halston thought it was going to be forever, like Troilus and Cressida. And it wasn't."

DONALD P. KELLY, Esmark's chief executive officer, was not David Mahoney. Unlike Mahoney, Kelly didn't care about designers or the social columns. Kelly was a Chicago legend whose rise in business had been so clever that "pulling an Esmark" had become a business buzzword for doing a canny deal. A former bookkeeper and data processor who grew up on Chicago's tough South Side, Donald Kelly sat on an empire worth an estimated $6.3 billion in annual sales, and its divisions were among the top ten advertisers in the U.S. Esmark included processed foods, toiletries, hair-care products, chemicals, fertilizers, girdles and bras, and automotive consumer products. In the four years since Kelly had become chief executive officer of

Esmark he had acquired thirty-four companies and sold a dozen others off. He was probably best known in the business world for resurrecting a moribund meat-packing company called Swift and Company and turning it into the largest firm of its kind in the U.S.

"Kelly doesn't mess around with operations, they'll be glad to hear," Donald Kelly (using the third person) told *Fortune* magazine about himself soon after buying Norton Simon Industries. "We view this step as a unique opportunity. Many of [NSI's] operations are logical extensions of our lines of business." Kelly wanted the Avis Rent-a-Car division even before Norton Simon bought it, and Norton Simon's Hunt and Wesson divisions would dovetail nicely with Esmark's Swift and Company; the United Can Company, an $11-million-a-year operation which already made the cans for Hunt and Wesson, could do that for Esmark foods, too; and the highly profitable liquor company, Somerset Importers, which imported Johnnie Walker scotch and Tanqueray gin, was a perfect balance for their foodstuffs.

But where did Max Factor and Halston Enterprises and McCall's Patterns belong? Factor had "management problems"—five different presidents in nine years—and McCall's sales had decreased by 50 percent in recent years because of waning interest in sewing. And Halston didn't seem to fit into *any* niche. The closest company in Kelly's jumbo conglomerate to all that high-toned fashion stuff was International Playtex, a division best known for its intimate apparel like bras and girdles; for its baby products; and for its rubber gloves and tampons. In fact, Playtex's second largest customer of private-label bras and girdles was JCPenney. So in late September of 1983, Esmark announced that three Norton Simon companies, Max Factor, McCall's Patterns and Halston Enterprises Incorporated, would now report to Joel E. Smilow, president and CEO of International Playtex. Suddenly Halston had become part of a bra and girdle company.

Kam Kammerschen resigned shortly after Esmark bought Norton Simon Industries, but one of his last responsibilities was to show Donald Kelly around Max Factor's assets. As they walked along Fifth Avenue toward the Olympic Tower, Kammerschen tried to prepare Kelly for what he was to see. "I told him there was no way to understand it and that the business was heading for oblivion because Halston was out of control because of a drug problem. I said the Penney thing is about ready to blow up and we've tried everything short of firing the guy to make it work."

Kelly listened glumly and said he understood, but all the forewarning in the world couldn't have prepared him for the salon in the sky. "I remember the look on his face when we walked into the Olympic Tower," said Kammerschen. "All those mirrors . . ." And there was Halston, looking serene and calm at his throne in front of St. Patrick's, imperious yet gracious to Kelly as he greeted him from behind black sunglasses. Halston showed Kelly around his domain, and Kelly nodded and smiled. "I mean, talk about being mystified!" said Kammerschen. "All this glitter and glamour and no bottom line . . ."

In September of 1983, Kelly told some Chicago stockbrokers about his visit with Halston at the Olympic Tower. "He kept calling me 'Mr. Kelly,' " he told the amused businessmen, "but I didn't know what his real name was. What do you call him— 'Mr. Halston'?" As far as the mirrored palace went, "All I've got to say is that it was a very impressive office for a small amount of profit." Kelly added, "It's a long run for a short slide."

To the victor belong the spoils. One source close to the situation claims that the Esmark people quickly stepped in and took all the box seats that the company bought on a seasonal basis for sporting events, but left unused the tickets for the ballet and the opera. Also, soon after Donald Kelly's visit to the Olympic Tower, Mrs. Kelly and her sister and daughters went to Halston's ready-to-wear showroom at 550 Seventh Avenue to buy some clothes. Mrs. Kelly was shown a suit she liked and she asked how much it was. When she was told it cost $700 she said, "I mean, how much is it wholesale?"

"That *is* wholesale," she was told.

"Oh *no*," a shocked Mrs. Kelly responded. "My husband wouldn't like that. I've never spent more than four hundred dollars on a piece of clothing in my life." They left the showroom without buying a single thing.

Yet even Donald Kelly came to appreciate the Halston flair. As Halston marketing executive Mike Pellegrino said, "Our volume was small, but we had a large image." A few months later Kelly seemed to resign himself to Halston's extravagance. "All those expenses are not necessarily fluff," he told a reporter, pointing out that Esmark also employed lobbyists in Washington, D.C. "We pay them a tremendous amount," he said of the lobbyists, "but how do you bottom-line it? They don't produce anything." And then, prophetically, he said, "Halston is a name, but how long is he going to be a name if he doesn't continue to do such things?"

"THE PRISONER
OF SEVENTH AVENUE"

The New York Times Magazine
March 1987

"**I**n the turmoil of these takeovers," said Linda Wachner, one of Max Factor's several presidents during that period, "little pieces always fall out. What happens if the little pieces are a person's life? It's a hell of a lot different than if it's just a little piece of 'Ashtray, Inc.'" Up at the Olympic Tower, "H" didn't see his life or his business as Ashtray, Inc. From his towering perch, "H" saw himself as king of all he surveyed, still with the upper hand in his struggle, and he became determined to fight the corporate mentality with its restrictions and directives. "I'll show those bastards who they're fucking with," was his battle cry.

The man Halston would be fucking with was Joel E. Smilow, fifty, the president of International Playtex. With an estimated $784 million in annual grosses, International Playtex was a highly profitable company for Esmark, and the company's hard-nosed chief executive officer was an entirely different kettle of fish from Kam Kammerschen, Lichtenstein, or Mahoney. He was a gruff, blunt, and difficult man, not given to compromise. Once he made up his mind, he was implacable. *Fortune* named Smilow one of the "Top 10 Toughest Bosses in America," and *The Wall Street Journal* called Smilow "a Kelly protégé." Smilow was also a tireless, self-made multimillionaire who had built International Playtex up over eighteen years with his bare hands from a small bra and girdle business into the worldwide leader in women's intimate apparel. In the early days of Playtex he was known for personally crisscrossing the U.S. and prowling beauty parlors and drugstores to find local brands to build up into national products. His company, said one analyst, was built "on pulling rabbits out of hats." Among other businesses, Smilow had in recent years acquired Danskin dancewear, French Carita hair products, and Almay Cosmetics. In 1981 he had snapped up Jhirmack hair products and turned the $6-million-a-year business into a $80-million operation within a few years. Smilow also had a reputation for shaving off divisions or lines that were unprofitable. "Few who know Smilow think he'll stay more than six months with any division that doesn't show promise," warned *Women's Wear*. "His history shows an impatience with bleeding companies."

Smilow heard all about the problems with Halston Enterprises, and he immediately asked for a business presentation from the company, "the kind of thing we would have normally presented prior to a takeover," said Michael Pellegrino, who was responsible for putting together the marketing side of the meeting. In September 1983, several core executives from Halston Enterprises went to the Stamford, Connecticut, office of International Playtex and presented budgets, future marketing strategies, and promotional plans to Smilow and Walter Bregman, Smilow's top executive at the company who would be overseeing Halston Enterprises for him. "We gave Smilow the opportunity to hear what goes on at Halston Enterprises, and it also gave him some insight into the unique way that Halston Enterprises functioned, on a more casual basis in relation to a larger corporation," said Pellegrino.

Smilow was incredulous. "This is how you operate?" he asked. Walter Bregman was more than a little amazed himself.

"It was out of control," Bregman said, "We saw that from the beginning. It was a crappy little company, and Halston was clearly egocentric. It was an ego trip that David Mahoney used to get into cafe society." The opinion up at Playtex was that Halston Enterprises had to be brought into line, the hemorrhaging of money with no returns had to be stanched, and the profitable Penney deal had to be saved from falling apart. Clearly, the way to do this was to put a strong manager in control of the company, somebody who could jump on the back of the tiger and tame it without getting eaten, somebody with clear-cut authority to do the job. And Smilow had just the guy to do it, a "company doctor" named Carl Epstein.

IN THE BEGINNING, Halston *adored* Carl Epstein. Carl Epstein *amuused* him. Epstein was Halston's "Little King," a diminutive man with a tight smile for whom Halston actually once made a crown and wrapped in a robe. Halston stood there grinning sardonically, towering over Epstein, as the two were photographed at the Olympic Tower together for posterity. With his small, twinkling blue eyes and balding pate, Epstein struck a Napoleonic figure; indeed, Halston had met his Waterloo.

Carl Epstein, fifty-seven years old, had worked closely with Smilow as the general manager of the Danskin dancewear division of Playtex. He had been with Playtex for ten years in various jobs, including general manager of family products, vice president of the girdle and bra division, and president of the BVD underwear concern. He had also left the company for a time to go into business on his own as a consultant, a "company doctor" as he once referred to himself. During that time he had worked for the Donut Corporation of American, a tuna-fish canner, the Rapid American Corporation, and over thirty other companies, tinkering, improving—or dismantling. In fact, his reputation in business was for the surgical paring down of troubled companies as well as for building them up. There is still much controversy over whether Epstein was sent in to close down Halston Enterprises or to strengthen it. Joel Smilow maintained, "I sent him to revitalize the company," and indeed, the real triumph for Epstein would have been to put the company back on top. Many times Epstein himself told employees, "I was only supposed to be here a few months . . ."

Epstein was from Boro Park, Brooklyn, and he liked his work because at heart he was a tactician. He loved the military and war history and had even applied to West Point as a young man. His hobby was collecting "edged weapons" and firearms from the Civil War period, and in the den of his house in New Jersey he kept a collection of swords, daggers, bayonets, and bullets. Yet this tough, pragmatic man with his finely tuned sense of justice and honor also had a huge, vulnerable heart and respect for the creative spirit that verged on the awestruck. Privately, Epstein felt honored to be asked to work with Halston, whom he believed was a bona fide genius and great artist.

But others contend that Epstein was sent in "to housebreak the genius." Said Paul Wilmot, "Carl Epstein came in like a Boy Scout. He was running around like it was going to be too fabulous for words. But when you looked closely at him you realized he was a hard-nosed businessman who found himself in this nonbusinesslike, glamour-oriented world."

Epstein immersed himself in Halston and his company to become expert at its operations. He had long hours of conversation with Halston himself, whom he came to respect as a "brilliant intellect," according to one of Epstein's colleagues. He read Halston's publicity scrapbooks and newspaper clippings, watched tapes of Halston on TV talk shows, and studied videotapes of the made-to-order and Halston Originals collections over the years. He studied the Penney deal and the existing licensing contracts with a fine-tooth comb and got to know every cost factor and expenditure incurred by the company. He reviewed the health-insurance policies and studied the employee benefits. He also personally interviewed practically everybody in the place to find out exactly what it was that they did for the company, including D. D. Ryan and Bill Dugan. When Epstein later had a conversation with Halston about his immediate staff, insiders said that Halston surprised Epstein by complaining bitterly about them. Epstein couldn't understand why D. D. Ryan worked at the Olympic Tower at all, and when he asked Halston for her job description, Halston reportedly said, "geisha." When Epstein asked Halston why he kept people on his staff, Halston looked surprised for a second and then said, "Because they *amuusse* me."

Epstein also learned that the antics of Victor Hugo *amuused* Halston, too, and that Epstein was expected somehow to deal with Victor's frequent and unwarranted presence in the showroom. Epstein was baffled by Victor Hugo and Halston's tolerance of him. "Carl was a nice Jewish guy in his sixties from Teaneck, New Jersey," said one of the design room assistants. "He had never come across a gay Venezuelan, coked-out, incomprehensible window decorator before." Allegedly, one day Epstein caught Victor walking out of the showroom with a sequined dress worth many thousands of dollars. Epstein ordered Victor never to come back to the showroom, and Victor threatened to tear apart the offices and break every mirror in the place, shouting, "This isn't *your* office." Said one observer, "Carl didn't know whether to call people in white coats or the police." Afterwards, Epstein reportedly kept an edged sword in his office for protection.

On another occasion, Victor had a family crisis, and he arrived at the showroom in frantic need of a large amount of cash. Halston locked himself in his office and refused to see Victor, who shouted and paced in the reception area for a while, demanding to see Halston. Eventually, he stormed into Carl Epstein's office and demanded that Epstein write a check to him for several thousand dollars. Epstein said he wouldn't give him a penny of company money and ordered him off the premises. Victor started jumping up and down and screaming at Epstein at the top of his lungs, *"I fuck Halston, not you! I fuck him, not you!"* Halston, who could hear the screaming in his office, sent a check out to quiet Victor down.

Although Epstein was quite aware of the need to keep Halston's image-making machinery well oiled, he was shocked at the profligacy of Halston's spending: he seemed to have no regard for cost or schedules whatsoever; and certain employees appeared to be drawing handsome salaries for no reason at all. Expensive bolts of fabric were ordered and left to collect dust in storerooms. Halston used limousines to ride a single block or gave the use of limousines to employees for job-related jaunts, and monthly limousine bills were running as high as $5,000. The workroom tailors were used to make personal clothes or furniture slipcovers for Halston and his friends on company time and expense, and Halston's costumes for Martha Graham's ballets seemed to take precedence over the Halston III JCPenney line. Also, not only was there a private cook, Viola, for the kitchen at the Olympic Tower, but sometimes, when Halston was in Montauk, Viola would prepare dinner for Halston at the Olympic Tower. The food was then rushed by limousine to the airport, where it was flown via small plane to East Hampton and then driven the rest of the way to Halston, who was ensconced in Montauk on the tip of Long Island. Perhaps the most shocking bill of all was the monthly florist tab—mainly orchids for the office and 101—which was running close to $40,000 a year.

Diplomatically, instead of forbidding any one specific expense or practices, Epstein tried to rein Halston in. Said Mike Pellegrino, "Anything is acceptable to a degree of the volume that the company is doing, and although Halston was involved in image and taste, there was a limit. I think in the case of Halston there were privileges allowed to people, budget privileges and perks, that were not balanced. I think Carl brought a more democratic attitude into a situation that for many years was perhaps not so democratic, but more of a monarchy. For many years, Halston was used to having his way, and then all of a sudden, someone said 'No,' or someone said 'Yes, but only this much.' "

For one thing, Halston would now have to produce expense-account substantiation, and his bills from the Bermuda Limousine Company were to be considered a personal expense. And the Martha Graham costumes could not be fabricated in the workroom on company time.

Halston sputtered with outrage. How *dare* Epstein tell him how to run his company? He couldn't believe Epstein had the gall. He'd been in business for thirty years and no one had ever, *ever* told Halston how to run his company. This little "kike," as Halston began to refer to Epstein, was not going to last long around the Olympic Tower. Halston would have him *banished*.

Epstein's primary concern at the time was that the Halston III JCPenney line continue to meet its production schedule. Since Patricia Alexander still had a good rapport with Halston, she was now made vice president of Halston III, where her main task was to facilitate the flow of designs and approvals from Halston. But while Halston had been able to pump himself up to peak performance for the debut collection when all the public attention was focused on him and so much seemed to be on the line, for the second, anticlimactic, collection he began to display his usual lack of interest in licensing programs. There were endless boards and swatches and sketches of apparel, but no samples to be shown for it, no finished work. A new merchandiser was hired to help, but Halston soon fired him, as well as at least two complete design staffs. As the weeks drifted by, the design room became increasingly disorganized. Phone messages to Halston by the hundreds were left unanswered. Because foreign manufacturers needed a longer "lead time" to ship finished goods, the Penney apparel had to be switched to American manufacturers at a much greater cost. At one point, Halston agreed to a meeting with William Howell, the head of JCPenney, to discuss possible ways of improving the chaotic situation, but reportedly Halston kept Howell waiting for forty-five minutes. Then when he finally let him into his office, Howell brought with him as a present for Halston a model of the original JCPenney delivery truck for his desk. Halston harangued Howell for half an hour before he left, and the delivery truck wound up in the wastebasket.

Finally, in March 1984, a thirty-eight-year-old designer named John David Ridge was hired to organize and run the design room, and briefly it looked as though things were actually going to work out. It was D. D. Ryan who recommended Ridge. She had known him when he was head of the workroom for Brooks Van Horn, a renowned New York costume supply house that executed many of the costumes for Broadway and New York ballets and operas. A graduate of the Pratt Institute, Ridge had also founded the costume design department for the Juilliard School and executed the costumes for many Broadway shows, including the Tony Award–winning production of *Dracula*. He had recently been in Great Britain working in the London theater and had only just returned to New York when D. D. Ryan ran into him at a New Year's Eve party and told him about a job running the design room at the Olympic Tower. Ridge had already heard rumors about how difficult Halston was to work with, but he was in some ways particularly well suited to the job because he not only knew how to run a large design room but he was also accustomed to "ghosting" or interpreting costumes for other designers. The hope was that there would be no ego problems with Halston.

Ridge was amazed at the scene that greeted him at Olympic Tower. "It was very much *The Wizard of Oz*," he said in what had become a familiar refrain. "Halston pretended he was in control of the Olympic Tower, but he wasn't." Yet there didn't seem to be anybody to say the emperor had no clothes. "It was a bunker mentality," said Ridge, "totally cut off from reality. Halston went from the Olympic Tower into his limousine to 101 and back again. It didn't seem to matter how far behind he was. They were still working on the summer line, which had to be in the Penney stores in six weeks." One of the first people Ridge met at the Tower was Victor Hugo, who sat and talked with him for an hour in the design room. When Hugo left, "I finally asked one of the assistants, 'Who is this person?' and they didn't know what to say to me," said Ridge.

Ridge found the large workroom well staffed and "first-rate," but filled with people who were "frightened as rabbits" of Halston. There was a vestige of the design staff that they had made Halston hire to do the Penney line, but "they never designed anything," said Ridge. "Every single thing had to be designed by *H* himself. He used to say, 'Everyone is just on-the-job training.' There was absolutely no one who could be as good as he was, and he had to design every single thing that went out for Penney. He had Bill Dugan with him all those years, but Bill never designed anything. Occasionally he would let Bill pick out a fabric and then later ridicule it. He would be horrible to Bill and mean to D. D. Ryan. They were both sweet people, but absolutely petrified; you know how a cornered rabbit or fox gets so frightened that they can't move. D.D. would sit there at night with a drink, smoking her cigarette, saying 'Oh, *H,* you're so wonderful.' Halston complained about D.D., but he would never fire her. He would say, 'She has no money, she has no place to go, I have to give her this job.' "

Ridge said the tailors would sometimes go for days without any work, waiting for Halston to design something, or spend weeks making Halston a sport jacket or slipcovers for his friends. "We used to joke that sometimes the tailors would sit there and pretend to be sewing with no thread in their needles just to look like they were busy," said Ridge. In general, Halston wouldn't show up for work until early afternoon, and then there would be much posturing and trips to the bathroom until about 6 P.M. when his energy was stoked and he would begin work—and cocktails as well. In just two or three hours he would be sitting back in his chair, eyes glazed, his cigarette ash dropping to the carpet, which now had scores of burns among the little *H*'s.

There are some who disagree, at least in great part, with this description. Halston's friend, artist Peter Wise, who also helped with Halston's orchids at home and in the showroom, saw Halston three times a week for many years, and he never remembered him seeming incapacitated or drugged.

The only project that seemed to invigorate Halston was designing the costumes for Martha Graham's new ballet, *Sacre du printemps,* which was opening that March at the New York State Theater in Lincoln Center. Yet even for his beloved Martha Graham he waited until the week before the costumes were due to start work on them. The concept for the costumes was for both the male and female dancers to be covered by foot-wide bands of stretch fabric strategically placed across their bodies. The weekend before the opening, Halston suddenly decided to send out for Ace bandages. "We cornered the market in Ace bandages," said John Ridge. "They bought thousands of boxes of Ace bandages, and they tried to paint them and sew them on the dancers, but when the paint dried it all flaked off. Having worked in costume design most of my career, I realized they were using the bandages for lack of knowledge, and I went out and got them real stretch material on which they could paint."

The costumes arrived in time for the opening and they were a huge success with both Graham and Halston. Halston was so grateful to Ridge that he gave him a signed Warhol poster as a gift. Three other signed Warhol posters would follow in gratitude for various other situations that Ridge pulled back from the brink, including the organization and design of the early fall line. One of the posters read "Thank God for you, John." Nevertheless, the tension was so great at the Olympic Tower that Ridge began dreading work in the morning, and after a few weeks, he went to see Carl Epstein and told him he was thinking about quitting. "You may not know this," he said to Epstein, "but you have a drug addict on your hands. I mean, there's a serious cocaine problem there."

Epstein said it was rumored but that no one knew for sure, and he asked Ridge not to quit. They needed Ridge. "Don't leave yet," Epstein said, "because things are going to change."

Ridge hung on. He helped Halston start work on the next collection of Halston Originals for fall of 1984. "They were so far behind," said Ridge. "It was crazy, just crazy. *H* would come into work with the headache that ate New York. He would then sit in his office and no one went near him for the first two or three hours, if you could possibly avoid him. He would bully and yell and reduce people in the workroom to tears, every day, like clockwork. By four or five o'clock he would get coked up enough and call me up in the design room and say, 'Let's fit.' "

Halston insisted on going over each and every piece for the Penney line, complaining all the time, "How can I give them new things, everyone wants new things, but they don't know how to make the old ones."

Every hour or so, said Ridge, "We would all get excused for a minute, and Halston would close the door and he would disappear into his little bathroom and have some more coke or a joint or two. About fifteen minutes later the doors would open again and we would go back in." By about eight o'clock at night Halston would be too impaired to work anymore. "His hands would shake so much that he would have to point while I cut the fabric," said Ridge. "Sometimes, though, late at night, I'd see a little bit of brilliance come out. His ideas were brilliant. Sometimes he would be draping things and it would be wonderful. I'd think, 'Boy, what it must have been like before all of this . . .' "

Halston's paranoia was increasing as well, as he became concerned again that his phone conversations at home and in the office were being taped. He worried about this with his brother as well as his friends. Indeed, Bert Keeter, who was fired by

Carl Epstein and who is bitter about his working experience there, claims that "Carl Epstein had all these tapes of Halston that he was recording that Halston didn't know he was taping." Keeter claimed that Epstein played a tape for him on which Halston says, "I'll show those bastards. They don't know who the hell they're fucking with."

On May 2, 1984, at the showing of the Halston Original collection at the Olympic Tower, Halston was so drunk and high that he was "flying off the walls," according to John Ridge. Carl Epstein had to hide Halston from reporters and TV news cameras to prevent him from embarrassing himself and the company. This kind of frightening public display was a new threshold that Halston had descended to; soon afterwards Epstein placed a personal phone call to the former First Lady, Betty Ford. Epstein explained the situation to Mrs. Ford and asked what the company could do to get Halston into the Betty Ford Clinic in Rancho Mirage. Ford reportedly said there was nothing that anybody else could do, that Halston himself had to want to be helped and he had to come forward personally and admit that he had a problem. Reportedly, Epstein let it be known to *all* the employees of Halston Enterprises that the company would be sympathetic if anyone wanted to enter a rehabilitation facility for drug or alcohol addiction and that their jobs would be guaranteed, and—in some cases—their salaries would be paid for six months. Halston's response to this was "I have no problem."

Others around Halston were more in touch. During the summer of 1984 Liza Minnelli saved her own life. On July 11, 1984, depressed and dangerously addicted to drugs and alcohol, Minnelli dropped out of *The Rink*, the Broadway show in which she was then costarring with Chita Rivera. "There was a while there when I felt like somebody had a gun on the party I was at and kept hijacking it to different places," she said of that period. " 'Now we're going to Bianca's!' And all the same people went there. You know, it's like a cartoon, this little group moving around. And that can be very tiring. And I was working. So I could never do anything until after work. So I missed a lot of what was going on, and I also arrived sober at a lot of places where people were already ahead of me. But I'd catch up. I'd catch up."

Two days after Minnelli dropped out of *The Rink*, Liza's half sister, Lorna Luft, flew with her out to California where Minnelli checked herself into the Betty Ford Clinic for detoxification and treatment. Over the next few years, a new Liza Minnelli emerged. The transition wasn't apparent at first, because she acted just as kooky and fun loving as she ever had, but over the years it became clear that Minnelli had licked many of her addictive demons. She was more self-confident and centered. She joined Alcoholics Anonymous and attends meetings faithfully. Her new self-respect gained her the respect of her peers, and her stock with the public was on the ascendant. She finally stopped being the doomed daughter of Judy Garland and began to fulfill the promise of her own stardom, alongside the likes of Frank Sinatra and Sammy Davis, Jr. Like many of her former friends from the fast lane, Minnelli began to discover that "being sober was hip," as she said.

But not Halston. The day after Minnelli signed herself into the Betty Ford Clinic, Halston showed John David Ridge a check for a substantial contribution to the clinic as a gesture of support for Liza. "Isn't it wonderful there's a place like that for people who need it," he said to Ridge, waving the check in the air. "The rest of us have to get on with earning a living."

IN THE MEANTIME, in a move most alarming to Halston, Halston Enterprises Incorporated, along with a financially ailing fragrance company named Orlane, was split off from Max Factor and paired together as a separate division of Playtex. From the Chicago offices of Esmark, as well as the Stamford, Connecticut, office of Playtex, word was quietly put out on the street that

Halston Enterprises and his money-making fragrance might be up for sale (although it was at first denied). However, there was a catch: Orlane carried with it a $20 million debt. In other words, if you bought Halston fragrance, you had to take not only Halston himself but Orlane off their hands as well. Although Smilow and Epstein and Esmark denied any pending sale, evidently representatives from several companies discussed buying Halston/Orlane from Esmark, including the fragrance company of Jacqueline Cochran, Inc., as well as Daniel J. Manela of McGregor Corporation, which also owned Fabergé. There were also discussions about selling Halston/Orlane to JCPenney, who reportedly had a "right of first refusal" clause in their contract with Halston if his company was ever sold. But Penney's position was "We will only buy this company if Halston wants us to buy it," said Walter Bregman, who was in charge of the negotiations. That March of 1984, at an Esmark shareholders' meeting held in Los Angeles, Donald Kelly and Joel Smilow assured stockholders that all was well within the company and there were no intentions to sell Halston/Orlane off. Said Esmark corporate gadfly Evelyn Davis, "It's very significant Halston is not at this meeting. He was always at the NSI meetings. His absence here is significant."

Indeed, that very month Halston first consulted with a litigating attorney named Malcolm I. Lewin, a partner in the law firm of Morrison Cohen & Singer. "Nick" Lewin, as he was called, was a fast-talking, native New Yorker with an accent that avowed his having grown up on Amsterdam Avenue in Manhattan. A married man, with a house in the suburbs of New Jersey and two college-age daughters, Lewin was a tenacious, but sometimes provocative, advocate whose stated legal philosophy was that he would rather negotiate than sue. But that didn't mean Lewin spoke softly and carried the big stick of a lawsuit. He was aggressively tough and sometimes intentionally abrasive. "Halston hired Lewin," said one Playtex executive, "because he was tough and because he was Jewish, and Halston thought he'd get one of their (Smilow and Epstein's) own to go 'sic 'em.' From the start, Lewin was building a dossier in anticipation of a lawsuit. That's a very strategic approach."

Said Lewin, "Halston was having a problem with Playtex, and they were personified by Joel Smilow and Carl Epstein. The first time I sat down with Halston to listen to his problems, he was all over the lot. The poor guy was in a lot of distress. They were basically freezing Halston out, pulling the company out from under him and trying to emasculate him."

As for the drug rumors, on a personal level, Lewin found Halston to be justifiably emotional, but completely in control. Lewin said he never saw any drugs or any signs of drug abuse. He never saw or spoke to Halston in a drugged or inebriated condition. There were many early-morning meetings and phone calls over the duration of their professional relationship, and Halston was always on time and completely sober according to Lewin. "I heard the rumors," he said, "and I saw no evidence of it. If somebody said to Halston, 'I hear you're on drugs,' Halston would answer, 'That's funny, just outside at the elevator someone said that you were on drugs.'—which is a perfect way of disarming somebody dealing in gossip and rumor."

Lewin began a long and exhaustive study of the "bible," the massive original 1973 Norton Simon Industries contract. Lewin read it scores of times, and as he read and reread the letters and documents he noticed that each time there was a copyright issue—for instance, a manufacturer pirating the name Halston, or a manufacturer trying to counterfeit clothing—and the Norton Simon lawyers wanted to litigate to stop it, Halston was asked to sign an affidavit saying that Norton Simon Industries owned his copyright. The reason for this, claimed Lewin, was that Norton Simon never received a "grant of authority" from Halston on his name *itself* and that Halston was still the primary owner of the trademark. This argument became known as the "man and his mark" theory.

According to Lewin, "They never got an assignment of his name. They got all the businesses that existed in 1973, they got an employment contract with him and several other things, but they didn't own the complete trademark. Imagine the trademark is a handful of sticks. The guy who's got them all owns the trademark. But in this situation Playtex owned some of them and Halston owned some of them. When the two of them were together working happily ever after in the Norton Simon years, Halston's and Norton Simon's sticks all sat in the same place."

To Lewin's mind, the situation was that there was "co-ownership" of the trademark. When this issue was raised with Playtex attorneys, however, it was scoffed at. In fact, few closely associated with the situation felt that Lewin's argument held any water. Even Halston's supporter, David Mahoney, who negotiated the contracts to begin with, said that Lewin's interpretation was wrong. "Halston sold the company who happened to own his name," was the way Mahoney put it. Still, Lewin clung to his own interpretation of the contracts.

This point was left moot for the moment as the situation became even more embroiled. Esmark's debt at that moment was growing increasingly unwieldly. Word on the street was that Kelly was anxious to unload it, and by May of 1984, the investment firm of Kohlberg Kravis Roberts made an unsolicited offer of $55 a share for Esmark in a deal totaling more than $2.3 billion. Kelly agreed to KKR's offer, but only days later Beatrice Foods, another giant Chicago food conglomerate, waded into the waters with a bid worth $1 more per share. "Fifty-six is better than fifty-five," said Donald Kelly, and a few days later the deal was done—sweetened to $60 a share, in what totaled a $2.8-billion transaction. Donald Kelly, on whom so much had seemed to depend only a short while before, was gone in a flash, "crowded out" by the new owners, as *The Wall Street Journal* put it. Kelly didn't seem too upset. It was reported that after receiving a severance fee of close to $2 million, he had fake business cards printed up that said, "Retired. No Business, No Worries, No Plans, No Problems, No Money, No Prospects."

By the summer of 1984, Halston was officially owned by Beatrice Foods, another hulking foodstuffs and consumer products company with annual sales of $9.3 billion. That, combined with Esmark's $6 billion annual gross, would make it the world's largest food conglomerate. Beatrice was headed by fifty-nine-year-old James L. Dutt. This time around, however, Halston never even got to meet Dutt, or the following chairman, William Granger, or was there any interest. By now, Halston had become just a grain of sand on a big beach. "They have 428 businesses, or something like that," Halston said of Beatrice, "and we haven't sat down yet. We'll get together soon. I'm sure."

He shouldn't have been so sure.

UP AT THE OLYMPIC Tower, Planet Halston wrenched free of its orbit and went off into space. On June 18, 1984, Halston suffered a massive blow to his morale when *Women's Wear Daily* gave his second JCPenney collection a damaging and negative review. "Halston wasn't doing *anything* by now," claimed Ridge. "He was just copying his own things. It was the most dreadful line." *Women's Wear* called the new line "Halston diluted to a pale substance and a flimsy representation of the designer's work . . . marred by its fabrics . . . and undermined by its inattention to fit." Halston stormily blamed it all on the inept assistants and interference from JCPenney. And again, on July 3, in an article titled "Retailers Rate Designers," several unnamed retailers ripped into Halston. "I don't think he is as salable as he was four or five years ago," said one. "He has a look, and right now this may not be its day . . ." Said another retailer, "His salability is very limited. He's not been as creative a force recently as he was in the early seventies." Privately, John

Fairchild agreed. "He started to get repetitious. He didn't do anything new."

The same month that Beatrice bought Esmark, Carl Epstein fired the first shot in what would turn into a full-fledged war with Halston. Representatives from Penney's advertising departments were trying to get Halston to approve an advertising campaign, and Halston was having none of it; it was the wrong look and the wrong models and the wrong photographer, and everybody at Penney was just incompetent. "There were convoluted approval forms (for the advertising), and Halston didn't want to deal with it," said Ridge, "so Carl approved it and sent it back."

Halston was furious. No one, *no one,* had ever *dared* to countermand his orders before. He demanded Epstein's presence in his Olympian office and read him the riot act. But Epstein had no apologies. He told Halston that the exigencies of the situation demanded that the advertising be approved, and that if Halston fell lax in his responsibilities in the future, the same thing would happen. Now the full wrath of the J.E. temper was unleashed, and according to one observer, the walls shook. "He called Carl every slimy anti-Semitic name and made every nasty comment that you could possibly think of," said Ridge. Halston had picked up the gauntlet, but now Epstein's ego had been wounded as much as Halston's, and there developed an unspoken subtext between them concerning besmirched honor.

Halston didn't seem to realize how offensive his anti-Semitism was. He even said to Lewin, "Epstein is something of a kike."

Lewin blanched and replied, "That word is not in my vocabulary."

Halston didn't seem to understand. "Isn't that what you call those kind of people?" he asked.

"Not around me, it isn't," Lewin said.

Another major contretemps with Carl Epstein arose over a new "master licensing agreement" with a large Mexican manufacturer. An extraordinarily lucrative offer had been made to Halston Enterprises for the complete distribution of all Halston products to be manufactured and sold in Mexico. Precious little extra work would have been required of Halston, and Epstein was projecting a possible $30 million income from the project if it went as well as expected. Reportedly, Halston wanted nothing to do with the Mexicans because he did not care for certain of the principals involved. Halston told Epstein to cancel the deal, and he complained to Joel Smilow about it at International Playtex. Allegedly, Smilow called Epstein and told him Halston had complained behind his back, and now it was Epstein's turn to be furious. "He called Halston in on the carpet," said a Playtex employee, "and warned him not to go over his head again, that it wouldn't work, that no matter what Halston pulled, business was going on as usual." Halston stormed out of the Olympic Tower and went home for the day, while the Mexican contracts were signed as planned.

Still, Carl Epstein, Ridge, and Patricia Alexander struggled to get the Halston III JCPenney line out for summer of 1984. "The ultimate corporate imperative," said one executive, "was not to go to court with JCPenney for nonperformance." But now Halston seemed to tune out altogether, and whether it had to do with spite or fury or because he was too incapacitated to work, he fell months behind in his deadlines. "With finally getting the fall line out I thought we'd go right into resort," said Ridge. "Well, I was wrong. It was as if H turned off after that. It took him weeks before he started even thinking about the resort line. Halston thought that just like all the other licensees, if he ignored them, Penney would just go away. That was a big mistake. Penney was a different animal than all the other licensees."

In the heat of the summer, events began to accelerate. That June, Epstein called a meeting at 9:30 on a Monday morning in the conference room with Halston, Ridge, Alexander, and Don Friese from Halston Originals. As a matter of routine, every head of every division of the company had to present a yearly business plan, and Epstein was beholden to enlist Halston's help in developing the plan. No one was sure if Halston would show up at such an early hour on a Monday morning, but he was there and seemed to be clear as a bell. At the meeting Epstein presented Halston with three strategic choices: Epstein's so-called Action Plan, in which Halston would agree to give up varying degrees of control. Halston listened, the color rising in his face, and then excused himself. Epstein suggested Halston take a week to think about it and scheduled a meeting for the following Monday morning. Halston never showed up for the meeting. Instead, he wrote a letter to Hercules Sotos at Playtex saying that he was unable to collaborate any further with Carl Epstein and demanding, in effect, that he be removed. The letter was ignored.

On July 24 Halston came in from Montauk to attend a 2:30 P.M. meeting at the Olympic Tower with Malcolm Lewin, Joel Smilow, and Playtex General Council Joel Coleman about the future of the company. The meeting took place around Halston's lacquered red table, and supposedly the first thing that Smilow did when he sat down at the table was to push aside Halston's white orchids and say, "I need to see you better." From that moment on, Halston was ready to strangle him. As the meeting proceeded, Halston was given several alternatives, similar to the ones Epstein had already outlined. In substance, the choices were: they could sell off Halston Enterprises to somebody Halston approved of, namely Linda Wachner, who was then president of Factor; or, Halston would have a limited involvement with Halston Enterprises, he would continue to collect his salary, but they would hire as many designers as they wanted to do the Penney line whether Halston approved of it or not; or he could have no involvement at all and they would do the Penney line themselves and shut down Halston Originals and his Made to Order operations.

Halston told them to sell it to Linda Wachner. Although

there is mixed opinion among those close to Halston about whether or not he really liked Wachner, he felt he would have some control over her. She was a tough but savvy business executive who understood Halston's personal needs and peccadilloes and had a flair for the glamorous and dramatic herself. "She came from the same school of management as Halston," said Walter Bregman. That wasn't to say he couldn't be just as mean to her as to anyone else. Once, before car phones were ubiquitous, Wachner had her limousine driver pull over to the side of the road so she could call Halston. When Halston learned from his secretary that Wachner was calling him from a phone booth, he said, "Tell her to call back in twenty minutes," and then laughed. In any event, Wachner was Halston's choice for his new owner.

The following day, July 25, Linda Wachner tried to buy Max Factor and Halston from Playtex for $270 million. It looked as though this deal would go through, but then forty-eight hours later, without warning Halston, Smilow rejected Wachner's bid for reasons that have never been publicly explained. Bregman claims the credit terms were not strong enough, and Wachner subsequently resigned her position at Max Factor a month later. Whatever the reasons for rejecting Wachner's offer, Halston felt miserable that the deal had fallen through and he was still under Smilow's thumb. Somehow he blamed himself for messing up the deal. According to Lewin, it was at this point that Halston's optimism about finding a solution to his problems was crushed.

The same day Wachner's offer was rejected, a meeting was called in the Olympic Tower among Epstein, Alexander, and Halston, reportedly to discuss and approve forthcoming advertising campaigns. Allegedly, Epstein wanted to discuss finances, not advertising, and Halston consistently refused to be drawn into such a conversation. The meeting culminated in Epstein's slamming a set of accounting books down on the desk in front of Halston, which caused everyone to jump an inch out of their chairs. On July 27, Halston wrote to Smilow and said that he was accepting his offer to take a few weeks off, and he headed out to Montauk.

Halston's favorite niece, Lesley Frowick, the eldest daughter of his brother Robert, had moved to New York to get into the fashion business and Halston had given her a job as an assistant. While Halston was "vacationing," Epstein suggested that because Lesley Frowick might be uncomfortable at the Tower without him there that she seek a leave of absence without pay. Subsequently, when she returned to the office one day unannounced, Carl Epstein challenged her presence there. A tense scene ensued in the waiting room in which Epstein said that Lesley should either come into his office to discuss her future employment with the company or he would consider her insubordinate and that she should resign. Reportedly, Lesley Frowick said that Epstein fired her for insubordination.

By the first weeks of August, with Halston isolated out in Montauk, word raced through Wall Street and Seventh Avenue that Halston had been forced out of his own company. "Rumors about Halston were flying fast and furious last week," *Women's Wear* said, and then went on to quote several of them, including "Halston is out." They also quoted a "friend" saying, "He's just gone away for a rest. Halston needed a rest." Another anonymous source said that "they even wanted him to move out of the Olympic Tower," and yet someone else said that Halston would remain with the company, but only as a figurehead. "They're going to bring in another designer to do the collections."

When contacted at the Montauk compound by reporters, Halston was irate to learn he was the scandal of Seventh Avenue. "Is that what they're saying?" he demanded. "Well its not true, no way." As for rumors that he was "leaving" his own company: "I have no plans for that," he said, "none at all, but I also don't have a crystal ball." And as for the stories about screaming fights with his new bosses at Beatrice, Halston had no comment.

In New York, Epstein dismissed the reports of trouble at the Olympic Tower as "sheer nonsense."

On Tuesday, August 21, John David Ridge "temporarily" assumed Halston's responsibilities as designer of the JCPenney line. Ridge also finished the resort collection for Halston Originals, and Don Friese put it into production. On the same day, D. D. Ryan and Bill Dugan "resigned" from Halston Enterprises.

By now, the Penney executives were furious that nobody at Playtex seemed to be able to control the situation up at the Olympic Tower. Penney was paying nearly $3 million a year for Halston's services, and clearly it was not Halston who was designing the Penney line. The sales of the line were bottoming out and Penney had invested tens of millions of dollars in the building of in-store Halston boutiques and a national advertising campaign. Now Lewin was casting aspersions that perhaps allowing John David Ridge to design the Penney line, and then advertise it as Halston merchandise, not only broke the truth-in-advertising laws, but was outright fraud. Then came an ultimatum. "The Penney people came to Playtex," said Ridge, "and told them, 'We sell millions of dollars worth of your bras and girdles a year, and we will not buy from you anymore unless you fix this problem with Halston.'"

That summer, Beatrice Foods had its own announcement to make: Joel E. Smilow was leaving International Playtex after a transition period. Smilow himself was not immune to the politics of big business, and his presence wasn't as appreciated by James Granger as it had been by his mentor, James Kelly. Smilow's position would be filled by Walter Bregman, and a man named Frank Grzelecki from outside the company was the named new divisional executive vice president. Hercules Sotos was now named president of International Playtex. By the end of the summer, Halston would have three parent companies in just over a year, three chief executive officers, four divisional vice presidents; his fragrance had four presidents, and Max Factor, also four presidents.

Ever mindful of avoiding a lawsuit for breach of contract with Penney, or worse, losing their business, Wally Bregman and Playtex's general counsel, Joel Coleman, tried to come to some compromise with Lewin and Halston. "Halston's personal and physical skill was diminished," said Bregman, "but we cared about the perfume, and we knew it would get sucked off the counter if Halston disappeared, so we tried to make a deal." Bregman remembered Halston's curious habit during negotiations of leaving the room every half hour or so. "He always wore black," said Bregman, "and we'd be having a progressive conversation and then he would leave the room and come back in three or four minutes with white stuff over his black turtleneck. Suddenly he would have a huge personality shift. I guess I was naive as to what was going on."

In late September, after a series of heated but determined negotiations, they were able to strike a remarkable deal—remarkable mostly because of its seeming generosity on Bregman and Playtex's part. In short, Playtex reportedly had agreed to split the company with Halston. Playtex was getting the profitable parts—the fragrance and the Penney license, but Halston was getting back the parts he could rebuild—his ready-to-wear company and his couture line. He could manufacture anything he wanted to under any other name except Halston, and if he wanted to use the Halston name, Playtex was perfectly willing to license his own name to him. To satisfy the Penney deal, Halston would remain chief designer in name, although he wouldn't stop them from hiring little designers to put out the line. Probably the whole Penney operation would be moved away from Halston into another location altogether.

The very next day, Tuesday, October 2, with the plan only vaguely outlined in what Halston said was a "letter of intent," Halston and Lewin were accused of leaking the deal to *Women's*

Wear Daily. The news was trumpeted with front-page headlines and a memorable centerfold-sized photograph of Halston inside, a little worn-looking but still lanky and handsome in his light tan Ultrasuede jacket giving the V-for-victory sign to the camera at the Olympic Tower, triumphant at last. "I think it's a rebirth," said Halston. "It's an upbeat, happy sort of thing. It's a new frontier." He also vehemently denied that Ridge would be designing the Penney line for him. "He's in charge of the workroom," Halston said. "He may have done some things while I was away, but I didn't look at them." Halston also claimed that the new deal allowed him to use his name "for any kind of clothing above the Penney price points," and that "the whole body is open to me, accessories, furs, loungewear, you name it."

Then suddenly something went wrong. First of all, Smilow, sitting out his last few months with the company, was affronted that the news had appeared in the press before it was a "done deal." In fact, when they tried to confirm it, Smilow said that the terms of the deal are "very personal and private considerations. It would not be appropriate for me to comment." Lewin denies that he and Halston leaked the story and claimed that Playtex already had drawn up a press release about it. Also, the deal that Halston had outlined to *Women's Wear* wasn't exactly the same deal that Playtex thought they had made. According to one insider, the trouble was that "[Halston and Lewin] made a deal and then they announced it in the press, and then they went back and they wanted more."

Mike Pellegrino agreed: "The next day I understand Halston came back and wanted more. Then he got it—a percentage of the licensing business, which wasn't part of the discussion initially. Then he wanted to buy his dress business back and they were willing to negotiate on that, then all of a sudden the story changed to more the next day."

"They kept moving the goal post," said Walter Bregman. "Even Lewin said to me, 'At this point, fellows, even I can't tell you when a deal is a deal.' "

Lewin says this is not true. "The structure was set, but there were continuing negotiations about peripheral items, issues about insurance, and some separate issues of fringe benefits, about parity with some of the presidents of other divisions." Lewin and Halston reasoned, for instance, that since other division presidents had full-time use of a limousine, why not Halston? Lewin claims that the other side was "torturing" Halston with some of the demands. For example, they allegedly were demanding that Halston agree not to appear in any "I Love New York" commercials because Beatrice was a well-known Chicago-based company. But the major reason why Lewin claims the deal fell apart was that the more they looked into it the more it became clear to them that the company had been so stripped of its physical plant and key employees that it would take a huge amount of money and a long time to build it back. In effect, they claimed that Playtex had destroyed the value of the firm. Naturally, this claim is hotly contested by the other side, who felt the company was leaner but more efficient and likely to be more profitable in the future.

In the meantime, Halston had returned to the Olympic Tower and was making life miserable for all the "traitors" who were helping Ridge and Epstein get out the Penney line, screaming in the hallways and throwing bolts of fabric around. Many thought his behavior was more pitiful than frightening, because he was clearly so tormented at the idea of losing control. It was his *baby* they had taken away. It was his *name* they were polluting with the designs of a lesser talent. And they seemed to enjoy watching him suffer so. Yet it was his own fault. He had painted himself into a corner. He had badly miscalculated his position and power, and the situation he found himself in was much of his own doing. Mercifully, it was decided that the Penney design team would move out of the Olympic Tower and away from Halston, temporarily to the 550 Seventh Avenue offices of Halston Originals, and everyone involved began to pack things in corrugated boxes and cardboard file cabinets. The moving operations tormented Halston even more. He began to spend hours every day picking through each box to discover some sketch or sample and scream, "They're stealing from me!"

It was at this point that Halston also had a major falling-out with perhaps his last trusted friend at the company, Patricia Alexander. Halston asked Alexander to publicly declare her allegiance to him and not go off with the Penney design team. In effect, by so doing, she would be putting her job in jeopardy without any guarantee that Halston would ever solve his entanglements with Playtex. Alexander, a divorced mother of two with her own considerations, turned Halston down in as gentle and polite terms as she could muster. Still, Halston went off the deep end with her. He launched into a four-star J.E. temper tantrum, attacking her loyalty and friendship and ethics. From that moment on, Halston told her, he considered Alexander nothing more than another "traitor." Apparently he felt so deeply betrayed by her that he continued to harangue her at home, sometimes calling her as late as 4 A.M. to tell her off bitterly.

Finally, there seemed to be a light at the end of the tunnel for Halston. A meeting was held on the night of October 12 at Halston's office in the Olympic Tower attended by Hercules Sotos, Wally Bregman, Nick Lewin, and Howard Chase. At this meeting a proposal was discussed that was so sweet, Halston couldn't possibly refuse. There was to be a new consulting agreement under the terms of which Halston would receive $750,000 a year plus 6 percent of all profits. Penney was going to pay $375,000 of his salary and Playtex $375,000. In return for the $750,000, he would only have to give 10 days a year of his time to Penney, and 10 days a year to Playtex. The other 345 days he could do as he pleased. Left unsaid was: Just get out of our hair.

Carl Epstein was purposely excluded from the meeting, as were Ridge and Alexander, to help keep Halston calm. While the meeting was going on, Epstein waited in his own office for the results. As the hour grew late, Epstein made himself a cup of coffee and discovered he was out of milk. He decided to venture over to Halston's side of the offices to see if there was milk in the kitchen refrigerator. But when Epstein got to the door of the south wing, somehow his key wouldn't work in the lock. He didn't have to look far to discover a building locksmith methodically going from door to door and changing the locks to expensive locks from France, with keys that were next to impossible to duplicate. When Epstein demanded to know who had told him to change the locks, the locksmith said, "Mr. Halston."

Epstein burst into the meeting in Halston's office. "What is the meaning of this?" he demanded loudly. Everyone turned to look at him. He pointed at Halston and growled, "How dare you change the locks to Beatrice property?" Lewin was speechless—he had no idea his client was going to change the locks. The meeting erupted into chaos and within minutes it was over, and so was the wonderful deal Bregman had offered. "It was clear that Halston was too unstable and unable to cope to make a deal," said Bregman.

The next morning, Epstein sent home all the employees when they arrived at the office. He phoned John Ridge and Patricia Alexander and told them to meet him at the Playtex headquarters in Stamford, Connecticut, for a showdown, not only with Malcolm Lewin, but with the Playtex executives as well; clearly, business could not be conducted up at the Olympic Tower under the present situation, and there had to be some sort of conclusion. This meeting turned into a marathon, which ran so late into the night it was eventually moved to the Playtex-owned offices of Almay in Manhattan. According to Ridge, he and Alexander simply told everyone that they found it impossible to work with Halston, and they would not. Either he had to go or they had to go. According to Lewin, Ridge and Alexander had "a two-hour tantrum, literally pounding the table and stamping their feet because they wanted Halston out."

Lewin told Herc Sotos, "Make your decision. Either put us

back in control of things or Halston is out and we'll conclude you locked him out."

He was locked out.

The following Monday, October 15, Halston appeared at the Olympic Tower with his niece, Lesley Frowick, and Bill Dugan and D. D. Ryan. They arranged for Halston's personal things to be picked up by a moving van and took with them whatever small possessions they could carry. "Everyone lined up to say good-bye," said one employee. "All the people from the work-room came out and his few loyal friends. There were tears as he went out the door for the last time. Viola and D. D. Ryan and Lesley cried. It was pathetic."

NOW IT WAS Halston who had been banished. The next time he wanted to design costumes for a Martha Graham ballet, he had to rent a loft and hire his own seamstresses. Still, he continued to collect a million dollars a year under the terms of his employ-ment contract, which didn't run out for three more years. The key to continuing to receive this salary was that he technically remain "willing and able" to work, and that it was the company who was stopping him from doing so. Naturally, Playtex would have loved to find an excuse to stop paying Halston a million dollars a year for doing nothing, and Halston's willingness to work was put to the test on several occasions. One of these times was an elaborate launch party planned for the Mexican licensing deal that he hadn't wanted to sign, the *Organización Mine, SA,* headed by Jaime Michan and Alfonso Nehmad. Scheduled for late October of 1984, just shortly after the "lock-out," the party was to be attended by Mexican diplomats and business executives and it was imperative that the Mexicans not realize what bad trouble the company was in. Halston was informed by Epstein that he was expected to attend. "He didn't want to go," remembered Lewin, "but we counseled him not to do anything to give them an opportunity to claim that he was in breach of his agreement. That was a constant refrain throughout the life of his agreement."

Halston attended, all right, looking more like a litigious businessman than a glamorous designer. He arrived dressed in a three-piece navy blue suit with a red tie, flanked on either side by his lawyer Malcolm Lewin and his partner Howard Chase, a scene that Halston later dubbed "Snow White and the two dwarfs." Trailing not far behind them was Halston's houseboy, Mohammed Soumaya, who was introduced as Halston's bodyguard and the former bodyguard for the king of Morocco. When Halston was asked why he found it necessary to come to his own showroom with both legal and physical protection, he smiled drolly and said, "I always travel with them. It's real fun. I'll keep doing it. I was a little apprehensive, but I happen to like these guys." As for Mohammed, Halston said, "I bring him everywhere."

The tension was so thick, the air seemed to crackle. Halston refused to participate actively in the event and stood quietly at the side of the room while Epstein did his very best to act as though nothing terrible was happening. The Mexican VIP's and diplomats politely came to where Halston stood to chat while Halston remained imperious and distant. When it came time to reenact the contract signing for the cameras, Halston declined and Epstein stood in for him. It was a true Mexican standoff.

In late November and early December 1984, there were several "sales" of dresses, blouses, accessories, and samples to fashion industry insiders. Dress stock was "wiped out" according to Lewin, for "a few bucks." Also sold were originals of unfinished goods and Penney merchandise and samples for "a pittance." Halston gowns brought a paltry $25 each. Halston attended the sale with Malcolm Lewin. When he saw the racks and racks of dresses," said Lewin, "It was the closest I ever saw him that I thought maybe he had tears in his eyes. He walked over to me and I don't know if he was talking to me or himself, but he said, 'These are all the dresses I did for Liza.' " Lewin told him to take the dresses, all of them, whatever he wanted, and Halston began to scoop up handfuls of them like a child let loose in a toy store. It was a pitiful moment.

When Epstein saw what Halston was doing, he rushed over to Lewin and said, "You know, you've got to pay for those dresses."

Lewin snarled, "Send me a fucking bill."

Epstein did, too, and Lewin challenged him to sue to try to collect on it.

In January 1985, the Halston Originals showroom at 555 Seventh Avenue was dismantled. Whatever fixtures and furnishings that hadn't already been carted away were being sold to the next tenant, a newcomer in the fashion business named Donna Karan. Halston, although he never went to the Seventh Avenue offices, decided he might want to keep certain sentimental things, and he and Lewin went to 555 Seventh Avenue together to see what was left. When they got there Lewin noticed several television monitors and a stack of half a dozen videotapes of various fashion shows of Halston Originals through the years. Lewin said to Epstein, "You promised you would give these tapes to Halston.' "

Epstein said, "They're duplicates and I'm selling them."

Lewin said, "What do you mean, you're selling them? These are Halston's fashion shows. You *can't* sell them."

"I'm *erasing* them," Epstein said, "and I'll get a couple of bucks for the blanks from Donna Karan."

Of all the many slights Halston felt he had to endure, the most aggravating for him was his inability to design dresses for Anjelica Huston and Geraldine Page to wear to the 1985 Academy Awards presentations. Anjelica Huston had been nominated as Best Supporting Actress for *Prizzi's Honor,* and Geraldine Page for Best Actress for her role in *The Trip to Bountiful.* Halston had been asked by both actresses to design gowns for them for the ceremony, which would be seen by one billion people in eighty-eight countries around the world. Coincidentally, JCPenney was one of the broadcast's many sponsors, and it would be a feather in their cap as well if Halston designed the gowns.

But Halston's presence was not desired up at the Olympic Tower. Epstein felt it would be disruptive suddenly to have him arrive and design two gowns. He wrote to Lewin and said, in essence, that if Halston wanted to design dresses for Huston and Page, Halston Enterprises Incorporated would be delighted to donate the fabric. But they wouldn't be put out in any way or incur any further expenses. And he certainly wasn't welcome up at the Olympic Tower; he'd have to find his own workroom and seamstresses. And, Epstein added, of course the company owned the rights to the designs, not Halston.

Halston never designed the gowns for the two actresses, and on March 26, 1986, both Geraldine Page and Anjelica Huston won the Oscar in their respective categories. Had they both been wearing Halston gowns, Halston Enterprises Incorporated, JCPenney, and Beatrice would have scored a major publicity coup. And Halston would have received a much-needed boost to his battered confidence and spirit.

If Halston was going to sue Playtex and Beatrice to get his name back, or clear the air, or end the torture, this was the moment. But Halston knew what such a step would entail. His adversaries would truck out witnesses about his drug use, they would testify about Victor Hugo . . . The detritus of his life would be paraded in a courtroom, and his name and his fragrance would be destroyed forever. No, there had to be a negotiated settlement. "There ain't too many winners in litigation," said Lewin, "and Halston did not think the courtroom was a forum in which he should air his problems."

Halston would live the rest of his life in a self-imposed exile, an Elba of his own creation. The man who was only as good as the people he dressed ended up not dressing anyone.

"THE FUTURE WILL BE
FASCINATING TO DESIGN.
I LIKE TO BE OUT WHERE THE
ACTION IS. I DON'T WANT TO
BE SITTING BACK ON PAST GLORIES.
I WANT TOMORROW'S GLORIES...
I WANT IT ALL."

Halston, 1980

I n late summer of 1985, Halston was hospitalized at the Memorial Sloan-Kettering Cancer Center in Manhattan where he was successfully operated on for a malignancy of the lower gastrointestinal tract. With his usual sense of propriety, Halston believed that it was unseemly for his health problems to be discussed in public or in the press. So, other than Nick Lewin, he did not tell any friends or business associates that he was sick. The only family member who knew of his illness at the time was Lesley Frowick, who still lived in New York. She visited Halston in the hospital every day and brought picnic lunches, complete with plastic ants, to cheer him up. "He was such an utterly private person," said Bob Frowick. "He never wanted anybody to know. We had a history of cancer in the family, colon cancer and liver cancer, and he didn't want any of that to come out in public. He wanted to drop out of sight for a while, take care of it, and come back. Essentially that's what he did."

Halston continued to deny he had been ill, even long after he had been discharged from the hospital and recovered. Naturally, denying his illness made the whole thing sound suspicious, and the nature of what was wrong with him was the subject of much conjecture at the Olympic Tower and at International Playtex—did Halston have AIDS? The answer was, at the time, no. When Nick Lewin, on a visit to Halston in the hospital, brought up the specter of AIDS, Halston's response was *"God forbid."* However, colon cancer was a serious enough problem that "scared the hell out of him," according to Lewin. Halston made a new will and named his brother Bob as executor. The cancer took a physical as well as psychological toll. Halston's younger brother, Don, remembered being shocked at how much weight Halston had lost when he next saw him. Eventually, up at the Olympic Tower, Carl Epstein learned the true reason for Halston's hospitalization when copies of Halston's health insurance claims were filed through the office, where his policy was paid by Halston Enterprises, Inc. Halston soon recovered, however, and the issue of his health faded into the background as he had hoped it would.

From the time he was deposed from his throne at the Olympic Tower, Halston began to spend more time at the Montauk compound that he rented from Andy Warhol. Halston liked the beauty and isolation of Montauk so much that he had bought nearly 100 acres of land in partnership with the model Lauren Hutton as an investment. The property, located between the Warhol compound and Dick Cavett's house to the east, was a wooded wonderland with bluffs overlooking the Atlantic. But there were also insurmountable problems with subdivision rights and town approvals, and there wasn't even an access road to the property—so it didn't look as though Halston would be building his dream house soon.

It wouldn't have been soon enough for Andy Warhol, who was in a perpetual state of anxiety over collecting the $40,000-a-year rent from Halston, especially since he had been told that he could probably get $80,000 for the house on the open market. Warhol complained frequently that Halston's rent was just barely covering the mortgage. But he never complained to Halston himself; it wasn't Warhol's style to confront anyone about money. At Halston's fifty-second birthday party that year at 101, Halston handed Warhol a piece of paper folded in the shape of a boat, which Warhol overeagerly assumed was the rent check. Warhol felt so guilty that he had not brought Halston a birthday gift that he gave Halston (and Victor, and Lesley Frowick) a piece of his stationery as a gift that said "IOU One Art," redeemable for an object of Andy's choosing at a later date. Warhol was stung when he got home and opened up the piece of paper Halston had given him to discover it wasn't the rent check but just a piece of paper that said "Happy Birthday" on it.

Warhol now felt more intimidated by Halston than ever. Sam Bolton, who worked with Warhol for five years and was Andy's frequent companion, said, "After the drugs took hold of Halston, Andy was very scared of him. He knew Halston could turn on him in a second." Bolton remembered going to 101 to see Halston with Warhol around this time, and Halston seemed almost stuporous as he pulled an amber gram bottle of cocaine from his jacket pocket and blithely passed it around the room for everyone to partake. Halston was also increasingly vituperative and vitriolic about his real and imagined enemies, and Warhol lived in fear that one day he would unintentionally say or do something to offend Halston. However, this didn't stop Warhol from his continued support and encouragement of Victor Hugo's shenanigans. By now, Warhol was one of Victor Hugo's last surviving patrons. Most of Halston's friends, including Bianca Jagger and Liza Minnelli, were disgusted and offended by Victor's continued abuse of Halston. Over the years Victor had lived many different places in between stints at 101, including a period at the Barbizon Hotel, which rented furnished apartments. Halston was angry with Victor again because he had discovered his Elsa Peretti silver candlesticks missing from 101, and Halston was convinced Victor had taken them and sold them for cash. Halston was about to change the locks at 101 when Victor calmed him down and said he had "just borrowed" the Peretti candlesticks and that they were in the Barbizon safe where he had left them as his security deposit.

Victor was still getting large amounts of money from Halston at various intervals, and when the flow was cut off, things invariably got nasty. On one occasion in Montauk, Victor and Halston had an argument during which Victor was so threatening that he chased Halston out of the Montauk house. Halston took a limousine back to New York and hired three bodyguards to protect himself and 101 from Victor until his rage blew over. When all else failed in terms of extracting money from Halston, Victor would resort to threatening to "ruin" Halston by exposing him in the press. Victor tried on several occasions to sell the story of his life with Halston (and Andy Warhol) to various sources, including R. Couri Hay, who wrote a gossip column for the *National Enquirer*. At one point, Victor even approached Halston's nemesis, Carl Epstein, and offered to testify or give evidence against Halston in Playtex's behalf in case of an eventual lawsuit in return for $10,000 cash. Victor Hugo also contacted the author of this book and asked to collaborate on a tell-all biography about Halston. At the same time, Victor was represented by an attorney who felt that he had a serious claim for a "palimony" suit against Halston. Some saw this as nothing more than extortion. The lawsuit never came about, in part because Halston offered Victor a cash settlement to avoid public embarrassment. In late 1985 a secret agreement was signed between Halston and Victor Hugo according to which neither party was allowed to talk about the terms, or even acknowledge the existence of the contract. Part of the agreement was that certain Warhol paintings and other objects were declared to be the personal possessions of Victor Hugo. Also, a considerable sum of money was paid to Hugo over a term of several years, said to be well into six figures. In return, Hugo was not to sell information about Halston, give interviews about Halston, or even visit him. He had been banished.

Alas, Victor Hugo ignored all three of these terms, and, in

fact, Halston encouraged him to ignore them. Within a few months, the money was gone, all seemed forgiven, and Victor was back in Halston's good graces. Everyone who cared about Halston was infuriated that he would forgive Victor yet again. But it was obvious that there was something that Victor supplied to Halston, some need he fulfilled, that gave Victor tremendous power over him. Besides, Halston liked the abuse.

While Victor filled the emotional abyss in Halston's life, the physical was being taken care of by Robert Rogers, an unassuming black man of medium height and build in his late twenties who was one of Manhattan's most successful male prostitutes. Originally from Gainesville, Florida, Rogers held a day job with the New York State Unemployment Insurance office. By night, Rogers was known as "Cuelar" and made $150 an hour with a call boy service named the Black Kings, which specialized in black men. Cuelar had achieved some modicum of fame as the model for a perennially popular line of greeting cards sold in adult bookstores and sex shops which bore the tag line, "Everything you ever heard about black men . . . is true!" As Cuelar's reputation as a courtesan grew, he opened his own call service and began advertising in two gay publications, the *Advocate* and the *New York Native*.

"Halston was very into black guys," said Rogers. "If he was prejudiced, he didn't discriminate when it came to sex. He had a strong sexual appetite, and he started giving me money without me even asking, two hundred or two hundred and fifty dollars." Cuelar says he saw Halston personally sixty or seventy times, but as the years went by, Halston wanted to up the ante. "He asked me if I knew of anybody else who was like me, a nice black guy who's well endowed. And I said I did. I sent that guy to him and he started to see him, at least once a week, sometimes twice a week. The guy would get one hundred dollars and I'd get fifty dollars for my referral. Between 1980 to 1983 I sent him many, many guys. Sometimes during the week, usually on a Wednesday, I'd go see him myself, but only for about an hour or so—he had a very tight schedule."

Halston's ultimate fantasy, according to Cuelar, was to have sex with a heterosexual black man, a blue-collar worker, if possible right off the street, and he was willing to pay dearly for it. Cuelar claimed to have waited at the 125th Street train station in Harlem and picked men out of the crowd at random whom he thought would be amenable to the suggestion that they earn up to $500 for performing a carnal act with a wealthy white man. Cuelar claimed it was surprising how many takers he could find at a subway station.

"I would say that Halston was eccentric," said Cuelar. "When you entered his place he would buzz you in, but he would be upstairs on the top floor and he would call from upstairs and say, 'Have a seat, I'll be right down.' He would come down always all in black and these silver clogs. He would descend the stairs very slowly and say, 'Welcome, would you like a drink?' A lot of guys couldn't hold a conversation, but Halston would just talk about current events, sports, and he would ask them questions about themselves. Then he would say, 'Would you like to go upstairs?' You were never in bed more than ten minutes. Several times we were in the bedroom watching TV and Elizabeth Taylor called for Halston's advice about her love life. I remember one time she was on the phone and there was a Burger King commercial on TV, and Halston's advice to Elizabeth Taylor was, 'Have it your way.' "

One night Cuelar got a call for his services from a man with a thick accent who gave his address 101 East Sixty-third Street. "I was shocked when he gave me the address. I said 'What's going on here?' It turned out it was Victor Hugo and he had heard about me from Halston. Halston was away in Montauk, so I went over there. Victor was always coked out of his head, so he wasn't interested too much in sex. He said, 'Don't tell Halston that we know each other.' I guess he had his reasons. I don't think Halston ever knew."

Cuelar did not remember Halston as being overly concerned about Acquired Immune Deficiency Syndrome, which had been identified as a sexually communicable disease by 1981.

"Nobody knew too much about it," said Cuelar, "and Halston didn't seem to be too concerned. But he wouldn't want to hurt anybody. He was a kind man who always wanted to help somebody. He helped a lot of people, there's no question about it. I don't think he had a mean streak in his body. I always worried about him because nobody was ever in the house with him to my knowledge. It was dangerous, I think. I used to wonder about that because he used to call up other escort services and they would send street guys over, and I was always curious if there was a bodyguard or somebody in the house in case somebody tried to rob him or hurt him. It was very, very dangerous for him to be in the situation that he was in."

IN THE SPRING OF 1986 a fresh whirlwind of business events blew into Halston's life that gave him "psychological whiplash," according to his brother Bob. In April Kohlberg Kravis Roberts, still lurking one step away in their pursuit of Beatrice, formed a company with investors called BCI Holdings and bought Beatrice in a headline-making leveraged buy-out deal for $6.2 billion, lumbering the company with a phenomenal $2.2 billion debt. KKR got a reported $45 million in fees for the deal, on which they were advised by none other than Donald P. Kelly, the former head of Beatrice. Now KKR brought Kelly back in as Beatrice's new chief executive, not so much to administer the business as to sell off pieces so that they could lower the debt. The real rub for Halston was not just that Kelly was back, but that he brought with him Halston's old *bête noire,* Joel E. Smilow, as head of International Playtex. But before this terrible news could even sink in, at the beginning of August 1986, Beatrice and Donald P. Kelly announced that an investment group lead by Joel Smilow was buying International Playtex from Beatrice for $1.25 billion. Simultaneously, Smilow was making a deal to sell Factor, Almay, and Halston to the Revlon Group, Inc., for $375 million. When the dust finally settled, in December 1986, Halston's fate rested in the hands of a completely new cast of characters headed by a man named Ronald O. Perelman.

Ron Perelman, corporate raider, so-called "greenmailer," and Revlon's chief executive officer, seemed an unlikely candidate to snatch Halston out of his business limbo. Yet of all the many executives who had held Halston's fate in their hands, Ron Perelman came the closest. Perelman was a paradox. He was an observing Jew who kept a strictly kosher household and preferred that pork products not be served at Revlon events, but he dined at Le Cirque several times a week and was fairly knowledgeable about rock music. The scion of a Philadelphia family that owned a $300-million miniconglomerate called Belmont Industries, Perelman arrived in New York in 1978 with a lot of cash and burning ambition. Within only a dozen years, at age forty-six, he had made himself into the third-richest man in America, according to *Forbes* magazine, with an estimated $3 billion fortune.

Perelman also had a reputation as a hands-on manager who was partial to buying companies that he had some personal interest in, and his crazy-quilt holdings included along the way such diverse companies as the Consolidated Cigar Company, the manufacturers of Muriel Cigars (which he smoked); Technicolor, the company that put color in movies; Pantry Pride, the Fort Lauderdale food service company; and the world's largest producer of licorice extract. When Perelman gained control of Revlon in 1985 after a bitter, $1.83-billion takeover battle, Revlon was a behemoth, with 42,000 employees worldwide and $2.47 billion in assets which included a lot of health-care products. Perelman pared the company down, sold off most of the holdings in health care, and put the emphasis on beauty products. Profits soared. Almay became the industry leader in hypoallergenic cosmetics. Perelman's marketing expertise is much vaunted, and reportedly it was he who enlisted the aid of internationally known fashion photographer Richard Avedon to create the "Most Unforgettable" ad campaign which focused on celebrities. Indeed, it turned out that Perelman was something of a celebrity buff. He liked the limelight and stardom, and reportedly he was the one who handpicked *All My Children* star Susan Lucci to replace Joan Collins in Revlon's Scoundrel perfume ads.

Perelman's first wife divorced him after she discovered he was having an affair with a florist; she received their Park Avenue apartment and $10 million in the settlement. In 1985 Perelman married Claudia Cohen, the television personality and influential gossip columnist who was something of a celebrity maven herself. Their wedding reception was held at Steve Rubell's new nightclub, the Palladium, where the entertainment was provided by the Pointer Sisters. Claudia Cohen was also a chum of Steve Rubell's, and therefore she had more than a passing acquaintance with—and understanding of—Halston. Not since Halston had been owned by David Mahoney was there an executive in charge who could better appreciate Halston's style and drama and social importance than Ron Perelman and Claudia Cohen.

Halston's relationship with Revlon started off promisingly. "I like Halston as a man," said Ron Perelman. "I think he's a uniquely talented individual. It's a very difficult thing, trying to mesh an entrepreneurial designer into a corporate setting, but we want to." Added Sol Levine, then president of Revlon, "All the other companies bought Halston for other reasons. They wanted Wesson Oil, they wanted Avis. We acquired Halston because we want it."

According to one Revlon insider, this was "bullshit," and Perelman really bought the company because he wanted Max Factor. "The pill was Halston."

Whatever the true reason, as far as Perelman was concerned, it was a new day and he was ready to make a new deal. He had no allegiance to Carl Epstein or John David Ridge, and certainly they were expendable if it meant getting Halston back.

Nick Lewin began his negotiations with Revlon by making a personal plea to Perelman's right-hand man and legal counsel, Howard Gittes, who was vice chairman of Revlon. "You've got to help me," Lewin said. "You've got to be more of a shrink here than a lawyer. Halston is coming to the bargaining table with a lot of baggage. On the one hand, he knows that Revlon isn't responsible for his problems, on the other, he feels beat up." Lewin said that Gittes understood the situation, and that he and Perelman were sympathetic toward Halston's needs. At one of the first meetings at Perelman's Madison Avenue offices, Lewin mentioned that film and opera director Franco Zeffirelli had asked Halston to design the costumes for an opera and Perelman's face lit up. "Great!" Perelman said. "That would be a great thing for him to do. I'll get the check to you in the morning!" Perelman also said he was willing to consider almost any new arrangement between Halston and Revlon, and that he was even willing to start Halston up all over again, back in the Olympic Tower if he wished, or in a new location, and Halston even spent the day with one of Perelman's representatives scouting possible sites for a new salon which Perelman said Revlon would buy for Halston. In anticipation of coming to a deal with Revlon, Halston even formed a new company which he named RHF (he joked that his new company should be named "Frowick's Frocks").

"The Revlon guys, in common parlance," said Lewin, "were *mensches.* They were tough, but ready to deal. They said, 'Listen, we put our cash down and we don't look back.' They said that Halston wouldn't have to come in and pose for pictures for Penney and turn Halston's life into a dog-and-pony show. They respected him for not being a whore, and they said to tell him that his checks would be in the mail every month." Those checks would be for far less than he had been accustomed to—his yearly salary would drop to $250,000—but he would be free to do practically whatever else he wanted to. It was strictly a consulting deal. Plus, as a sweetener, along with several other perks, even if Halston died, certain moneys would be paid to a beneficiary for several years, in this case, Martha Graham. "Was it ever a sweet deal," said Lewin.

Then something happened between Halston and Ron and Claudia Perelman that made them uncomfortable about him. During the summer of 1987, the Perelmans invited Halston to their Lily Pond Lane beach "cottage," a huge oceanfront mansion along billionaires' row in East Hampton. Reportedly, Perelman and Halston got along so well that sometime during Halston's visit Perelman took Halston aside and said, "Listen, let's get rid of the lawyers and make a deal." Halston, encouraged, said he would see to it that they came to terms. Then, shortly thereafter, Halston insisted that the Perelmans come visit him at the Warhol compound out at Montauk. It was allegedly while they were out at Montauk that something transpired that turned the Perelmans off. The following Monday at his office, Perelman said he discovered that Halston was a "sleazeball," according to a former Revlon executive. Halston privately blamed Perelman's distaste on Steve Rubell, whom he called a "yenta" because he was allegedly carrying tales between Halston and Claudia Cohen. Whatever the reasons for Perelman's conclusion that Halston was a "sleazeball," relations between them soured. Halston went to Perelman's office on his own for a meeting and left rankled and disturbed. He claimed that at the outset of the meeting Perelman lit a big cigar, took his shoes off, and put his stockinged feet on his desk in Halston's face and said to him, "I hear you're a prima donna."

Still, the new contracts were reportedly only one or two paragraphs away from being signed when Halston told the syndicated gossip columnist Liz Smith about the pending deal and she ran a small item about it in her daily column. This not only infuriated Perelman, it also did not sit very well with Perelman's wife, Claudia, either, who was scooped on an announcement to which she felt some proprietary rights. To show their ire after this leak in Liz Smith's column, Perelman and his minions canceled twenty-six meetings with Halston and his attorneys.

Negotiations drifted. Meanwhile, the dueling with Carl Epstein continued long distance, and in June of 1987 Epstein held a fashion show at the Olympic Tower with clothes designed by John Ridge for the Japanese and Mexican licensees. ("Minus Halston, Revlon Puts on a Fashion Show," said *Women's Wear,* who did not review the clothing.) Halston watched from the sidelines as Ron Perelman began to revitalize Almay, creating a new market for hypoallergenic cosmetics with the company, which saw sales topping $100 million. Max Factor started introducing new lines as well, including a new line of clear mascara which became a best-seller and a line called California Fragrances, which blossomed into one of the healthiest fragrance lines in the business. As Halston's name disappeared from public view, his original fragrance sales began to fall sharply, and despite his objections, Revlon released a second woman's fragrance on the market, called Halston Couture. Halston detested everything about this new perfume, from the scent to the bottle to the packaging. The fragrance soon flopped, much to Halston's consternation and secret satisfaction. It felt like slow suicide.

THROUGH MUCH OF the second half of the 1980s, Halston was conspicuous by his absence on the New York scene. Months went by without anyone seeing or hearing from him. He made only rare public appearances. "There really isn't much to celebrate," he would say when people asked why he didn't go out anymore. "People are always asking, 'What happened?' 'How are you?' It can be very difficult. I have no answer." In February 1987 he appeared at the Metropolitan Club in Manhattan looking ruddy and fit in his black tie and dinner jacket for a dinner dance benefiting the Hereditary Disease Foundation held to launch a new perfume by the Italian fashion house of Krizia. At the party he ran into many of the society women who were his former customers and who hadn't seen him in years. Several of them stopped by his table to ask how he was feeling and congratulated him on how well he looked.

Halston seemed oddly discomfited. "I imagine they're saying how well I look because they heard these horrible stories and rumors about me," he said to his tablemates, which included the former president's granddaughter, Anne Eisenhower, as well as Kathleen Simon and newspaper columnist Richard Johnson.

"What kind of stories?" Anne Eisenhower asked.

"Stories . . . like that I'm doing heroin," Halston said, laughing. Everyone at the table laughed with him, but the laughter was strained.

That same February of 1987, Halston hired Lisa Zay, a secretary who had worked with him at the Olympic Tower, to come to 101 several days a week and help him with correspondence and keep his paperwork current. Zay, twenty-eight years old, worked out of the fourth floor at 101, and during the next two years, she said, "I never witnessed any sort of drug use. I heard the rumors, but personally, I have never seen any drug use . . . He was always okay, and he kept very busy. There were business details and dealing with his lawyers. He went to lunches and to the theater a couple of times with Liza Minnelli. He adored Martha Graham more than anyone, and often went to her rehearsals and just sat and watched." It was also in 1987 that Halston began a surface renovation of 101, including some painting and new carpeting.

Halston spent a great part of that year at the Warhol compound in Montauk. Victor Hugo, never far away for long, rented a house twenty minutes from Halston in East Hampton. Victor's modern rented house was a messy place filled with stacks of Warhols leaning up against the walls—paintings, drawings, and lithographs that Victor had obtained over the years. Although by now AIDS was a grim health reality and methods of transmission of the virus were well known, Victor's wild orgies and sex scenes continued unabated, sometimes with partners imported from Manhattan, about 100 miles away. Victor continued to meet with Halston as well, and every week or so he would bring checks for various amounts of money, signed by Halston, to the local gay bar and restaurant, the Swamp and Annex, to cash.

On February 22, 1987, Halston was shocked and deeply grieved to learn that Andy Warhol had died unexpectedly after routine gall bladder surgery at New York Hospital. Warhol had always been petrified of hospitals since he almost died in 1967 after having been shot by feminist Valerie Solanas at his Factory. The story insiders were telling was that he died of fright when he woke up in the hospital and his nurse had left the room. Whatever, for reasons that are still the subject of litigation, his heart gave out. It was a huge blow to Halston, for Warhol suddenly to be gone, so unexpectedly. But it was an even bigger shock when, shortly after Warhol's death, the artist's estate tried to raise the rent on the Montauk property. Halston didn't see why the rent should go up just because Warhol had died. In fact, according to one Warhol insider, Halston felt that with all the improvements and new furniture he had put into the compound, the rent should be lowered. But the pressure was on to double the rent, and Halston angrily abandoned the Montauk house in the spring of 1988, taking with him the furniture he had put in.

For Halston the summer of 1988 was the first time in over twenty years that he hadn't had a place on either Fire Island or Long Island. That summer he uncharacteristically traveled for five weeks in Europe. It was an easy, rambling trip, spent revisiting favorite places, spending some time with his brother, Bob, who was then the senior Foreign Service officer at the American Embassy in Brussels. Halston even managed a *petit rapprochement* with Elsa Peretti in Italy, and while he was visiting her, for laughs, they called Joe Eula and all three of them chatted on the phone together and gossiped, just as if it were yesterday.

While Halston was off in Europe that summer, his employment contract with Revlon quietly lapsed. Now he was no longer an employee of Halston Enterprises, Inc., or being paid $1 million a year. Up in the Olympic Tower, all the licenses were allowed to run out, including JCPenney. Halfhearted negotiations dragged on with Ron Perelman and Howard Gittes all through the winter of 1988. Finally, in May 1989, Gittes gave Nick Lewin a deadline: they had to have a new employment contract signed by the end of the month or the deal was off. "It was the weekend I had to go away for my daughter's graduation," said Lewin, "and I wrote to Gittes asking him to extend the deadline two more weeks. We recycled. Then it became June, and that's when the show took place."

"The show" was a "Halston" made-to-order fall and winter collection shown up at the Olympic Tower on June 25, 1989, and it outraged Halston. He had adjusted to the fact that Ridge was designing the Penney line and Halston Originals and the licensees, but to attempt to show a *couture* line that was the exclusive province of the *artiste* was unforgivable. The clear inference was that John David Ridge had now stepped into the master's shoes. "It's not like it's just some unknown designer they're copying," Halston fumed to *Newsweek* magazine. "You have a lot to live up to if you want to play Halston." As for his business problems, he said, "I can never get out of the name of Halston," he said. "It's who I am. [Revlon] can sell it tomorrow. To me, it's more personal." He went on to say, "I had the good fortune of having the most fashionable women in the world come to me. Together we changed the mood of fashion. That's not forgotten. When I design again, it will still be Halston, whatever I call it."

At the Olympic Tower, Carl Epstein told *Women's Wear Daily*, "We don't want to create the impression that anyone is coming in to replace Halston." Revlon's public-relations man, Dan Moriarity, added, "We want to let people know the house of Halston is alive and well. We hope he will rejoin us."

According to several Revlon employees, Perelman and Gittes didn't know that the made-to-order show was going to take place at the Olympic Tower, and they were sandbagged by Carl Epstein and John Ridge, who were allegedly planning to try to make Ridge into a star. According to insiders, Epstein and Ridge knew their own days with Halston Enterprises, Inc., were numbered, and they were trying to make best use of their time by launching Ridge on his own career. Sources close to Carl Epstein refute this story vehemently and claim they knew exactly what was going on at Revlon. Whatever the motivation for the "Halston by John David Ridge" show was, Halston announced that he would no longer consider signing contracts with Revlon. "They just weren't forthright with me," said Halston. "How could I trust them after that?" He even wrote Perelman a note saying that negotiations were off.

But by then, it was all just bluster and bluff on Halston's part anyway. He knew he would never sign the contracts. He knew he wouldn't live long enough to fulfill them.

SKYLAB IS FALLING

At the start, he was determined to fight it, to stay healthy until new treatments for AIDS could be found, to fight for every second left to him. When he saw he was losing the battle, however, he opted to die quietly and with dignity. This was the last great Halston show, done with class. He wanted no sympathy, no show of concern from friends. The last thing he would have tolerated was pity. He was better than brave, he was noble. When Liza saw how much weight he had lost and asked if he was sick, he said, "Nonsense!" and when Victor Hugo saw a telltale lesion on Halston's neck, he denied it was there and covered it with makeup. Rather than shatter his dignity, nobody challenged him. "He didn't want people to worry," Liza said. "He was magnificent."

He first tested positive for the AIDS virus in November 1988, when he began to notice early symptoms of the disease, including night sweats and a mild temperature. Two months later, in January, Bob Frowick was passing through New York on his way to Washington, D.C., where he was to be honored for his years in the Foreign Service by Secretary of State George Shultz. He stopped in New York for dinner with his brother at

101, and that night Halston "told me what he was up against," said Bob, who was struck by his brother's casual bravery. Halston, however, was full of optimism that he had many years left. A healthy diet, rest, exercise, and a new antiviral wonder drug called AZT were the formula. After all these years, Halston had even given up smoking cigarettes. "He had this indomitable will," said Bob, "as well as a lifetime of a strong body."

On April 21, 1989, with rumors of his illness swirling throughout the fashion industry, *Women's Wear Daily* ran a ghoulishly ironic interview with Halston entitled, "Halston Haunts Seventh Avenue." "Halston lives," the article began. "His clean-cut, all-American style showed up at every major New York collection. His spirit is everywhere." The gist of the article was that fashion had gone full circle, and that Halston's look was back and fresh, and the legacy of his work was seen in the collections of all the young designers, including Calvin Klein. So where was Halston now that they needed him? "I'm in a position to do whatever I damn please," he said.

Yet Halston could take little delight in the *Women's Wear* tribute. A month later, in May, came a blow that virtually wrecked his fighting spirit. It developed that when Andy Warhol was alive, he had called writer Pat Hackett every morning and dictated a diary about his adventures. Warhol had started the diary as a tax record for the Internal Revenue Service, but the daily retelling of his life soon turned into a soap opera in which Halston was one of the main characters. *The Andy Warhol Diaries,* as the 897-page book was titled when it was published that spring, stripped Halston bare. Over 200 detailed entries were made about Halston and Victor Hugo throughout the book, including stories of Halston's turbulent relationship with Victor, of Halston and Victor's drug use, of Halston's drag party in 1978, of long visits to the bathroom with Liza Minnelli. ("Maybe Liza's ripped her dress and Halston's going to sew it for her," Warhol mused.) In one passage, Warhol recounted the tale of one of Victor's orgies at 101, right down to the greasy

fingerprints on the walls. In another segment, Klinton Spils-
bury, the handsome, six-foot-five-inch actor who played the
Lone Ranger in the Hollywood remake, tells Warhol how he got
drunk one night at Studio 54 and woke up the next morning in
bed with Halston. In another entry, Liza Minnelli rings the
doorbell to Halston's house one rainy night while Martin Scorsese waits outside and says to Halston, "Give me every drug
you've got." Halston hands her a huge supply of various drugs,
just as though he's running a drugstore, including "a bottle of
coke, a few sticks of marijuana, a Valium, four Quaaludes,"
according to Warhol, and Minnelli goes off into the night with
Scorsese. Bianca Jagger—who got off relatively lightly in the
book—nevertheless sued the publishers in Great Britain, and
Halston threatened to sue in the United States. When Pat
Hackett, the editor of the diaries, ran into Victor Hugo at a
party, he seemed unfazed. When she asked him if he was angry
he shrugged and said, "Darling, that's show business!"

Halston was less magnanimous. As he watched the book race
up the best-seller lists he became so angry with the Warhol
estate for publishing it that he dumped almost all his Warhols
onto the market at wholesale prices so he would never have to
see them again. What he didn't sell he gave away to the Des
Moines Museum of Art.

The publication of the diaries took a terrible toll on Halston.
With his dirty laundry hung out for all the world to see, what
little spirit he was able to muster in the face of his illness was
destroyed along with the last shreds of his dignity. Soon after
the publication of the Warhol diaries his health began to deteri-
orate rapidly, and a month later he was rushed to New York
Hospital for his first major AIDS hospitalization for an oppor-
tunistic pneumonia, *Pneumocystis carinii,* complicated by
Kaposi's sarcoma lesions in his lungs. Halston's brother Bob,
tipped off by the houseboy, Mohammed, that Halston was
direly ill, rushed to New York to see if he could help, pretending
to Halston that it was just a coincidence that he was there. "I

was absolutely shocked to see what bad shape he was in," said Bob. "He had deteriorated greatly since January, and I didn't think he'd survive more than a very short time. He'd lost weight, he was weak, and he could hardly breathe. He was just in miserable shape. Some of the doctors didn't feel he had very long to live, just weeks." Yet, incredibly, he slowly fought his way out of it. "The IV feeding helped bring him back," said Bob, "but from that point on he went into this descending health syndrome in which he would be all right for a while and then he'd get quite sick. He'd go into the hospital and be brought back a bit, but he could never get enough strength back to get back to where he was before he reached that lower plateau. Later on he'd sink again and just keep going down like that."

By July another shock: Steve Rubell, who had looked sickly and thin for several years, yet who consistently insisted both to the press and in private that he did not have AIDS, died suddenly of complications from hepatitis and septic shock at Beth Israel Hospital at age forty-five.

In September, Halston was hospitalized a second time for pneumonia, and, tipped off again by Mohammed, Bob Frowick returned to New York to be with him. "Halston was ticked off that I was there," said Bob. "I pretended it was just a coincidence I was in New York, but he knew. This time he didn't look as bad as he did in June," said Bob. Still, he was very ill and weak when he returned to 101, and he languished in bed watched over by Mohammed and a private duty nurse.

That fall, with Halston too weak and infirm to defend himself or his property, Victor Hugo descended upon 101 and took up residence. Despite the fact that Halston was dying in his bedroom, Victor was up to his old tricks. One night he rang up Robert "Cuelar" Rogers at two in the morning and invited him over to 101. Rogers arrived at the town house in the dead of night and remembered hearing the silence of the huge house broken by the wrenching sound of Halston's sickly cough as it echoed through the place while he and Victor had sex in a guest room.

Bob Frowick, outraged at Victor's behavior, as was Mohammed, had Victor thrown out of the house. They hired armed, twenty-four-hour-a-day security guards to keep watch over Halston's valuables and to keep Victor Hugo at bay. When Victor was finally asked to leave the house that September, it was the last he and Halston ever saw of each other.

AS THE END drew near Halston turned increasingly toward his family. He sold his land in Montauk and his beloved town house in Manhattan for $5 million to Fiat heir Gianni Agnelli. Halston planned to be out of 101 by the end of January 1990, and with his usual, burning sense of optimism, he began to look for property in Santa Rosa, California, somewhere high up on a mountaintop, where he would build a dream house. Halston's sister, Sue, and her husband, Bud Watkins, had moved to Santa Rosa, about twenty miles north of San Francisco in the picturesque hills of the Sonoma Valley. Coincidentally, Bob Frowick's two sons and his daughter, Lesley, had moved to the San Francisco area as well, and when Bob retired from the Foreign Service, he, too, bought a house in Santa Rosa, just minutes away from where his sister lived. It was at Bob's new house that Halston's final Thanksgiving took place. It was a spectacular holiday for them all. Don and his wife came in from Gainesville, the house was filled with cousins and children, and it was the first time that the entire family had assembled in one place since 1957. There was much hugging and kissing and toasting, and for a brief but magical day, being in Bob Frowick's house, redolent of the smells of turkey and stuffing and ringing with the sounds of family laughter, transported Halston back to those golden days of his youth, when all the world seemed strong and secure—and he was Roy Frowick again. Secret tears were shed behind his back that day, but in front of him the family kept up a brave and cheerful front.

★ ★ ★

Halston found two AIDS specialists to consult in San Francisco, Drs. Charles MacDonald and Robert Rodevin; then he went back to New York in early December to make final arrangements to have have his personal possessions and some odd pieces of furniture shipped to Santa Rosa. Just before the Christmas holidays of 1989, he arrived back in Santa Rosa, expecting to return to New York on December 30 to spend one last New Year's Eve at 101 East Sixty-third Street with the New York people he loved. But he never made it back to Manhattan. "Around Christmas Day," said Bob Frowick, "he started to get sick again. He went into Pacific Presbyterian Hospital on the twenty-ninth of December and he was there over the New Year and for much of January. He lost a lot of weight at that point, and he was never able to gain it back again. He was pretty infirm by then."

Released from the hospital on January 16, he checked into a $1,000-a-day suite at the Mark Hopkins Hotel under the name of "Mr. Condencia." He spent much of the month of January working on his will. He thought about his bequests very carefully, according to Bob Frowick, and spent hours figuring them out. "He did many things to provide for the family," said Bob. "I told him that he was doing things very nobly. He was quietly thinking about each individual's situation, and he tried to do something to elevate all our lives' possibilities." On February 2, 1990, the R. Halston Frowick Trust Fund was established and Bob was appointed executor. This trust is private, and the value and contents have never been made public. The only publicly named recipients of bequests other than Halston's immediate family were Mohammed Soumaya, his loyal houseboy; Halston's secretary, Lisa Zay; and the Medical Research Institute of San Francisco.

Although by some estimates Halston's estate should have been as large as $20 million, Bob Frowick said the true value was only a fraction of that. "He made quite a lot of money in his time," he said, "but not the same kind of money that the big conglomerates who owned him were making. Also, he hadn't had any income since the summer of 1988, and he had liquidated his assets and had spent lavishly for years and given lavishly to Martha Graham, and in the end, there wasn't any great fortune there. What he had essentially was the money that he was immediately tapping from the sale of his house and his art."

Still, there was more than enough to buy a $200,000 black Rolls-Royce Silver Cloud, so on those good afternoons he could tour the countryside and go out for picnics. For a while he still called New York to keep up with friends, but then he let go of New York, too. Liza would call him at the Mark Hopkins and say, "Are you okay? Are you okay?" And he would insist he was. "He would say, 'I'm buying a mountain, I'm buying a car'— and this and this and this," Liza said. "He was always so vital, eventually you stop asking 'Are you okay?'"

In February 1990, the *National Enquirer* ran the first published story about Halston's illness, breaking the news with the brazen headlines *"LIZ IN SHOCK:* Her Designer Pal Halston Is Dying of AIDS." The story went on to delineate his physical decline over the last few months and quoted an insider as predicting he had only six months left to live. "He's been living out his last days like a hermit—sitting in a wheelchair in a $1,000-a-day suite at the ultra-elegant Mark Hopkins Hotel," said the *Enquirer.* Halston was tormented by the story, and he blamed it on a leak by a member of the hotel's staff. He immediately checked out of the hotel and moved to Santa Rosa to live with his sister, Sue, for a while.

The next few weeks were idyllic, considering how sick he was. When he was up to it he still cooked, chicken soup and stews. And during the day on sunny March afternoons, he sat on the fenced-in patio of Sue's house and sketched plans for a new patio for her. Sometimes they took drives up and down the coast, to see the Pacific Ocean, or the redwoods. "But he wasn't in Santa Rosa very long," said Bob, "before he called me urgently one day and said we had to go back down to the hospital right away, and we did. That was the last time that we had. He just couldn't make it . . . his lungs . . . he had too much stacked up against him."

Halston was as elegant and dignified as he met his death as he had been in life. He spent his last few days sitting up in bed in room 670 of the Pacific Presbyterian Medical Center. He was always dressed in silk pajamas, wearing a bright red Halston robe, and several times a day freshly pressed, fine linen sheets were put on his hospital bed. It was a pleasant enough room for a hospital, with a small sofa and a large window with a view of San Francisco Bay and the Golden Gate Bridge in the distance, and on every table, as always, there were clay pots of white orchids.

"He was quite lucid up until the last few days," Bob Frowick said. "When he was alert he was extremely alert, and he had very strong mental faculties that never left him" But he suffered so greatly in his last few days that the family felt it was a blessing for him to let go. He died in his sleep on March 26, 1990, at 11:21 P.M. He was fifty-seven years old.

Halston's death made international headlines, including the cover of *People* magazine, which said, "He lived so fast his first and last names blew off in the propwash." From the start, Halston's family bravely resolved to make the cause of his death public. "We think it is best for all concerned to know the reality," Bob said at a press conference the family held to formally announce Halston's death from Kaposi's sarcoma as a complication of AIDS. "We profoundly hope it has a positive impact on the public." While Sue and Don choked back tears in front of a phalanx of TV cameras and print reporters from around the world, Bob quietly told the assembled press, "The family mourns the loss of a magnificent and deeply respected brother and friend. We shall miss him."

A simple, $1,200 funeral was held for Halston at the Halstead N. Gray-Carew & English funeral parlor. His body was cremated, and the remains were put into a $55 container. On Friday afternoon, March 31, church services were held for him at Calvary Presbyterian Church on Fillmore Street in San Francisco. The funeral was attended by Liza Minnelli, Berry Berenson Perkins, Dennis Christopher, Pat Ast, Mohammed, Lisa Zay, Bill Dugan, D. D. Ryan, Karen Bjornson, and Pat Mori. A drag queen holding a red rose and wearing a Halston dress wept on the steps of the church as the mourners passed by. Later, a small reception was held in a suite at the Mark Hopkins Hotel where hors d'oeuvres and drinks were served.

Victor Hugo did not attend the funeral in San Francisco, or the gala "celebration" memorial that Liza Minnelli held for Halston in New York at Alice Tully Hall at Lincoln Center on June sixth of that year. Victor Hugo was not welcome at either event, and he knew not to show his face.

Two months before Halston died, yet another contract with Victor Hugo had been drawn up. This agreement allegedly pledged that Hugo would not contest Halston's will or in any way bring embarrassment to his estate. Again, Victor promised not to sell the story of his seventeen years with Halston, or to give interviews about him. In return, he was allegedly given an additional six-figure sum in several payments. A few months later, Victor Hugo had spent almost all the money and was selling interviews about Halston for cash. He lives in hotels in Miami Beach and New York and continues to sell off the vestiges of his hoard of Andy Warhol paintings and drawings.

After Halston's death, Revlon at first confirmed that it was their strategy to continue using the Halston name, and that whatever licensing programs still existed as well as a small line of Halston Originals would continue under the stewardship of John David Ridge. However, things did not work out as smoothly as had been hoped between Revlon and Carl Epstein and Ridge, and on September 1, 1990, Revlon officially closed Halston Enterprises Incorporated and shut down the Olympic

Tower offices. Halston Enterprises, for all purposes, ceased to exist.

Carl Epstein retired from business and continues to live in New Jersey. John David Ridge pursues a successful career as a costume designer for theater and ballet.

LIZA STILL CRIES when she thinks about Halston.

Years after he died, she remembered a story about how kind and smart he had been with her, even when she was at her craziest. It was during the period when she was still drinking and drugging heavily, and in her wild paranoia she was convinced that the satellite called Skylab was going to fall on her head. The weekend that Skylab was actually scheduled to fall Liza took refuge with Halston out at the Montauk compound. She was terrified when she arrived, but Halston had good news for her; he had been watching TV and the scientists had determined that Skylab was going to fall in the Indian Ocean—five thousand miles away from them. But that wasn't good enough for Liza. She didn't care what the scientists said; she was certain Skylab would fall on *her* head.

Halston smiled that perfect smile at her and took her by the hand and led her outside to the wooden porch. He pointed to a spot on the lawn about three hundred feet away and said, "Look, that's where Skylab is going to fall, and we're going to sit here and wait for it." He pulled over two lawn chairs and they sat and held hands as the sun went down. Later, he went inside and cooked dinner for them, which they ate on the porch as they waited for Skylab. Finally, late that night, when it was announced that Skylab had crashed in the Indian Ocean, Liza was able to fall asleep.

"The last time I saw Halston was about five days before Thanksgiving," Liza said. He wanted to have Thanksgiving dinner at 101 with Liza, but since he was due in Santa Rosa for the big family reunion, he and Liza had a "faux" Thanksgiving dinner in New York. "He had that kind of a spirit," Liza said. " 'It's not Thanksgiving? We'll make it Thanksgiving.' "

He looked awful by then. He was coughing and smoking cigarettes again and he had lost a great deal of weight. His face was slicked with bronzer. Yet Halston had Thanksgiving dinner with all the fixings prepared for Liza, including stuffing and cranberry sauce. After dinner, they were sitting at the table talking, and Liza started complaining about her life in general. "I was saying *this* was so hard," said Liza, "and *that* was so difficult, and *that* was difficult."

Halston listened to her thoughtfully, smoking a cigarette, and when Liza was finished with her lament, he said softly, "Gee, I think about *my* life, and I've just had a *wonderful* life. Always. I was always a success. I've always had the best workers. I always had the nicest friends. I always had everything I wanted." He smiled his perfect smile at her. "I've had a *great* life," he said.

Liza stopped complaining. When she kissed and hugged him good-bye that night, he promised he would be back by Christmas or New Year's, but they never saw each other again.

On the night that Halston died, just one minute before the Academy Awards show went on the air, at 9 P.M. New York time, Liza got the call that Halston had lapsed into a coma. She was sitting in her kitchen in her apartment, the kitchen where she and Halston used to sit around eating pot roast family style, and as Liza hung up the phone the Academy Awards show went on the air, with an audience of a billion people all around the world.

"Through the shock and the grief," said Liza, "—out of nowhere—comes the Halston perfume commercial. Suddenly, Halston was on every satellite hookup in the world, and I thought, 'Damn right!' "

INDEX